# Radical Gestures

JAYNE WARK

# Radical Gestures

## Feminism and Performance Art in North America

McGILL-QUEEN'S UNIVERSITY PRESS
Montreal & Kingston • London • Ithaca

ISBN 978-0-7735-2956-4 (cloth)
ISBN 978-0-7735-3066-9 (paper)

Legal deposit third quarter 2006
Bibliothèque nationale du Québec

Printed in Canada on acid-free paper.
Reprinted in paperback 2009

This book has been published with the help of a grant from the Canadian Federation for the Humanities and Social Sciences, through the Aid to Scholarly Publications Programme, using funds provided by the Social Sciences and Humanities Research Council of Canada.

McGill-Queen's University Press acknowledges the support of the Canada Council for the Arts for our publishing program. We also acknowledge the financial support of the Government of Canada through the Book Publishing Industry Development Program (BPIDP) for our publishing activities.

---

Library and Archives Canada Cataloguing in Publication

Wark, Jayne, 1956–
Radical gestures : feminism and performance art in North America, 1970 to 2000 / Jayne Wark.

Includes bibliographical references and index.
ISBN 978-0-7735-2956-4 (bnd)
ISBN 978-0-7735-3066-9 (pbk)

1. Feminism and art–Canada–History–20th century.
2. Feminism and art–United States–History–20th century.
3. Performance art–Canada–History–20th century.
4. Performance art–United States–History–20th century. I. Title.

N72.F45W37 2006  700'.82'097109045  C2006-900267-3

---

This book was designed and typeset by studio oneonone in Sabon 10/13

To Peter
who makes all things possible

and to Claire and Lucy
for their endless patience and understanding

and to my mother, Lynn
who supported us all

# Contents

# List of Illustrations

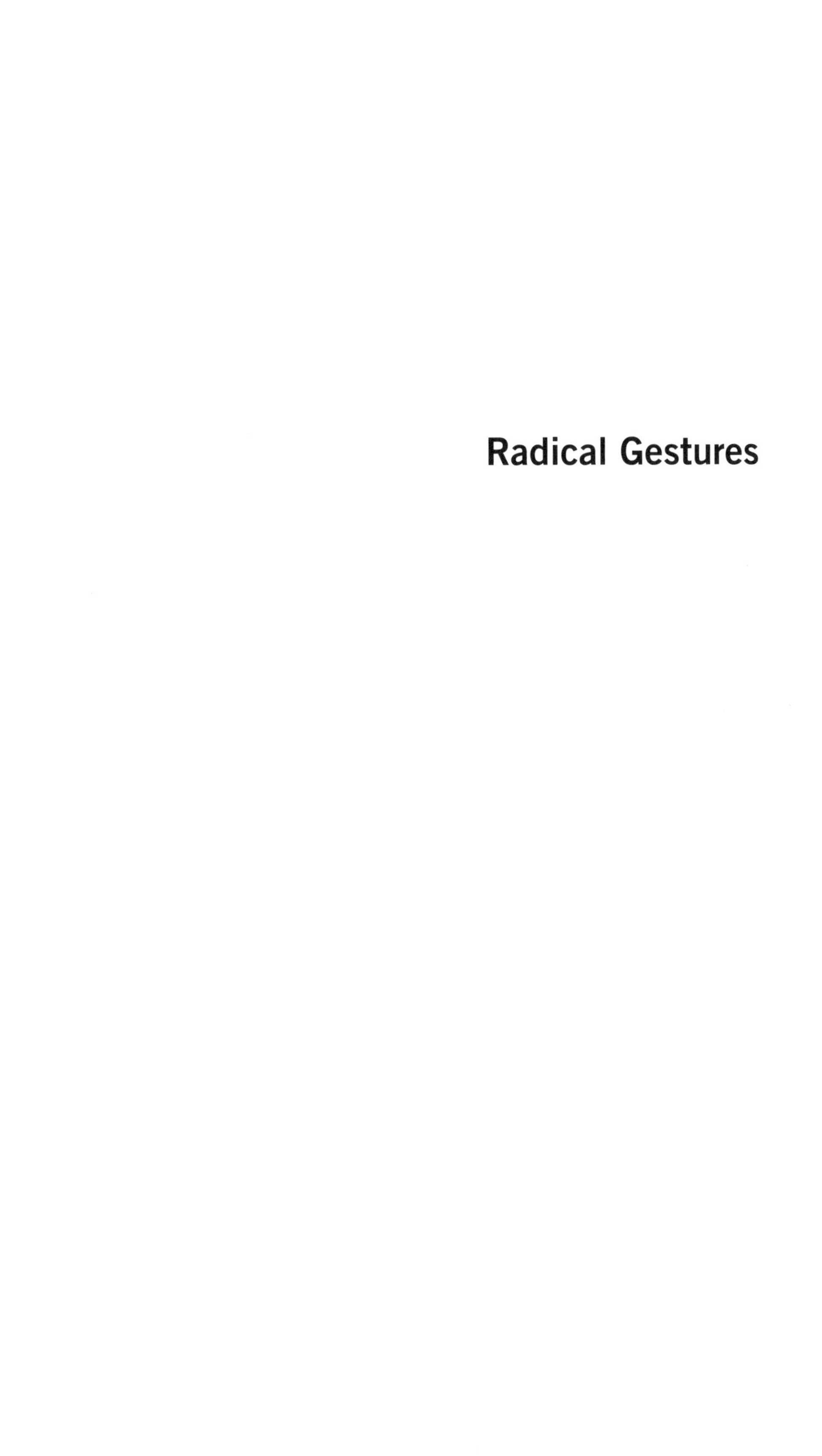

# Radical Gestures

# Introduction

In 1968 Robin Morgan and a troupe of feminists stormed into and disrupted the smooth proceedings of the Miss America beauty pageant in Atlantic City by crowning live sheep as Miss America(s) and throwing hair curlers, false eyelashes, bras, and girdles into the Freedom Trashcan.[1] Although no bras were actually burned, this assault on one of the clearest symbols of gender differentiation incited the media to portray feminist activists as crazed "bra burners" and to dismiss their anger as sexual frustration.[2] Undaunted, feminist activists of the early 1970s stepped up their struggle to gain control of women's bodies and women's lives not only through changes to legislation and medical practice, but also, as the invasion of the Miss America pageant demonstrated, by addressing how the dynamics of sexual hierarchy were played out within the symbolic and ideological structures of cultural representation.

By the early 1970s, a feminist consciousness had begun to spread pervasively throughout the art world as well, precipitating a confrontation with established values whose long-term effects are still felt today. Although women artists, critics, and historians reassessed and challenged the underlying and unspoken assumptions about gender, sexuality, and creativity in a wide variety of ways, this new feminist consciousness found one of its most distinctive manifestations in North America in the practice of performance art. Indeed, the relationship between feminism and performance art since the 1970s has become so inextricably linked that it is inconceivable to speak of one without reference to the other. The central argument of this book is that feminist performance played a decisive role in negotiating a new relationship between art and politics by bringing about what feminist scholar Janet Wolff has called "the contestation of the social arrangements of gender" through cultural intervention.[3]

One common objective of this contestation was simply to achieve professional recognition, an accomplishment that had previously been denied to all but a few "exceptional" women artists. But if gaining entry into the art world was a precondition to engaging in a discourse on feminist concerns, this did not mean that all women artists who sought professional recognition did so on the basis of making feminist claims for their work. Indeed, some women at the time were ambivalent or even hostile to the idea that gender has anything to do with art making. Others took the view that the very fact of their being women would make their work self-evidently different from that of their male peers. These ideas persist today, especially among some younger women who feel that, at best, feminism has accomplished its objectives and that, at worst, feminism conveys an unfashionably negative context for the reading of their work. In the words of Canadian artist Charmaine Wheatley, who has recently achieved some notoriety for her impromptu striptease performances in commercial strip clubs: "We make work from our own perspectives and naturally gender and cultural background affects the way we see things, but I get bored when people start off talking about feminist politics when looking at my work. It's disappointing, insulting and feels like a rejection or an unwillingness to really connect or understand the ideas I am sharing with the audience."[4]

As Wheatley's remarks make clear, not all art by women is feminist art, nor do all women consider themselves feminists, nor, for that matter, does making art from a feminine point of view necessarily result in feminist art. This book operates on the premise that feminist art is by definition political. I concur with Rosi Braidotti that feminism is "the movement that struggles to change the values attributed to and the representations made of women in the longer historical time of patriarchal history (*Woman*) as well as in the deeper time of one's own identity."[5] I concur also with theatre historian and theorist Janelle Reinelt, who wrote: "Feminism must be defined with a political edge; its application to performance is and must be a political act."[6] This book examines feminist art as that which manifests the conscious intention of remedying the effects and conditions of sexism in our culture. It is therefore not a study of performance art made by women but rather a study of the work of those women who used performance to bring an awareness of feminist concerns to the practice of art making, thus explicitly proposing the idea that art could be a form of political practice.

The idea that art could be political was in itself a radical concept in the late 1960s and into the 1970s because the art world was still dominated by the belief that the purpose of art was either to transcend or to provide an alternative to the crude exigencies of social struggle and political strife. It was a time, in other words, when the critical alignment between art and politics that had catalyzed the historical avant-gardes of the early twentieth century no longer had currency. But as women began to consider the implications of the feminist axiom that "the personal is political," they realized that no aspect of life, art included, is exempt from politics. They began to see the claim that art was a "neutral" aesthetic field uncorrupted by politics as an ideological device with which to maintain the status quo both within and beyond the art world. In challenging these ideas, feminism has played an instrumental role in forcing the contemporary art world into an awareness of how its premises of autonomy and neutrality conceal assumptions of power and authority. The foundations for and the beginnings of this process are outlined in chapter 1, which examines the development of radical politics in North America in the 1960s and the questions that began to arise in the art world, as the social crises deepened around 1970, about whether art and artists had political responsibilities. In contrast to the widespread ambivalence expressed over these questions, the emergence of feminism in the art world at this historical moment led to a new understanding of the political and of how the art world was in itself already political. From the conventional Leftist focus on classes and masses, feminism shifted the focus to a concept of the political as emerging from and merging with the personal. In this way, feminist artists enabled the kind of direct engagement between art and the politics of everyday life that had seemed so daunting to their male peers at the time.

Chapter 2 addresses the origins and development of early feminist art. It considers the conditions under which a feminist consciousness began to emerge in the art world and the strategies devised by women artists to change their circumstances. These strategies operated both at the level of activism, through the establishment of feminist communities, organizations, and pedagogy, and at the level of ideology, through critical engagements with the values, precepts, and ideals that then prevailed in both art and society. As practitioners in a visual field, these artists were particularly attuned to the role of representation in maintaining ideological attitudes that denigrated women or excluded women's experiences as having any relevance to the professional and public practice of art. The significance of this point cannot be underestimated, for, as Simone de Beauvoir said, "Representation of the world, like the world itself, is the work of men; they describe it from their own point of view, which they confuse with the absolute truth."[7] As a form of representation, art, like verbal language, is not a neutral vehicle for the expression of preexistent meanings but rather a system of signs through which meaning is produced, received, and negotiated. This chapter addresses the question of why performance was the method of representation used so frequently by feminist artists in their efforts to renegotiate their relationship with the world. Many explanations have been offered for why performance by women became so distinctive as a *feminist* practice, but one of the most salient was formulated by feminist art critic Lucy Lippard in 1976: "When women use their own bodies in their art work, they are using their *selves*; a significant psychological factor converts these bodies or faces from object to subject."[8]

The distinction Lippard made between women as objects and subjects is elaborated upon in chapter 3, which focuses on how early feminism defined its political objectives and on how these objectives were articulated in early feminist performance art. It begins by examining how the initial project of "second wave" feminism attempted to account for the basis of female subordination by theorizing the concept of sexual difference.[9] Since women had not been omitted accidentally from participation in patriarchal discourse and culture, feminist analysis addressed the question of how difference functioned to maintain and justify social hierarchy along sex/gender lines. And once sexual difference became the basis for understanding what made women's experiences distinct from men's, this difference also became the "essence" that united women in their struggle for emancipation. By surveying the work of de Beauvoir with reference to more recent theoretical thought, this chapter will address the complex debates that have ensued regarding the question of who constitutes the "subject" of feminist emancipation. While many early feminist performance artists produced work that sought to discover the "true" femininity that lay concealed behind the oppressive façade of patriarchal culture – a topic explored in this chapter through works that aligned femininity with the body, nature, and spirituality – such ideas have subsequently been repudiated not only for naively presuming that bad images of women could simply be replaced by good ones, but also for being insensible to the differences that exist *between* and *among* women. Although feminists in the 1980s and 1990s have made valuable and necessary critiques of such essentialist thinking, the tendency to categorize all 1970s practice under this rubric has come to have a deleterious effect on our understanding of early feminist art and politics. As I argue in this chapter, a strategic form of essentialism was necessary at the time in order to develop feminism as a political practice with which a wide spectrum of women could identify. At the same time, however, I argue that it is wrong to construe all 1970s feminist practice as monolithically essentialist and to dismiss it wholesale on this basis.

The fallacies underlying such assumptions about 1970s feminist art are addressed in the subsequent three chapters, which link the activities and approaches of artists in the 1970s to those of artists working in the 1980s, the 1990s, and the present. In order to underscore the many continuities between early and later feminist art, these three chapters follow a thematic organization that nevertheless allows for the presentation of this body of work within its changing historical and theoretical contexts. These chapters identify the principal concerns preoccupying feminist artists during these years and examine the approaches and methods used to enact these concerns in performance. Chapter 4 considers the role of language-based forms in feminist performance. Although the existing literature on feminist performance has tended to prioritize work centred on the actions or images of the body, the widespread use of autobiographical and narrative structures documented in this chapter provides clear evidence of how significant these strategies of storytelling were for the articulation of how the personal was indeed political. Chapter 5 addresses the theoretical concept of "performativity" and traces how it was manifest in feminist explorations of roles and transformations from the 1970s through to the present. This chapter addresses how the formations of identity, agency, and subjectivity were interrogated not only at a personal level, but also in relation to social codes and structures. The final chapter takes up the theme of the body and its representations, which is alluded to throughout the book but examined here in more depth and detail in relation to how women's bodies have been an embattled terrain over which feminist artists have struggled to gain control. This chapter examines how feminist performance artists contested long-standing assumptions about the hierarchical relations between sexuality and creative agency, how they generated transgressive strategies of resistance to both aesthetic and social discriminatory conventions, and how they asserted their own embodied particularities within social and cultural discourse. It concludes with some provisional explanations of how and why feminist performance continues to be both relevant and challenging to contemporary art practice.

Some final notes must be made regarding how performance art has been addressed in the literature and how it is defined for the purposes of this study. As historian Roselee Goldberg has observed in her survey *Performance Art from Futurism to the Present*, performance art is an extremely permissive, open-ended, and anarchic medium that "defies precise or easy definition beyond the simple declaration that it is live art by artists."[10] Although this permissiveness and resistance to definition that has always characterized performance art is reflected in the liberal scope of the literature on the subject, this literature does tend to fall into three broad, albeit sometimes overlapping, categories.[11]

One category comprises the literature generally preoccupied with the ontological status of performance. On the one hand, there are studies that regard performance art as a strategy for undermining art's traditional prioritizing of painting and sculpture. This approach addresses the relationship between performance and the objects or quasi-objects it uses or produces as the residual trace of an ephemeral event, as seen in Henry Sayre's 1989 book *The Object of Performance: The American Avant-Garde since 1970* and in two major exhibition catalogues from the 1990s: *Outside the Frame: Performance and the Object, A Survey History of Performance Art in the USA since 1970* and *Out of Actions: Between Performance and the Object, 1949–1979*.[12] On the other hand, there are studies explicitly concerned with performance art's ephemeralness, although these studies tend to part ways around questions of "liveness," presence, and absence. For example, some early accounts of performance, such as those by Ira Licht, Rosemary Mayer, and Cindy Nemser, asserted that its unique quality is its ability to do away with objects and other intermediary devices so that the "presence" of the artist/performer is fully apprehensible to the audience.[13] More recently, Peggy Phelan's book *Unmarked: The Politics of Performance* has similarly insisted upon the liveness of performance, but she argues that what this more precisely offers is evidence of lack or loss of presence because the transitory nature of performance undermines any secure relation between subjectivity and the body. Phelan also argues that performance cannot be saved, recorded, or documented without betraying "the promise of its own ontology" and thus relinquishing its politics as a form of resistance to the economies of reproduction.[14] Other theorists and historians have argued, however, that ontological priority cannot be given to the live event. Kathy O'Dell and Amelia Jones, for example, have addressed the role of representation and documentation in performance, while Philip Auslander and Anne Wagner have examined how the "rhetoric of presence" in performance is constructed in relation to anxiety about "mediatization."[15] This debate over liveness and documentation continues today, as seen in Catherine Elwes's article in the March 2004 issue of *Third Text*.[16]

While overlapping somewhat with these ontological approaches, another category of literature on performance art takes the body as its focus and examines how it operates in performance as a form of artistic language that "speaks" about ideas or experiences not by embodying them in objects but by communicating them to audiences either directly or by means of documentation of the event or action. This approach primarily addresses performance art that interrogates questions of subjectivity, identity, and social relations as they are marked on or enacted by bodies as metaphors for psychic, cultural, and institutional codes and signifiers. Studies in this vein would include Phelan's book discussed above as well as such studies as Lea Vergine's *Il corpo come linguaggio* (1974) and, in the late 1990s, Kathy O'Dell's *Contract with the Skin*, Amelia Jones's *Body Art: Performing the Subject*, and Rebecca Schneider's *The Explicit Body in Performance*.[17]

A third category of literature on performance art encompasses studies of feminist performance. Again there is some overlap here because several of the books already mentioned are largely (Phelan, Jones) or wholly (Schneider) focused on feminist performance. But apart from these studies and Moira Roth's *The Amazing Decade: Women and Performance Art in America, 1970–1980*, most of the literature on feminist performance has been in the form of journal articles or essays in anthologies, exhibition catalogues, and books on feminist art as a whole.[18] In addition to studies of feminist performance as an art practice, many studies also examine its role from the perspective of either theatre or its more inclusive corollary, "performance studies."[19] The feminist research that has been done in theatre and performance studies includes important texts by Jill Dolan, Elin Diamond, Janelle Reinelt, Kate Davy, Sue-Ellen Case, Lynda Hart, and others, including Phelan and Schneider.[20] This body of work, much of which has informed this current study, addresses a number of concerns and preoccupations that are shared by feminist performers working in art and theatre contexts, such as questions of identity and subjectivity, embodiment and representation, role-playing and authorial agency, and spectatorship and relation to audience.

Notwithstanding these shared concerns and the blurring of boundaries that has occurred in the last forty years or so with respect to disciplines and categories in the arts, performance has taken shape as a distinctive practice within the visual arts and thus differs from performance in the context either of theatre or of productions within the domain of performance studies. For one thing, performance in the visual arts has its own history, models, theories, and debates, dating back at least to Jackson Pollock's "action paintings" of the late 1940s and including Allan Kaprow's important assessment of their legacy in the 1950s as well as Michael Fried's defence of Modernism against the "theatricality" of Minimalism in the late 1960s.[21] For another thing, most artists who do performance also produce other kinds of visual art and identify themselves as visual artists.[22] Finally, the venues that support or show their work tend to be art galleries, and the critics and historians who write about their work tend to be art critics and historians, as indeed is the case in most of the studies cited so far, the only exceptions being those by Phelan and Schneider. By contrast, those who write from a performance-studies perspective generally exclude art-based performance, focusing instead on work produced within the context of experimental theatre, especially in New York.

The scope of this study, therefore, is restricted to those forms of feminist performance that have responded and contributed to the discourse of performance as a practice within the visual arts. The definition of performance art is expanded here beyond Goldberg's conception of it as "live art by artists" to include not only live performance done either for an art audience or for a nonart public, but also private performances documented through photographs or written accounts, certain photographic works that incorporate an aspect of performative self-display, and numerous video tapes, some of which were documents of live performance and some of which were produced as video tapes in their own right. Generally speaking, the primary criterion used for determining whether or not a given work would be considered here is whether the artist engaged in some form of performative action, pose, gesture, or event. This book examines feminist art and is written from a feminist perspective; just as feminist art has worked to bring about historical change for women, the overarching intent of this book is to bring about change in the way we see and understand history.

# 1

# Art, Politics, and Feminism in the 1960s

## RADICAL POLITICS IN THE 1960S

The spectacular disruption of the Miss America pageant by Robin Morgan and her feminist cohort was only one of a series of events that marked 1968 as a year of unrelenting social crisis and turmoil. After the military disaster of the Tet Offensive in February, the American public and government were divided as never before about whether to end their role in Vietnam. President Lyndon B. Johnson's announcement, on 31 March, that he would not seek nomination for a second term led to a brief relaxing of antiwar protests. Then, on 4 April, Martin Luther King was assassinated in Memphis, and any lingering commitment to nonviolent resistance within the civil rights movement seemed to go to the grave with him. Rioting broke out across American cities, and three weeks later came the student occupation of Columbia University, events to which the police and National Guard responded with ferocious violence. Europe also erupted in May, most famously in the *événements* in Paris, where students were joined on the barricades by artists, actors, writers, and filmmakers, as well as by workers who launched a general strike that almost brought down the de Gaulle government. The rebellion spread quickly through Western Europe and into Communist Poland, Czechoslovakia, and Yugoslavia, only to be put down by the onslaught of Soviet tanks and guns.[1]

Over the summer, the situation worsened in the United States. After presidential candidate Robert Kennedy's assassination on 5 June, and with no end to the war in sight, the protest movement's pent up frustration was destined to be unleashed at the Democratic Convention in Chicago in August. Fearing a reprise of the Paris uprising on his own turf, Mayor Richard Daley called in a force of twelve thousand Chicago police, five to six thousand National Guardsmen, and six thousand US Army troops. From 25–30 August, Chicago exploded in a clash of billy clubs, Molotov cocktails, rocks, tear gas, Mace, and rifle butts, with much of the mayhem caught by television cameras. The appalling violence shocked the politicians, journalists, and public, who generally saw Daley's security forces as most culpable. Many in the antiwar movement were also repelled by the Chicago debacle, and they saw the presidential election of Richard Nixon in November as certain to prolong America's involvement in Vietnam and thus the social strife at home.

Throughout the turbulent years from 1968 to 1970, the antiwar and antiracist protests continued, and membership in the Students for a Democratic Society (SDS) swelled. But even though the protestors sometimes numbered in the millions and included all manner of citizens, not just student radicals, Nixon's policy of "Vietnamization" proceeded apace.[2] With the bloodshed continuing in the face of such widespread protest and despite such economic and human cost, it seemed more and more evident that the war was not just a misguided mistake, but also a symptom of a profoundly corrupt system. For several militant new groups emerging from within the SDS, the main organization of the New Left, the only solution was full-scale revolution. The most extreme faction was the Weather Underground Organization. Its slogan "Bring the war home!" was given ironic meaning on 6 March 1970 when several members blew themselves up manufacturing pipe bombs in a New York townhouse.[3]

For those in the New Left committed to change by political rather than violent means, this event was the culmination of a deepening sense of moral collapse. It forced them to confront a dilemma that went to the core of the student movement. This movement, which comprised the first generation affluent enough to hone its socially critical faculties *en masse* at universities, had begun its struggle by fighting on behalf of oppressed others. Advocating revolution seemed to offer a way to assuage liberal guilt by transforming it into radical action. But, as Todd Gitlin has noted in his political memoir of this period, there was no revolutionary crisis in America. It would have to be manufactured "from on high" by privileged intellectuals.[4] And with groups like the Weather

Underground commandeering its vanguard, the inevitable outcome could be only further isolation from any potential or credible allies – for example, the working-class multitudes. Although the student movement continued to participate in antiwar protests into the early 1970s, its larger goal of building a great new society had proved unattainable. The sense of defeat and betrayal – from within and without – was bitter and profound.

The essential problem faced by the New Left was that its vision of the collective good was, with the exception of the antiwar protest, which engendered widespread sympathy, utterly irreconcilable with the interests of the vast majority of Americans. In this sense, the roots of its political failure are as old and familiar as the origins of socialism itself and its utopian ideals. By positing any given model of the "good society" as the common objective, the Left has all too often disregarded inevitable divergences of outlooks and values among different social groups and thus confused "rowing with steering."[5] Concomitant with this, the New Left faced the additional dilemma that it imagined itself to be the instrument of change, while disparaging itself, as Gitlin wrote, for not being "the *real* instrument of change."[6]

The anguish and frustration over the inability to bring about substantial social change was not confined to those groups directly involved in activist politics. The heightened awareness that resulted from the political protests and debates of the 1960s had also led many artists to confront complex questions about the position of art within the relationship between culture *and* democracy. It had forced artists to reconsider existing assumptions about the function of art within a society and the role it played in sustaining the status quo through what Edward Said has called the "twinning of power and legitimacy," whereby one force obtains "in the world of direct domination, the other in the cultural sphere."[7] As this book will discuss, the rethinking of the relationship between culture, power, and politics by women and other new social groups would eventually have deep reverberations for art practice in the following decades. But those artists grappling with the question of political responsibility in the late 1960s and early 1970s first had to face the conundrum that, as Jonathan Harris put it, "fine or 'high' art could not be mobilized within the re-politicized conjuncture of 1968."[8] The reasons for this conundrum and how artists came to terms with it (or did not) require some further elaboration.

## THE QUESTION OF ART AND POLITICAL RESPONSIBILITY

American artists had spoken out against the war since the mid-1960s. On 27 June 1965 a full-page ad appeared in the *New York Times* with the headline "End Your Silence." It included a lengthy antiwar statement and the signatures of five hundred artists.[9] A few artists also made the war the subject of their work, as seen in James Rosenquist's *F-111* (1965), May Stevens's *Big Daddy Paper Doll* (1968), and Nancy Spero's *War Series* (1967), while Andy Warhol's *Red Race Riot* (1963) and Robert Indiana's *Alabama* (1965) had touched upon the problem of racism. In addition to fundraising, the art community made two other major contributions to the antiwar effort: the Peace Tower, built in Los Angeles in 1966; and the Angry Arts Week, organized in New York in 1967 (and repeated in Boston and Philadelphia), which featured the *Collage of Indignation* at New York University's Loeb Student Center. Artists also planned a boycott of Chicago art galleries after the fiasco at the Democratic Convention there in August 1968 but were persuaded by dealer Richard Feigen (whose schedule now had a gaping hole in October due to Claes Oldenburg's withdrawal) to do a show of protest art instead. Of those who participated, very few dealt directly with the issue of Mayor Daley's sanctioning of police brutality at the convention, and many simply submitted works in their usual style.[10] In the spring of 1969, a new organization called the Art Workers' Coalition (AWC) organized a demonstration at the Museum of Modern Art (MOMA), but its purpose was to demand changes in museum policy rather than to protest the war.[11]

There is no question that many artists felt the kind of anger and shame about the situation in America that had fuelled the radical student movement. As the crises deepened toward the end of the decade, the question of whether and how artists might respond took on an increased urgency, but there was no clear consensus. Some artists, like Sol LeWitt, categorically denied that any art with political content could be significant as art: "I do not think that I know of any art of painting or of sculpture that has any kind of real significance in terms of political content, and when it does try to have that, the result is pretty embarrassing."[12] In the same 1968 article in *Metro*, Don Judd maintained that anti-hierarchical and unconventional art could have political implications by resisting America's dominant values and social structures. Allan Kaprow, creator of the performance mode known as Happenings, felt that such performative events could adopt the strategies of political protest, but he did not think that art should serve specific political causes. Nevertheless, his ambivalence was poignant in that he also spoke of his "anguish and helplessness knowing that we cannot directly affect the course of politics."[13]

After the turmoil of the next two years, culminating in the May 1970 police shootings at Kent State and Jackson State Universities of students protesting the US invasion of Cambodia, the situation seemed dire. In January 1970 the AWC had produced a poster protesting the My Lai massacre. After the MOMA, who had agreed to distribute the poster, withdrew its support, the AWC organized two demonstrations in front of Picasso's *Guernica* in the MOMA.[14] On 22 May, Robert Morris and Poppy Johnson led an Art Strike against the Museum of Metropolitan Art, demanding that it close for a day in protest of the atrocities earlier that month. By the fall, the editors of *Artforum* had come to feel that the question of art and political responsibility was significant enough to be featured in the pages of this major art magazine. In the September 1970 issue, they published "The Artist and Politics: A Symposium," which included the following statement, along with responses from twelve artists:

> A growing number of artists have begun to feel the need to respond to the deepening political crisis in America. Among these artists, however, there are serious differences concerning their relations to direct political actions. Many feel that the political implications of their work constitute the most profound political action they can take. Others, not denying this, continue to feel the need for an immediate, direct political commitment. Still others feel that their work is devoid of political meaning and that their political lives are unrelated to their art. What is your position regarding the kinds of political action that should be taken by artists?[15]

Among the respondents who felt that art and politics should not mix were artists as diverse as Walter Darby Bannard – a confirmed Modernist and old friend of Clement Greenberg – and Lawrence Weiner, who was then on the cutting edge of Conceptual art. Bannard said: "Political things should not affect the making of art because political activity and art-making have never mixed to art's advantage, and my guess is that most artists are better off out of politics."[16] Weiner was just as adamant: "So-called Art whose original intent and most often content is political or social does not concern me as an Artist. They are for me only varied forms of sociological propaganda."[17] Ed Ruscha's position was similar: "I have excluded political science from my program ... I isolate myself and my work continues smoothly with no involvement in any issue. As an American citizen though I have no trouble seeing how bad things are ... [yet] I don't think an artist can do much for any cause by using his art as a weapon."[18] Robert Smithson was perhaps the most eloquent in expressing contempt for what many regarded as an utterly corrupt "system": "My 'position' is one of *sinking* into an awareness of global squalor and futility. The rat of politics always gnaws at the cheese of art. The trap is set. If there's an original curse, then politics has something to do with it. Direct political action becomes a matter of trying to pick poison out of boiling stew ... The political system that now controls the world on every level should be denied by art."[19]

Smithson's advocacy of denial should not, however, be seen as an abandonment of politics. Like the other artists associated with Minimalism, his work was informed by strategies of refusal and negation. On one level, the Minimalists' "blank form," seriality, industrial materials, and so on were clearly intended as critical refusals of the aesthetic ideals of postwar Modernism (figs 1.1 and 1.2).[20] Certainly, Minimalism irritated Modernists like Michael Fried, who mounted a sustained and cogent attack against Minimalism in his 1967 essay "Art and Objecthood."[21] But on another level, the Minimalists' antagonism was also toward the larger social sphere, with whose values they saw Modernism aligned. As Minimalist artist Robert Morris wrote in "Notes on Sculpture," which appeared in the same issue of *Artforum* as Fried's essay: "Such work [Minimalism] ... would seem to have a few social implications, none of which are negative. Such work would undoubtedly be boring to those who long for access to an exclusive specialness, the experience of which reassures their superior position."[22] Morris's inference here is that Modernism had become identified as both a symptom and a legitimatization of the orthodoxy and hierarchical authority of the "Establishment." As the Minimalists saw it, Modernism's elitist aesthetic priorities impeded the formulation of an art practice capable of engaging with the disturbing social and political realities of the period. Even more insidiously, it served as a means by which these realities could continue to be repressed by supporting the status quo in both art and the larger society. The Minimalists' goal was both to expose this complicity and to invest their own work with connotations that linked it to those larger social and political realities.

In the *Artforum* symposium, this sense of political commitment among the Minimalists was clearly evident, as in Carl Andre's terse statement,

"Silence is assent."[23] Jo Baer was also unequivocal: "I think the time for political action by artists is now ... and should be taken in the art world and in the world at large. Political action need not inhibit art-making; the two activities are dissimilar, not incompatible. In fact all art is eventually political. As the carrier of esthetic experience, art is a powerful effector of choice and action." But as for the question of how this commitment could be made evident in art, she could only refer allusively, as Morris had done, to the way materials and formal arrangements could have "political implications that bear on the sovereignty of the subject and the nature and ramifications of self-determination."[24] In his statement, Don Judd said that his own work, which he made from a position of "opposition and isolation," also had such implications. But by also observing that "one reason for the popularity of American art is that the museums and collectors didn't understand it enough to realize that it was against much in society," Judd was admitting that whatever political meaning its creators ascribed to such implications went largely unnoticed by those who held financial and administrative power in the art world.[25] In making this admission, Judd effectively put his finger on the crux of the problem facing artists who were concerned with reconciling vanguard art practice with political responsibility.

Part of this problem was how the legacy of the avant-garde had been reconceived in postwar American art. The most important text to have articulated a theory of the avant-garde in this context was Clement Greenberg's "Avant-Garde and Kitsch," first published in 1939.[26] The thesis of "Avant-Garde and Kitsch" was that art should adopt a position of critical detachment in order to avoid being the instrument of either partisan politics or capitalist corruption. When Greenberg first wrote his essay, he was responding to the conditions of the 1930s, when he saw art being absorbed, on the one side, into the tendentious politics of the period and displaced, on the other, by the popularity of mass-cultural forms. For Greenberg, both these debased forms of culture were kitsch, and they served together as a corrupt ideological ploy to manipulate the masses. At the time, Greenberg was writing from a political position on the Left, and the main point of his essay was that ambitious, avant-garde art must be preserved so that it might survive into that time when a new socialist culture had arrived.

In effect, what Greenberg argued was that art must retain its autonomy in order both to preserve itself and to maintain its ability to function as a form of critical practice. During the Cold War tensions of the late 1940s and 1950s, however, Greenberg, like many intellectuals at

1.1 Carl Andre. *Lever*, 1966. 137 firebricks, 11.4 x 22.5 x 883.9 cm assembled; brick: 11.4 x 22.5 x 6.4 cm each. National Gallery of Canada, Ottawa.

the time, abandoned his commitments to the Left and became a booster of American culture.[27] Over time, his notion of autonomy as a strategy for critical resistance eventually gave way to a neo-Kantian model of "disinterested" aesthetic discrimination as an end in itself. In his *Critique of Judgment* (1790), Immanuel Kant had set out the aesthetic principle that, in order for art to be of universal significance, it must be detached from the contingencies of life. As Kant put it, "The delight which determines the judgment of taste is independent of all interest," meaning that judgments must not be affected by any motivation that is not strictly aesthetic.[28] In 1961 Greenberg, who had by then become perhaps the best known American art critic, expunged the original allusions to socialism when he republished "Avant-Garde and Kitsch" as the opening essay to his book *Art and Culture*.[29] That same year, he also published "Modernist Painting," a key essay articulating his Kantian ideals. Greenberg asserted here that art must be "self-critical," a practice by which each given art form must establish its own "characteristic methods" by eliminating any and all effects borrowed from other art forms so as "to entrench it more firmly in its area of competence."[30]

Although Greenberg's increasingly prescriptive, formalist, neo-Kantian views did not hold complete sway over the art world in the 1950s and 1960s, as indicated by the emergence of such countervailing practices as neo-Dada, Pop, Fluxus, and especially Minimalism, none of these art forms really challenged the essential principle that art should remain autonomous and apart from the contingencies of social life and politics. For this reason, when the German critic Peter Bürger published his seminal book, *Theory of the Avant-Garde*, in 1974, he was critical of such practices. Bürger's view of the avant-garde was very different from Greenberg's. Whereas Greenberg – like Renato Poggioli, who had also written about the avant-garde in 1968 – saw the avant-garde as constituting a resistance to convention and orthodoxy by means of innovative and experimental forms, Bürger defined the avant-garde in relation to its social role.[31] Bürger argued that the Aestheticist movements of the late nineteenth century, with their dedication to "art for art's sake," represented the apogee of autonomous art within modern bourgeois culture. This autonomy effectively relegated art to isolation within its own institutional

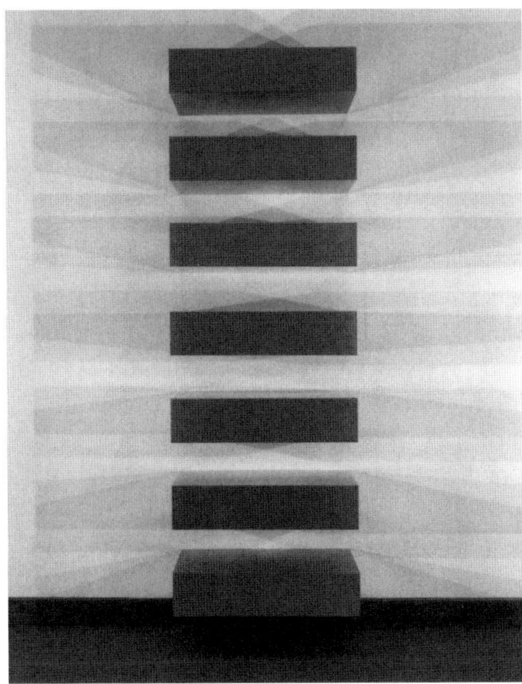

1.2 Donald Judd. *Untitled*, 1966, reconstructed. Galvanized iron, 23 x 101.6 x 78.7 cm each element – installed vertically on wall with 23 cm intervals. National Gallery of Canada, Ottawa.

sphere, and this "apartness from the praxis of life" was itself an admission of art's inability to have any transformative social role. As Bürger argued, the historical avant-garde movements of Futurism, Constructivism, Dadaism, and Surrealism recognized this problem and set out to destroy the autonomy and institutional isolation of art by "reintegrating art into the life process." Bürger acknowledged both that this was a risky endeavour because it could result in the loss of critical distance and that, ultimately, "the political intentions of the avant-garde movements (reorganization of the praxis of life through art) were never realized." For Bürger, this failure was particularly tragic because, when postwar artists resumed the use of avant-garde techniques and strategies, they did so without avant-garde intentions. This rendered them merely a "neo-avant-garde": "[T]he neo-avant-garde institutionalizes the *avant-garde as art* and thus negates genuinely avant-gardiste intentions ... [since it] is autonomous art in the full sense of the term, which means that it negates the avant-gardiste intention of returning art to the praxis of life."[32]

Although Bürger's text remains pivotal for discussions of both the historical and the "neo" avant-gardes, it has not gone unchallenged. Benjamin Buchloh, for example, contested Bürger's foundational premise that the goal of the historical avant-garde was to destroy the institution of art. Buchloh thus negates this premise as a valid critique of the postwar neo-avant-garde artists. In Buchloh's view, all avant-garde practice should be defined as a continually renewed struggle over the definition of cultural meaning, the discovery and representation of new audiences, and the development of strategies to counteract and resist the tendency of the ideological apparatuses of the culture industry to occupy and control the spaces of practice and representation.[33] Hal Foster similarly defended the postwar neo-avant-garde artists by arguing that they did not merely repeat the historical avant-garde's goals and strategies as hollowed out aesthetic gestures. Foster argued, for example, that the neo-avant-garde did not invert or abandon the critique of the institution of art but instead worked to extend it in order to reveal its operations. He added further that the neo-avant-garde addressed the relationship between art and the praxis of life not by collapsing the two but rather by testing the conventions of each with reference to the conventions of the other – that is, by testing the limits of art in relation to the commodity and industrial forms of bourgeois capitalism within the specific context of the postwar period.[34] These are persuasive arguments that point to the need for new narratives of the history and theory of the avant-garde, but as revisions of Bürger's theory, they still do not account for two important factors upon which rest the central premises of the present study.

First, the neo-avant-garde's focus on the institution of art, combined with the lingering residue of the Modernist demand for artistic autonomy, meant that there was no tangible context in which to envision a practice that was aesthetically ambitious while also being socially or politically engaged. This was precisely the situation Judd referred to in the *Artforum* symposium by way of explaining his isolation as an artist from the political crises of the day: "Part of the reason for my isolation was the incapacity to deal with it all, in any way, and also work. Part was that recent art had occurred outside of most of the society. Unlike now, very few people were opposed to anything, none my age that I knew."[35] Second, as artists endeavoured to move out of this isolation, they confronted the other part of the problem identified above by Judd. That is, however much the postwar neo-avant-garde artists challenged the status quo of Modernist cultural authority by engaging with the everyday objects and industrial procedures of late capitalism, the fact that they did so primarily by making aesthetic refusals and negations in a highly specialized formal language meant that the constituency to whom such strategies were legible as having "political implications" was restricted to art world insiders, and as Judd said, was even invisible to many museums and collectors. Moreover, in their discussion of Minimalism's strategies of aesthetic negation, Charles Harrison and Paul Wood noted that, "far from being 'meaningless,' strips of felt or piles of industrial waste may come to 'mean' anything – and who is to say?"[36] Given this, it is not surprising to learn that Judd, although advocating that all artists should be politically involved, ultimately conceded that "art may change things a little but not much."[37]

The circumstances for Conceptual art were not markedly different. Although Conceptualism's purview extended beyond Minimalism's preoccupation with challenging the prevailing modes of production – to the extent that Conceptualism aimed instead to undermine the authority of the entire institutional apparatus in which art was displayed, received, and commodified – it, too, was restricted to an insular form of critique. Conceptual artist Joseph Kosuth might have declared in 1975 that it was "the art of the Vietnam era," but as Blake Stimson has shown, Conceptual art's claim to having finally brought radical art and politics into convergence in the manner of the historical avant-garde artists is ultimately untenable.[38] For one thing, Conceptual art, like

Minimalist art, was still driven largely by an Oedipal urge to kill off the Modernist fathers.[39] For another thing, far from weakening the institution of art in any fundamental way, Conceptual art effectively opened it up to a wide new range of cheaper products; as Robert Smithson cynically commented in 1972, the art institutions were now getting "an aesthetic bargain."[40] Finally, if self-reflexive critique was Conceptual art's defining strength, it was also a limitation, for as Alexander Alberro has noted, it gave rise to a situation in which Conceptual art carried "the implicit message ... that art can only make meaningful statements about itself and the systems that determine its limits."[41]

Even the mode of Conceptual art known as "institutional critique," which sought to expose how the institutions of art were complicit with the ideological structures that determine all aspects of social and cultural experience, was constrained in its ability to reprise the *engagé* relationship between art and politics that had characterized the historical avant-garde artists. Hans Haacke certainly went further than most with works like *MOMA Poll* (1970) and *Shapolsky et al. Manhattan Real Estate Holdings, A Real Time Social System as of May 1, 1971* (1971), which revealed how members of the boards and administrations of the MOMA and the Guggenheim Museum were affiliated respectively with war profiteering and slumlord housing, thus making explicit the extent to which the art world was inherently bound up with the politics of the real world.[42] Haacke's overt references to politics were exceptional at this time, however, and may at least in part be accounted for by his German background, which perhaps gave him a more immediate familiarity with the political strategies and intentions of the historical European avant-garde artists. Most American artists were reticent to make such direct political references in their work. Thomas Crow has attributed this reticence to the elevated "conceptual demands of advanced art practice," which made artists face a "stark choice ... between the demands of 'the Movement' and the demands of a career in art, however radically conceived."[43] For his part, Benjamin Buchloh has argued that Conceptual art, as distinguished by "its acute sense of discursive and institutional limitations, its self-imposed restrictions, its lack of totalizing vision, [and] its critical devotion to the factual conditions of artistic production and reception," was permeated by a dystopian "disenchantment with those political master-narratives that empowered most of '20s avant-garde art."[44] Either way, what is evident here is a profound ambivalence about art's capacity to bring about liberating change.

## FEMINISM AND THE REDEFINING OF POLITICS

At precisely this historical moment, however, new forms of political understanding began to enter the art world, primarily through the agencies of the feminist and civil rights movements. Although broadly aligned with the New Left, the emancipation struggles of these agencies revealed the limits of class-oriented politics in accounting for how oppression and ideological control are embedded within all forms of social institutions – from the public sphere of the art world to the privacy of home and family – and are experienced both socially and at the subjective level of the individual. The feminist movement thus provided women – and women artists – with a context in which to articulate their individual and collective concerns within a reconceived notion of the political. For feminist artists, this resulted most significantly in a new conception of the relationship between art and politics. As Peggy Phelan has observed, whereas the civil rights, New Left, student, and antiwar movements had employed art as a form of propaganda for their political arguments rather than as a field for the expression and exploration of their convictions, art became for feminists "the arena for an enquiry into both political and personal revision; art was both extraordinarily responsive to political illumination and productive of it."[45] This meant that, unlike their male peers, feminist artists were able to see art not as compromised by, or in conflict with, their political goals, but indeed as the object of them. As they sought to negotiate a new relationship between art, life, and politics, they recognized how existing aesthetic practice was itself a form of gender oppression. As a corollary to this, they saw how art could serve as a powerful weapon for women's emancipation struggles, both within and beyond the art world. In order to understand how such ideas became manifest within art practice, however, it is necessary to understand their relation to the establishment of the feminist movement as a whole.

Given that the women's movement, in all its historical phases, was a struggle of opposition to tradition and convention, its resurgence within the milieu of the profound social upheavals generated by the radical movements of the 1960s was perhaps inevitable. Women were involved in activist politics in significant numbers from at least the early 1960s. In 1960 the Voice of Women/Voix des femmes was formed in Canada as a peace movement for the abolition of nuclear arms.[46] In 1966 both the Association féminine d'éducation et d'action sociale and the Fédération des femmes du Québec were founded, building upon the long tradition of women's political involvement in Quebec that had been established as early as the 1930s with such organizations as the Cercles des fermières and the Union catholique des fermières.[47] That same year, the National Organization of Women (NOW) was founded in the US, and the Committee on the Equality of Women in Canada was established. Aided by pressure from Judy LaMarsh, then secretary of state and the only female cabinet minister in the Liberal government, the committee persuaded Prime Minister Pearson to strike the Royal Commission on the Status of Women in February 1967.[48] Over the course of its two-year inquiry, the commission documented a sea change from initial public ridicule to recognition of the significance of the women's movement across the country.[49] In 1972 the National Action Committee (NAC) on the Status of Women was formed to pressure government to bring laws into conformity with the commission's 167 recommendations.[50]

As Micheline Dumont has observed, although such organizations had some success in achieving civic and legal rights for women, and although women in the 1960s theoretically had greater choices of social roles, the right to exercise these choices was contingent upon the proviso that they first fulfilled their roles of wife and mother. Once women had recognized that their right to self-determination only existed in this surplus space, provided that they did not violate the "so-called natural role of women," it soon became clear that the real basis for the inequities between women and men was deeply obscured within the social order.[51] Even the radical political movements of the 1960s were not free from these inequities. As one Frenchwoman wrote in 1969, "I was struck by the great words: liberation of peoples, liberation of women. My liberation consists of serving him after my work while he reads or 'thinks.' While I peel [*épluche*] the vegetables, he can read [*éplucher*] at leisure – either *Le Monde* or works on Marxist economy. Freedom only exists for the well-off ones and in the real world, the well-off one is the man."[52]

As American women in the SDS also realized, being part of a movement dedicated to egalitarian social change was no guarantee of equal treatment or recognition of their particular concerns. Women were certainly considered vital contributors to the movement and were actively sought out and recruited. But while their male peers were willing to treat them respectfully at a one-to-one level, they also "subtly demoted them to girlfriends, wives, note-takers, coffeemakers" and not so subtly pushed them aside during public political meetings or even jeered them with catcalls when they attempted to raise women's issues.[53] These tensions produced a sense of alienation among radical women that led in turn to the realization that policy changes to discriminatory laws would not in themselves alleviate the pervasive oppression they felt in both their public and private lives. As Sara Evans wrote in her history of the American women's movement: "As the public and private spheres interpenetrated, the inherited roles proved less and less adequate as sources of identity and self-esteem. Traditional definitions could not encompass, explain, or help women to cope with the new realities of their lives. Thus, only a movement that simultaneously challenged their roles in both the home and the outside workplace could have tapped the pain and anger of most women and moved them to action."[54]

The key element of this new women's movement was the formation of groups that provided opportunities to discuss "personal" issues that were seen as irrelevant to, and thus prohibited from, public and political discourse. But as women shared stories about rape, abortion, sexuality, socially prescribed roles, and female subordination, they began to understand their discontent and anger as fundamentally political. In Evan's view, this process was analogous to Marx's theory that, in order for a class to organize itself in the service of a future goal and act collectively on its own behalf, it must first become self-conscious of itself as a class.[55] As Evans described it, by substituting the agency of gender for that of class, these groups were able to use consciousness raising to transform the act of sharing personal experiences into a political instrument. Group members' rejection of old theories and reliance instead on their own experiences "evolved into a kind of phenomenological approach to women's liberation ... Thus consciousness-raising became both a method for developing theory and a strategy for building up the new movement."[56]

This group consciousness raising was important for several reasons. It helped dispel the illusion that women had achieved equality and, eventually, would lead women to question what equality might mean in a culture still defined by patriarchal values. It also helped women break out of the isolation that had kept them from recognizing their problems as collective ones, and as Rosi Braidotti has noted, it thus enabled women to become "valid and trustworthy interlocutors for other women" so that "the 'other' for a woman ceased to be necessarily the other sex."[57] Moreover, the process of group consciousness raising formed the theoretical basis of the crucial feminist concept that the personal is political. While this concept holds that personal experience matters, it does not mean that everything centres on the personal. On the contrary, it accords significance to that juncture where the personal and the political, the private and the public, the individual and the collective, the particular and the universal intersect and often clash. Although the separation of these categories is one of the defining characteristics of modernity, the feminist challenge of personal politics does not seek to collapse all distinctions between these categories but rather considers how each set of these categories has been ideologically constructed in relation to the other. By revealing the terms of such relationships, feminism aims to make visible the character and bases of women's subordination and thus to make way for the reconstruction of society's civil and political institutions. While this objective is motivated by the particular concerns of women, it is, along with other contemporary social movements, constitutive of what Johanna Meehan has described as "the universalistic demand for institutional change."[58]

The practical and theoretical models for political change established within the early women's movement would come to constitute the basis of the feminist art practices that began to emerge in the late 1960s. The politics of feminism enabled women not only to achieve unprecedented participation in the art world, but also to redefine the political in relation to art and thus to make art an agent of change in the larger world. In so doing, feminism brought a renewed relevance to the old question of art's relation to the praxis of everyday life. For those artists debating the question of autonomy versus social engagement around 1970, it is perhaps inevitable that – since intellectuals like Herbert Marcuse, Henri Lefebvre, and Louis Althusser would have been their key points of reference at the time – they saw autonomy as art's only viable position in the face of the overwhelming scale of the cultural, state, and bureaucratic systems of ideology described by these theorists.[59] The currency of such discourse at the time would also have helped women to understand how their own subordination had been produced and maintained by ideology rather than by force, but with the feminist shift of political focus from classes and masses to the personal as political, the possibility of a direct engagement between art and the politics of everyday life became much more immediate and therefore less daunting. The process by which this happened is the subject of the following chapter.

# 2

# The Origins of Feminist Art

## FEMINIST ART AND FEMINIST PERFORMANCE

The historical prejudices and prohibitions against the involvement of women as professional artists have been well documented by feminist art historians since the 1970s.[1] Although the old structural barriers had mostly fallen away by the twentieth century, incidents of blatant sexism existed well into the 1960s. In 1962, for instance, British sculptor Reg Butler could state in a public lecture: "I am quite sure that the vitality of many female students derives from frustrated maternity, and most of these, on finding the opportunity to settle down and produce children, will no longer experience the passionate discontent sufficient to drive them constantly towards the labours of creation in other ways. Can a woman become a vital creative artist without ceasing to be a woman except for the purposes of a census?"[2]

Even though such incidents became less commonplace during this decade, the hierarchy of sexual difference continued to be manifest in the guise of the Modernist aesthetics that dominated this period, especially through the writing of critics like Clement Greenberg and Michael Fried. Since Modernist judgments about art were ostensibly neutral and disinterested, they permitted the conclusion that if women artists were less successful than their male colleagues, this was evidence of their lesser competence as artists rather than of any prejudicial interests at work within the judgments themselves. Carefully obscured here was the fact that, far from being neutral, aesthetic judgments were invested in an ideological structure that positioned woman, as Griselda Pollock has argued, "as a negative term in opposition to which 'masculinity' established its dominance and exclusive synonymity with creativity."[3] In other words, while the lesser status accorded to women artists was ideological at root, any admission of this would risk exposing what Laura Cottingham has called the "masculine imperative" upon which aesthetic claims to disinterestedness actually relied.[4]

It was possible for a woman to achieve a modicum of success, provided she worked within the conventions established by men. As feminist writer Shulamith Firestone noted in 1970, "where individual women have participated in male culture, they have had to do so in male terms."[5] Indeed, artists like Eva Hesse, Agnes Martin, Jackie Winsor, and Dorothea Rockburne achieved considerable acclaim working within variations of abstraction and Minimalism. It was another matter, however, if a woman artist attempted to integrate her experiences as a woman into her work. One of the first women to bring attention to this situation was Carolee Schneemann, an artist who produced films and performances that celebrated the sensual and visceral energy of the body. Although she played an active role in the New York art scene in the mid-1960s, she expressed her anger and frustration at the refusal of her male friends, whom she called "the men's art team," to take her work seriously. She said that women were permitted to participate in the art world, but only so long as they did not "challenge and threaten the psychic territorial power lines by which women were admitted to the Art Stud Club, so long as they behaved *enough* like the men, [and] did work clearly in the traditions and pathways hacked out by the men."[6]

Schneemann's observations make it clear that if women were going to participate in art practice on their own terms, they were going to have to challenge aesthetic assumptions that art was neutral or disinterested. In short, as women artists became politicized by feminism, they had to reject the premise of autonomy that had prevailed not only in Modernist art and criticism, but also in Minimalist and Conceptual art. As Canadian art critic Monika Kin Gagnon observed, "to be a feminist producing art is to recognize that artistic production takes place within a social context; moreover, it is to recognize that artistic production will reflect a variety of gradually evolving shifts in strategy."[7] Beginning in the late 1960s, feminist artists took up the challenge of developing new artistic strategies that not only contested existing modes, but also opened up practices that had been previously nonexistent, marginalized, denigrated, or suppressed. Simply put, a new political praxis would need a new art praxis.

The form of practice that emerged at this time as most particularly associated with the burgeoning of feminism in the art world was performance. Numerous critics and scholars have addressed the question of why performance held such appeal for early feminist artists, but no singular and satisfactory answer has been proposed. It is often said that performance art's status as an innovative mode provided new spaces from which to speak and thus to challenge the dominant narratives and canonical values of current cultural practice. Performance artist Cheri Gaulke, for example, expressed the belief that "in performance we found an art form that was young, without the tradition of painting or sculpture."[8] This view continues to be reiterated even today. In a recent article on the history of feminist performance and video in Vancouver, Marina Roy wrote that – unlike painting, sculpture, film, and photography – video and performance "were so new that women felt they could truly make these media their own, without the historical baggage of male precedence."[9] While this observation is not exactly inaccurate, it is not sufficient to explain the complex historical relationship between feminism and performance art.

For one thing, performance art was not new in the 1960s and 1970s. Performance art actually has a long history, going back to the bohemian cabarets of the late nineteenth century and reappearing in various early-twentieth-century avant-garde movements, such as Futurism, German Expressionism, Dada, and Surrealism.[10] Performance never disappeared entirely, but not until the 1950s would it again be the focus of energetic activity. This renewed interest is usually attributed to the example of Jackson Pollock's drip paintings, or more specifically, to the photographic images of Pollock at work that were widely circulated in the early 1950s. These images appeared in Robert Goodnough's article "Pollock Paints a Picture," published in *Art News* in May 1951, and one month later, Hans Namuth's film, *Jackson Pollock*, which included scenes of Pollock painting, was screened at the Museum of Modern Art in New York.[11] The following year, art critic Harold Rosenberg published "The American Action Painters," also in *Art News*, in which he famously pronounced that "at a certain moment the canvas began to appear to one American painter after another as an arena in which to act ... what was to go on the canvas was not a picture but an event."[12] The impact of Pollock's example as a "performer" was made explicit six years later when the artist Allan Kaprow published "The Legacy of Jackson Pollock." Kaprow declared that Pollock had dealt a deathblow to painting as we know it and had "left us at the point where we must become preoccupied with and even dazzled by the space and objects of our everyday life."[13] Kaprow's response was to develop the performance practice called Happenings, which were based on expanding the gestural expressiveness of Pollock's painting to physical interactions with elements from the everyday world in order to bring art and life together in improvisational and participatory experiences. Pollock's example, and especially Kaprow's reading of it, would in turn be inspirational for a whole generation of artists who explored the possibilities of performance-based art practices in the 1960s.[14] Kaprow's ideas about the passage from painting to physical assemblages to spatial environments to performative Happenings, which was spelled out in his 1966 book, *Assemblages, Environments and Happenings*, was also highly influential for the realm of theatre.[15] As Richard Schechner has acknowledged, Kaprow's book was inspirational for his own ideas about experimental theatre in practice and theory, which have sought to expand the bounds of what theatre can be (ritual and healing as well as entertainment and education) and where it can happen (the street, park, and countryside as well as conventional theatre spaces) and to shift its disciplinary frame of reference from drama or theatre studies proper to "performance studies," which can encompass anthropology, environmentalism, psychology, semiotics, ethnography, and so on.[16]

As to the connection between Pollock's legacy and the question of why performance became so attractive to feminist artists, art historian Amelia Jones has offered some insightful suggestions in her book on body art. Jones proposes that the significance of what she calls the "Pollackian performative" is that it triggered "a profound philosophical shift [from a] modernist to a postmodernist conception of artistic subjectivity." This shift, which has its roots in French poststructuralist philosophy, posits the former as an (imagined) coherent and transcendent subject, and the latter as "a subject potentially dispersed, dislocated, and open to spectatorial engagement." In Jones's view, the images of Pollock at work were central to this transition because they made the artist's body visible. She argues that, in typical historical and critical texts on art, "the body of the artist, by definition (until recently) male, has been veiled: both central and hidden, both represented yet, on the surface of things, ignored."[17] This veiling of the artist's body served to uphold the Modernist pretext of neutrality and disinterest because unveiling the body would have meant revealing the (male) artist-genius not as universal and transcendent but as a subject particularized by gendered, raced, classed, and sexed identity. By making the body visible in the act of making the work of art, the "Pollackian performative" not only threw into doubt the supposed disinterestedness of the Modernist critical project, but also made it possible for the question of embodied subjectivity to become itself the basis for a newly politicized art practice by emergent feminist artists.

Jones's argument is compelling, but its usefulness for understanding the significance of performance to feminist art is limited, paradoxically, by her singular focus on the body. Undoubtedly, the body has always been one of the central elements of feminist performance, but the radical potential of performance cannot be confined to the manifestations of the body alone. As part of a political movement focused on historical change, feminist performance also offered critiques of representation that encompassed social codes and interactions not solely of or about the body. Moreover, the significance of narrative and text in feminist performance must not be underestimated, although it often is – perhaps because they are seen as mere supplements to performance as a *visual* arts practice. For feminists, however, the disruption of dominant narratives and the assertion of counter-paradigmatic narratives through storytelling of one kind or another was a powerfully politicized strategy of engagement. In fact, the use of narrative and autobiography has been so pervasive as to constitute one of the most definitive characteristics of feminist performance as a whole.

The conclusion that seems to emerge from the foregoing is that there can be no simple, monocausal explanation for why so many women were drawn to performance at a certain historical moment. Its lack of prescriptive confines was certainly a factor, as was its potential for making the body the site of a newly politicized understanding of subjectivity, but the broad appeal of performance for female *and* male artists also had to do with how it was positioned, along with other anti-object art forms, as a countervailing force against the market-driven, commodity-oriented ethos that dominated the art world in the 1960s.[18] Performance's broad appeal was also derived from its potential for the enactment of agency. Agency is the condition of being in action; that is, one who acts has agency, in contrast to one who is acted upon. As art historian Kristine Stiles defines it, performance is an "art of actions" in which both performer and viewer are acting subjects who exchange and negotiate meaning "in the real social condition of everyday life." Performance may thus instantiate the possibility for social and political change so that what is now the case may not be so in the future. For Stiles, "the extraordinary degree of interplay between action and politics which characterizes 'The Sixties'" was paralleled by artists' commitment to laying bare "the very real intersections already existing between aesthetics, activism, and culture."[19] Nevertheless, even though this commitment was an energizing force for much performance at this time, the extent to which it was made explicit rather than vaguely implied is debatable. As Robyn Brentano has argued:

> The relationship of avant-garde performance to the political realities of the 1960s is a complex issue ... While many artists were committed activists who participated in grass-roots activities, performances in the early sixties generally were focused on aesthetic innovation and lacked explicitly political content. There was a sense in the air that art would contribute to social change by changing consciousness and by operating outside the institutional confines of the art establishment where it could reach a non-art public.[20]

As women artists became politicized by feminism, however, the potential of performance as an "art of action" coincided with their growing sense of themselves as agents of social and political change. As an art form that features the living body, performance allowed women to place themselves, both literally and figuratively, at the very centre of their work and to assert themselves as the active and self-determining agents of their own narratives. By intersecting the personal with the performative, they were able to blur the distinctions between author and agent, subject and object. The tension and distancing this created between acting and lived experience allowed the performer to stand beside herself, as Rebecca Schneider has put it, and thus to "show the show" upon which rests the naturalizing imperatives and ideological constructs of sexual hierarchy.[21]

The pervasive use of effects to create this tension and distancing that we see in feminist performance recalls the theatre techniques of Bertolt Brecht. At the core of what Brecht called "epic theatre" was his famous concept of "alienation" (*Verfremdung*). This concept, which Brecht formulated in the 1920s by drawing from Hegelian philosophy, Marxian sociology, and the aesthetic theory of the Russian Formalist critics who flourished in the wake of the Russian Revolution, essentially held that, in order for audiences to become critically aware, they had to have their familiar understandings and expectations overturned through a process of defamiliarization or estrangement that would dialectically bring about a bewildered insight into their state of social alienation.[22] In contrast to the realist or naturalist styles of bourgeois theatre, where ideology is kept hidden, the objective of Brecht's epic theatre was to make ideology visible and thus to engage audiences in an active and self-aware process of ideology critique.

Although Brecht devised his techniques for creating "alienation effects" specifically for the theatre, they also had their parallels both in the montage cinema style developed in the 1920s by Russians Dziga Vertov and Sergei Eisentein as well as in the visual arts, where they followed a trajectory that went as far back as the invention of collage by the Cubists in 1912; intersected with the Russian Formalists in the work of Vladimir Mayakovsky, Kasimir Malevich, and other Russian avant-garde artists; resurfaced in the photomontage practices of the Dada and Surrealist movements; and survived, albeit in a form more aesthetic than political, in much post-Second World War art. In 1975 film theorist Laura Mulvey published a groundbreaking article, "Visual Pleasure and Narrative Cinema," in a special Brecht issue of the British film journal, *Screen*. Mulvey articulated both a psychoanalytic diagnosis of the spectatorial constructs of Hollywood-type cinema and a specifically feminist antidote for disrupting them by means of Brechtian alienation effects.[23] The implications of Mulvey's analysis of how women were positioned as fetishistic objects within the cinematic apparatus of the "male gaze" will be further discussed in chapter 6. Important to note here is that this article became the impetus for a discourse of feminist theory across a range of disciplines from cinema to art, theatre, and performance studies. Art historian Griselda Pollock, for example, published an important essay in 1988 in which she identified "Brechtian distanciation" as the key strategy of 1970s feminist art that worked to disrupt and reveal the ideological operations at work within the normative codes of representation.[24]

Feminist theorists and practitioners in theatre and performance studies also quickly grasped the critical potential of Brechtian concepts. But while their analyses have addressed the parallels between what Janelle Reinelt has called the "spectacularity of stage and screen," they have also focused on the specific conditions of female *bodies* in performance and on the possibilities for activating a critically engaged female spectator.[25] One of the first studies to map out a relationship between Brechtian and feminist theory in a theatre-specific context was published by Elin Diamond in 1988, the same year that Pollock's essay was published.

Like Pollock, Diamond not only drew upon Mulvey's analysis of the structures of representation and spectatorship, but also proposed ways in which Brechtian strategies for estrangement could disrupt ideology and bring about critical awareness. Particular to Diamond's analysis, however, was the focus she placed on the Brechtian concept of *gestus*, which she describes as "a gesture, a word, an action, a tableau by which, separately or in a series, the social attitudes encoded in the playtext become visible to the spectator."[26] Since the Brechtian actor achieves this *gestus* by demonstrating or "quoting" the character's behaviour rather than by impersonating or identifying with the character, this strategy has enormous potential for "alienating" gender in a manner that exposes its ideological constructs. As Diamond argues, because the Brechtian-feminist performer's body is thus *historicized* – that is, loaded with its own history and that of the character – she is not locked into the position of fetishistic objectification of her typical filmic counterpart as described by Mulvey. Rather, "this Brechtian-feminist body is paradoxically available for *both* analysis and identification, paradoxically within representation while refusing its fixity."[27]

This simultaneous yet paradoxical availability of the self-aware feminist performer also makes available the possibility of a self-aware feminist spectator. As theatre critic Jill Dolan argued in her 1988 book, *The Feminist Spectator as Critic*, the normative structures of spectatorship in cinema and theatre address the male spectator as an active subject while objectifying female performers and positioning female spectators as "passive, invisible, unspoken subjects."[28] Dolan identifies Brechtian alienation techniques as a way "to disrupt the narrative of gender ideology, to denaturalize gender as representation, and to demystify the workings of the genderized representational apparatus itself."[29] In this way, the Brechtian spectator, who is posited by Diamond, Dolan, Mulvey, Pollock, and others as a feminist spectator, is led "not to accept passively the representational conventions institutionalized before them, but to question the interactions and representations played out in the representational space."[30]

Brechtian theory became important for feminist performance studies in theatre because it provided a way to critique the traditional view of theatre, going back to Greek drama, as a mirror that reflects cultural and social organization. As Jill Dolan pointed out in an article first published in 1985, when theatre is assumed to be a mirror that reflects or imitates "real life," the polarized and hierarchical gender system it reflects is also presumed to be real. Echoing the conclusion that Griselda

Pollock and Rozsika Parker had come to in 1981 in *Old Mistresses*, Dolan asserted that representation was not a mirror at all but an ideological construct that mediates and re-presents the beliefs of those who create theatre, and she called upon feminists to investigate theatre's workings by treating it as a laboratory rather than as a showplace. In an epilogue added to this article in 1992 summarizing how feminist theatre criticism had emerged in the intervening years, Dolan cited Brechtian theory, especially as Diamond had developed it, as a particularly useful model for treating the stage as a laboratory.[31]

As Dolan also noted in her epilogue, her emphasis on performance rather than on dramatic literature and playtexts was still unique in feminist theatre criticism in 1992, a point Sue-Ellen Case concurred with in the Introduction to her 1990 anthology, *Performing Feminisms*.[32] The exception Dolan and Case both cited was Jeanie Forte's essay on performance art, which documented how performance that foregrounded the actual gender of the performer could raise critical issues about theatrical form and its social function.[33] This acknowledgement of Forte's essay was important not so much for her observations about specific performance art pieces, which did not really go beyond what Roselee Goldberg and Moira Roth had said, but rather for the way she identified the particular disruptive potential of performance art as stemming from the intersection of the body with the text: "The female body as subject clashes in dissonance with its patriarchal text, challenging the very fabric of representation by refusing that text and posing new, multiple texts grounded in real women's experience and sexuality."[34] Forte was not naively asserting that women's use of their own bodies in performance could simply turn them from objects into subjects but rather that their appropriation of authorial agency could create the kind of "dissonance with their representations" advocated by French feminists like Luce Irigaray and Hélène Cixous in their concept of "writing the body." In Forte's view, "Cixous's and Irigaray's strategies are much more vividly realized in the context of women's performance than in writing" because, if the body is itself "the 'text' by which identity is read, then women's performance art is always the positioning of a female body as subject in direct opposition to its patriarchal text."[35]

Notions such as the "presence" of subjectivity in performance and questions such as whether women's bodies in performance could ever completely avoid the threat of reappropriation within the dominant structures of representation have been much debated in theories of performance art. Nevertheless, as we will see, these writings by feminist theatre critics underscore the extent to which the signature use of their own bodies by feminist performance artists could offer a way to move beyond a sole reliance on text-based analysis. In Lynda Hart's view, this approach could be especially useful for repudiating the still pervasive assumptions that realist theatre was a reflective mirror or "mimesis" of reality. As Hart describes it, theatrical realism positions women as non-subjects in the "death-space" of absence, negativity, and unrepresentability. While cautioning that the desire to recuperate the feminine in performance has often led to the erroneous belief that the female body on stage can somehow be more immediate and free from the overdeterminations of realist or mimetic theatre, she proposes that feminist performance can at least offer a critical interrogation of "the body/text conflation of conventional mimesis" so as to achieve a "fluidity of movement simultaneously inside and outside dominant discourses."[36]

This body of discourse that developed in theatre studies does not answer the question of why feminist artists in the 1970s were drawn to performance any more precisely than do the other factors we have considered. What it does do, however, is underscore why feminist artists understood that the use of their own very real and material bodies could produce a powerfully subversive challenge to the presumed truth and authority of the culture's dominant texts – whether they were playtexts, representational "texts," or the ostensibly neutral and disinterested judgments embedded in the texts of contemporary art criticism. If in the end we cannot isolate any singular explanation for feminist artists' attraction to performance, we can perhaps more profitably argue at least that feminism and performance art became so inextricably linked because of the important contributions women were able to make to contemporary art practice through their involvement in performance. By making performance so conducive to their critical and political objectives, feminist artists were able to do what others had not – that is, to initiate a radically innovative practice that reengaged the aesthetic and the social after a long period of neo-Kantian autonomy and depoliticization.

## FEMINISM AND COMMUNITY

The feminist concept of the political as emerging from and merging with the personal was foundational to feminist art. The stress on the personal, however, is not to be confused with isolated individualism. On the contrary, in order for women to become politicized they had to combat the art world's mythologizing of the individualistic artist-genius. This meant that they had to become informed by what Rozsika Parker and Griselda Pollock described as "a political consciousness of the differential position of women in our society."[37] As elsewhere in the women's movement, this consciousness had to be developed in the context of groups and communities where the connection between the personal and the political could be empirically and theoretically understood. In the art world, however, such organizations did not begin to form until around 1969, with the Women Artists in Revolution in New York being one of the first. Although it was only with the formation of such groups and networks that an explicitly feminist art practice began to emerge around 1970, there is evidence of what we might call "proto-feminist" work being made in the mid-1960s in the context of the Greenwich Village cultural community in New York.

In her book on the Greenwich Village community, historian Sally Banes described it as a vibrant heterotopia that drew intellectuals and creative people from across the country to participate in its dynamic, alternative culture.[38] This utopian scene was quite open to the participation of women, and the venue that became its focal point, the Judson Memorial Baptist Church, has even become primarily associated with the cultural activities of women. The Judson Church is an active religious institution that wanted to make itself accessible to all members of its surrounding community. In the 1960s it housed an art gallery, hosted town-hall political meetings, ran an addicts' rehabilitation program, sponsored performance events, and was home to both the Judson Poets' Theatre and the Judson Dance Theatre. The dance theatre in particular flourished as an interdisciplinary meeting ground not only for dancers, choreographers, and musicians, but also – because of its policy of collaboration and openness – for visual artists, poets, and filmmakers. Begun in 1962 as a class recital for a group of choreographers who had taken a dance composition class with the musician Robert Dunn, who had studied with John Cage and taught at Merce Cunningham's dance studio, the Judson Dance Theatre functioned for two years as a cooperative based on weekly workshops. Its organizational model was uniquely collaborative and open to anyone who wanted to participate. The participation of nondancers was possible and desirable because the objective of the group was to strip dance of its theatrical stylizations and imbue it with the authenticity and immediacy of ordinary bodily actions.

The significance of the Judson Dance Theatre for the history of dance has been well documented elsewhere, but it was also important to the history of feminist performance in that it provided the first model in the history of the arts wherein women were the creative leaders.[39] Moreover, their principle of collaboration offered a counterpoint to the dominant mythology of the heroic individual genius, and their egalitarianism was an impetus to resist stereotypical expectations of gender roles. This egalitarianism was manifest in such works as *Word Words* (1963), a collaborative dance by Yvonne Rainer and Steve Paxton. Dressed in the minimal amount of clothing permitted by law (G-strings for both and pasties for Rainer), the dancers performed identical energetic movements that served as a refusal of sexual difference by stressing their androgynous similarity (fig. 2.1). It must be acknowledged, however, that as late as 1974 Rainer was ambivalent about the feminist implications that have been attributed to her choreography and insisted that her primary interests were "in a certain kind of sexually undifferentiated athleticism, in using the body as an object, just in terms of its weight and mass."[40] But even if Rainer's objectives and strategies were not explicitly feminist at the time, she and the other Judson women, including Simone Forti, Deborah Hay, Lucinda Childs, and Trisha Brown, became role models for succeeding generations of women artists in all fields because their formidable capabilities had enabled them, as Banes notes, to transform the field of dance "from a marginal, lower-status art form to a central arena – where all the arts met – for avant-garde expression of the early Sixties."[41]

The Judson spirit of egalitarianism was one example of how the gendered asymmetry that permeated the art world could be ameliorated. It could not, however, be easily eliminated. The first visual artist to address this asymmetry explicitly was Carolee Schneemann, who arrived in New York in 1961 and was soon drawn into the circles of artists associated both with Happenings and with Fluxus, a loosely formed, international group of artists influenced by John Cage's experimental music and the ideals of "democratizing" art by narrowing the gap between high art and everyday life. She also became involved in the Judson Dance Theatre, where she was able to experiment freely with her interest in the concreteness of materiality, both of objects and of bodies. Through her association with Judson, she became conscious of how gender was a determining factor not only of aesthetic interpretation and judgment, but also of social status within the art world. That is, the unequivocal acceptance and respect she received from the Judson group was in sharp contrast to the dismissive treatment she encountered elsewhere in the art world.

2.1 Yvonne Rainer in collaboration with Steve Paxton. *Word Words*, 1963. Photodocumentation of dance performance, 29 January, at Judson Memorial Church, New York. Photographs: Robert McElroy (top), Henry Genn (below).

The first work in which Schneemann exhibited her growing sense of gendered consciousness was an installation/performance done in her loft in December 1963 called *Eye Body: 36 Transformative Actions* (fig. 2.2). The setting consisted of large, expressively painted panels, broken glass and mirrors, plastic sheeting, photographs, and motorized umbrellas. Schneemann herself entered this chaotic and kinetic mélange, allowing snakes to writhe over her greased and painted body in symbolic reference to the sexual power she associated with ancient Goddess-worshiping cultures.[42] Notwithstanding its somewhat romantic, neoprimitive aspirations, Schneemann's *Eye Body* has rightly been recognized as a bold and courageous attempt to displace women's customary role in art as muse or model by instating herself as the active agent of her own imaginings and representations.[43] By doubling herself both as object and subject, image and image maker, Schneemann sabotaged the predictable expectations of even the most adventurous art practice of the day. Not that she received much credit for her efforts, however. In an era when the French Nouveau Réaliste artist Yves Klein could rise to international fame by using women as "living paint brushes" (so that he could "stay clean") in his *Anthropométries* (1958–60) and Ben Patterson could cover a "shapely female" with whipped cream and have her licked clean by men in a Fluxus performance called *Lick Piece* (1963), Schneemann was rewarded by being kicked out of Fluxus because her work was too "messy."[44]

Schneemann's *Eye Body* alludes to the concerns with visuality, representation, and embodied subjectivity that would be fully explored by feminists in the 1970s, but it is important not to overstate her work as prophetically in advance of its own historical locatedness, as Rebecca Schneider seems to do in writing that it "generated a turning point, a politicizing point, a feminist turn in her work."[45] The trouble with this claim is that it implies not just that Schneemann was cognizant of sexual discrimination, but also that she had begun to formulate a socially and politically conceptualized mode of response. The beginning of that kind of response was possible in 1963, as the publication of Betty Friedan's *Feminine Mystique* demonstrates, but there is little to suggest that *Eye Body* was much more than an individualistic assertion of self-worth.[46] For one thing, Schneemann herself has acknowledged the limitations of her understanding at that time, saying "I knew I was onto something, but I didn't know what exactly – I just knew this was really significant."[47] For another, if *Eye Body* really did signal a politicized, feminist turning point for Schneemann, then this is all the more difficult to reconcile with her involvement the following year in a performance by Robert Morris called *Site*, especially if account is taken of Schneemann's performance called *Meat Joy*, which was produced in the intervening period.

*Meat Joy*, which was performed in Paris and London in May 1964, and again in November at the Judson Memorial Church, was characteristic of the egalitarian ethos fostered by the Judson community (fig. 2.3). It was also an example of the early 1960s' fascination with a shameless glorification of sensory, gustatory, and erotic transgression, which was particularly evident in the campy experimental films of those years: Andy Warhol's *Kiss*, *Eat* and his notorious *Blow Job*; Jack Smith's *Blonde Cobra* and *Flaming Creatures*; Barbara Rubin's *Christmas on Earth*; and Jean Genet's *Un Chant d'Amour*.[48] *Meat Joy* began with the audience entering the darkened room while Schneemann recited her notes for the performance as well as slightly pornographic descriptions of dream images and fantasies.[49] Her voice was mingled with multiple soundtracks of rock and roll music, Parisian street traffic and market vendors, and French vocabulary lessons referring to body parts, odours, and human and animal characteristics. Then a group of male and female performers entered the space, undressed one

2.2 Carolee Schneemann. *Eye Body: 36 Transformative Actions*, 1963. Action for camera. Photograph: Erro.

2.3 Carolee Schneemann. *Meat Joy*, 1964. Photodocumentation of performance with raw fish, chickens, sausages, wet paint, plastic rope, and paper scrap. Photograph: Al Giese.

another, wrapped each other in paper and rolled around on the floor smearing themselves with paint. As the tempo increased, they introduced raw fish, chickens, and sausages and generally cavorted in a total immersion of primitive bodily sensations that defied all sense of propriety and public decorum. Jill Johnston, a critic for the *Village Voice*, wrote perceptively: "The fish in 'Meat Joy' could symbolize the watery matrix of our origins. It doesn't matter. The point of the meat and fish and paint was to demonstrate the sensual and scatological pleasure of slimy contact with materials that the culture consumes at a safe distance with knife and fork and several yards away in a gallery or a museum."[50]

In Banes's view, *Meat Joy* was "the apotheosis of libidinal plenitude" within what had become a well-established genre of scornfully anti-bourgeois films and Happenings at the time.[51] But it is also possible to discern an incipient feminism at work here. For one thing, the fact that

Schneemann undertook such a work must be read as a bold intervention in gendered power relations. As Michel Foucault has shown in his studies of social institutions, the body, especially the female body, has been systematically regulated and disciplined by strict codes.[52] In order to transgress these controlling regimes, either one must already possess power or one must appropriate power.[53] For male artists like Warhol and Smith, who dominated this genre of transgressive libertinism, the possession of that power was a given. But for a woman to author a sexualized work, especially one of such libidinous abandon, constituted a disruptive usurping of power. Furthermore, *Meat Joy* also accorded the manifestation of female sexuality a far greater degree of self-determination and openness than did other works in this genre. The women who participated in *Meat Joy* were not constrained by stereotypical conventions of female sexuality as either passive objects of the male gaze or as sexually voracious predators. On the contrary, they were as active, exuberant, and self-fulfilling as the male participants. Male and female did not act upon one another but were joined together along with their audience, who witnessed their erotic pleasures at such close proximity that the performers sometimes rolled into them in what Banes called an optimistic spirit of community.[54]

In contrast to the sensual abandon and communitarian spirit of *Meat Joy*, Morris's *Site*, which was performed at the Surplus Theatre in New York in 1964, was a rigorously disciplined and artist-centred performance (fig. 2.4). *Site* was devised by Morris during the period when he was closely involved with the Judson Dance Theatre both by making props and by participating in their dances, which bore many structural similarities to his own Minimalist aesthetics and enabled him to explore the "situational" nature of his sculpture in a temporal context.[55] *Site* contained many of the hallmarks of Minimalism, such as an emphasis on structure and form as well as a cool inexpressiveness. Its centrepiece was a reclining odalisque played by Schneemann as a virtual recreation of Manet's *Olympia*, although, as Schneider has noted, Olympia's black servant has been completely erased.[56] Wearing a mask and work gloves, Morris manipulated large panels of plywood so as to "frame" the Olympia tableau and make explicit the constructed nature of art. As Maurice Berger reads *Site*, its intent was also to drive "the formal problems of process into the ideological realm of labor and production" by making an analogy between the labour of workers (prostitutes and manual labourers) and that of artists.[57] Other historians, however, have remarked on the unmistakable gender-role

2.4 Robert Morris. *Site*, 1964. Photodocumentation of performance with Carolee Schneemann at Surplus Theatre, 5-7 May, New York. Photograph: ©Hans Namuth Ltd.

determinations of *Site*, whereby Schneemann's/Olympia's feminine role as the passive object of sexual desire – as both sight and site of the male gaze – is confirmed, while Morris aggressively asserted his own active, and therefore safely masculine, role as an artist.[58]

Given how Schneemann had already foregrounded her own artistic agency and embodied sexuality in *Eye Body* and had celebrated gendered egalitarianism in *Meat Joy*, it is difficult to understand why she allowed herself to be so passively objectified in Morris's piece. The fact that Schneemann does not discuss *Site* in her autobiographical book, *More than Meat Joy*, suggests that she subsequently disavowed her involvement in it. She did include a small photograph of it, but beside this she wrote: "My own private ... and ironical title was 'Cunt Mascot.' Cunt Mascot on the men's art team. Not that I ever made love with ANY OF YOU NO! I didn't feel perceived by our group – not even sexually."[59] As historian Henry Sayre has suggested, "One is forced to accept this as her gloss on the performance itself," which nevertheless seems to have catalyzed her process of discovering "the seeming imperturbability of the masculine position, a certain obdurate blindness born of power."[60] So if Schneemann originally participated in *Site* in the spirit of mutual cooperation that characterized the Judson milieu, it would seem that later, as her feminist consciousness deepened, she realized the extent to which it reinforced the gender hierarchy she had already begun to strive against with *Eye Body* and *Meat Joy*.

By the mid-1970s, Schneemann's view of her male peers as a repressive force that sought to stifle and demean her creative energies as a woman and as an artist was made abundantly clear in *Interior Scroll*, which she first performed at the "Women Here and Now" conference in East Hampton, New York, in 1975. After undressing and painting her body with broad strokes, Schneemann read from a long paper scroll extracted from her vagina (fig. 2.5). The text, which had been written for her film *Kitsch's Last Meal* (1973–77), described her meeting with "a happy man, a structuralist filmmaker" who disparaged "the personal clutter, the persistence of feelings, the hand-touch sensibility, the diaristic indulgence, the painterly mess" of her films. Discounting her as a filmmaker, he went on to say, "we think of you as a dancer."[61] As Schneemann read from this text pulled from her most intimate bodily cavity, the audience could not have mistaken the irony of word and image. The deliberate grotesqueness of her display defiantly asserted the corporeal reality of her body as a challenge to the objectifying gaze of the "happy man." As such, it enacted what Vivian Patraka has defined as "binary terror" – the terror unleashed when binary social or cultural categories are collapsed.[62] As Rebecca Schneider has interpreted Schneemann's work, this collapse is enacted by presenting the naked female body not only as the *object* of the work (as is usual in the established conventions of art), but also as the active creative *agency* of the work. Schneemann's display of her own body thus exposes the contradiction inherent in a culture that aligns creative agency with the male principle in opposition to the passivity of the female. As Schneider notes, what makes Schneemann's work so significant is that she does not simply access artistic creativity by making her gender invisible, which would leave unchallenged the pretext of artistic creativity as gender blind or neutral, but rather that she "inexorably entangles in a very 'messy' embrace" her presence both as explicit female body and as artistic agent.[63]

To be sure, Schneemann's defiant display in *Interior Scroll* came from a later period when feminist political consciousness had permeated the art world more thoroughly, but it is clear that the rudiments of such consciousness can be traced to the New York milieu of the mid-1960s. The Judson community, as an avant-garde group dominated by creative women, was certainly a major factor. So too was the presence of Fluxus, which attracted a considerable number of women artists, including Alison Knowles, Charlotte Moorman, Mieko (Chieko) Shiomi, Shigeko Kubota, and Yoko Ono. But although historian Kristine Stiles has claimed that "questions of gender and sexuality figure prominently in Fluxus actions," such questions were rarely posed in a way that addressed gender relations from an explicitly political perspective.[64] Yoko Ono's *Cut Piece* and Shigeko Kubota's *Vagina Painting* constitute two important exceptions.

Ono's *Cut Piece* was performed in Kyoto (1964), in New York (1965), and in London (1966) as part of the "Destruction in Art Symposium." In each case, Ono knelt alone on the stage and, placing a pair of scissors before her, invited the audience to cut off her clothing (fig. 2.6). Although audience members' reactions at each venue varied in the reserve or abandon with which they cut off her clothing, the implications of the piece always invoked tensions between exhibitionism and voyeurism, victim and assailant, sadist and masochist, subject and object.[65] While the spectacle of bodily abjection and debasement was a persistent current in Fluxus works, several of which involved the objectification of women at the hands of or in collaboration with men, such as Ben Patterson's aforementioned *Lick Piece*, Robert Watts's *Branded Woman's Thigh* (1962), and Nam June Paik's *Opera Sextronique* (1966), Ono's *Cut Piece* problematized such associations in prophetic, unique ways.[66] For one thing, as Thomas Crow has observed, its enactment of "women's physical vulnerability as mediated by the regimes of vision" heralded the emergence of modern feminist activism.[67] For another, the assumption of such a pose of female submission and obedience by a Japanese woman also revealed the extent to which gendered relations of power and subordination were inscribed within specific social, cultural, and historical conditions.

Whereas Ono's *Cut Piece* can be seen as passive-aggressive, Kubota's *Vagina Painting* was openly aggressive toward the gendered presumptions of artistic creativity still dominant in the art world at the time. Performed at the Perpetual Fluxfest in New York in 1965, *Vagina Painting* had Kubota squatting over a large sheet of paper and making drippy, gestural marks in blood-red paint with a brush attached to her underpants. The reference to Pollock's Abstract Expressionism was as unmistakable as the reference to female anatomy and biological functions. The result was a resounding clash between these two points of connection. In this way, *Vagina Painting* can be seen to demonstrate a prescient understanding of the conditions Amelia Jones would later

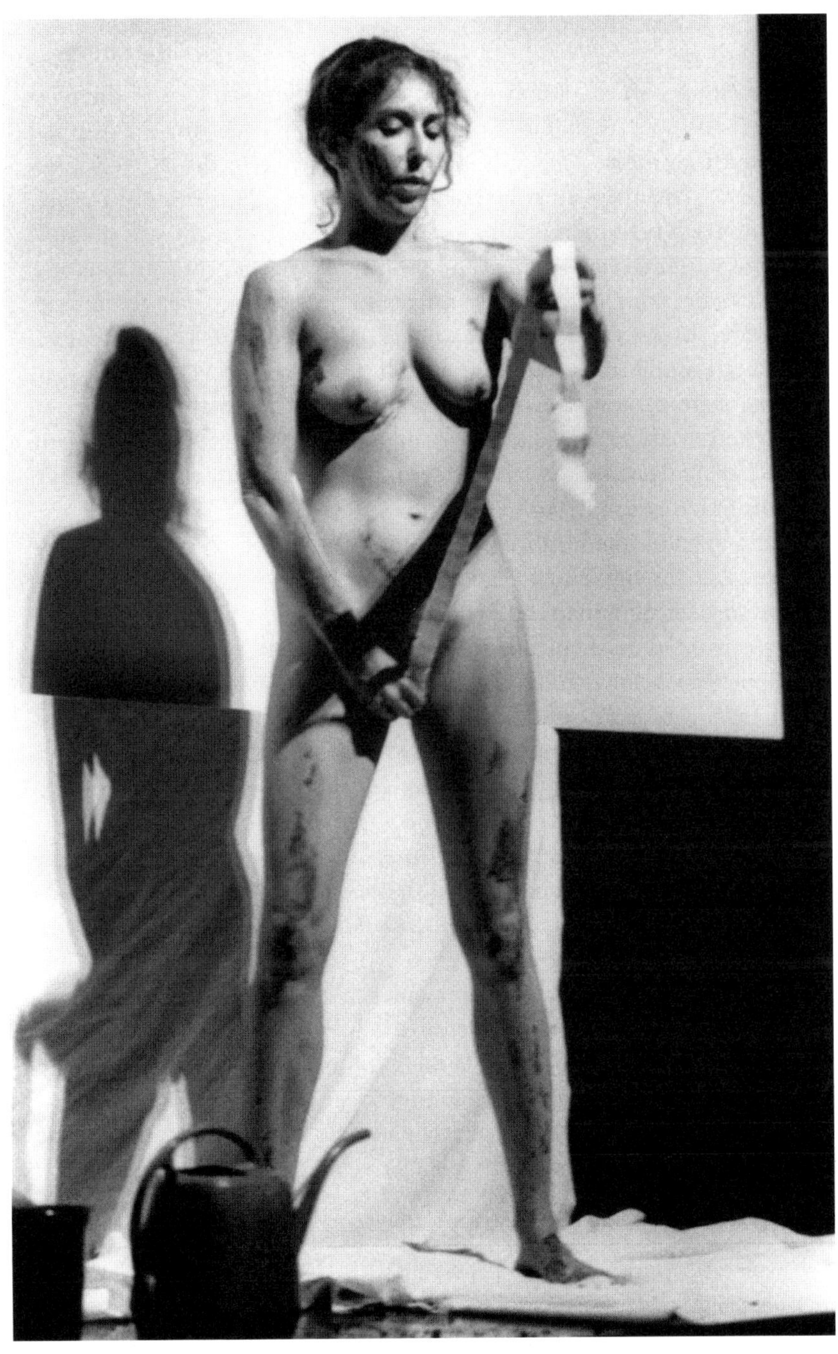

2.5 Carolee Schneemann. *Interior Scroll*, 1975. Photodocumentation of performance at the "Women Here and Now" conference, East Hampton, New York. Photograph: Sally Dixon.

elaborate upon theoretically in relation to the implications of the photographs of Pollock painting. As Jones put it, in order for the Kantian pretext of aesthetic neutrality and transcendence to do its work successfully, "The artist must be embodied as male in order to be considered an artist – placed within a (patri)lineage as originary and divinely inspired – but his embodiment (his particularity as a gendered and otherwise vulnerable, immanent subject) must be hidden to ensure his transcendence as disembodied and divinely inspired."[68] Kubota's *Vagina Painting* literally exposed what had been concealed within this gendered construct of artistic creativity. In doing so, it enabled Kubota to assert herself as both the agent of bodily display and the agent of artistic creativity in a gesture of "binary terrorism" as flamboyant and uncompromising as Schneemann's.

Although Ono and Kubota were more readily accepted in their artistic group than Schneemann perceived herself to be, these particular works were not deemed acceptable within what was an otherwise democratically open and aesthetically experimental collective. Stiles documents that Ono felt her work to have been rejected because it was "too animalistic," while Kubota recalled that her Fluxus colleagues hated *Vagina Painting*.[69] Both artists seem to have encountered the same situation that led Schneemann to complain that women were permitted to participate in the art world so long as they did not challenge the status quo or deviate from "the traditions and pathways hacked out by the men."[70] It would seem that, on the one hand, the egalitarian ethos of the Judson and Fluxus communities offered unprecedented opportunities for the participation of women artists, and this in turn led some women to express their frustration with the sexual hierarchies and prejudices still deeply entrenched in the art world. On the other hand, it was clear that, once women began to explore strategies for politicizing art along lines of gender (and sometimes race), they faced strong resistance from their male peers even in these most liberal and supportive mixed communities.

## ACTIVISM AND PEDAGOGY

As Rebecca Schneider has observed, the achievements of women artists over the following three decades did not come from knocking politely on the closed doors of the art world's institutions but from creating an "insistent scene of their own."[71] This process had two main trajectories.

2.6 Yoko Ono. *Cut Piece*, 1965.
Photodocumentation of performance
at Carnegie Recital Hall, 21 March, New York.
Photograph: Minoru Niizuma.

One was the formation of activist groups, while the other was the formation of the kind of feminist art community created by Judy Chicago and her cohort in southern California in the early 1970s, which will be discussed below. Important early examples of activist groups include the Women Artists in Revolution, which was affiliated with the Art Workers' Coalition, and the Ad Hoc Women Artists' Committee, which originated in October 1970 to contest the poor representation of women at the Whitney Museum's Annual Exhibition of American Art. Along with the Los Angeles Council of Women Artists and the West-East Bag, these groups provided support and advocacy for women artists, gathered statistics, and provided a liaison network for sharing information on actions, legal manoeuvres, methodology, and techniques.[72] In 1972 the women artists' cooperative Artists-in-Residence (AIR) was founded in New York to provide exhibition space as well as a venue for lectures and other public events.

In Canada women's art organizations tended to be focused less on political activism and more on the support and development of women artists and their art. Montreal's Galerie Powerhouse was founded in 1973 as the first gallery in Canada devoted to women's art and in many ways formed the Canadian counterpart to AIR. In addition to having two exhibition spaces, Powerhouse also served as a community centre and sponsored lecture series and workshops. Among its many projects was *Artfemme 1975*, a massive exhibition of women artists, which was coorganized with the Saidye Bronfman Centre and the Musée d'art contemporain de Montréal.[73] As Nell Tenhaaf has written in her recollection of the early days at Powerhouse, there was considerable tension over the question of whether their main objective was to show art made by women or to show art that was specifically feminist and critical in its outlook. Tenhaaf explains that these tensions were further complicated by the fact that Powerhouse had its roots in the anglophone community, which aligned itself with the North American feminist movement as a whole yet was surrounded by a francophone majority culture that was engaged at the time with its own complex identity issues.[74]

By the late 1970s, the Quebec francophone feminist community was beginning to organize its own networks, collectives, and events. One of the most important of these was the Théâtre expérimental des femmes, founded in 1979 by Pol Pelletier, Nicole Lecavalier, and Louise Laprade. Although their work was more in the realm of theatre than in the realm of performance art per se, its highly experimental nature and its focus on social issues and critiques of patriarchy provided a prominent feminist model in Quebec throughout the 1980s. The early 1980s were particularly significant for feminist art and culture in Quebec. In 1981 Silvy Panet-Raymond and Dena Davida cofounded the dance company Tangente, which played a major role in catalyzing the contemporary – and now highly influential – dance scene in Montreal. In 1982 the exhibition *Art et féminisme* was held at the Musée d'art contemporain de Montréal and was accompanied by a catalogue in which historian Rose-Marie Arbour outlined the relation of Quebec women artists to North American feminism in general.[75] That same year, performance artist Diane-Jocelyne Côté organized *Réseau art-femme*, a series of performance events and exhibitions that took place in four locations around the province, each one with a different title and theme.[76]

Elsewhere in Canada organizations for women artists and filmmakers also emerged during these years. In Vancouver, the emphasis was on video and film production, with organizations like Reelfeelings (1973), Women in Focus (1974), the Vancouver Women's Media Collective (1978), and Amelia Productions (1980) supporting both creative and documentary practices.[77] In 1972 a collective of filmmakers in Toronto, including Kay Armatage, Sylvia Spring, and Deanne Taylor, began planning for a festival of film, video, and photography by women and soon had a national organizing committee of 200 women. In 1973 the resulting Women and Film (1896–1973) International Festival began touring throughout nineteen Canadian cities.[78] These kinds of groups were crucial to the formation of an expanding feminist community of professional women artists. Their goal, which was to integrate women into the art world by contesting and reforming its existing structure, has been successful to a significant degree, although the Guerrilla Girls, with their disruptive actions and posters exposing sexism and racism in the art world, have made it their business to keep reminding us of its limits.[79]

Although such early activism played a crucial role in creating a feminist scene, the approach envisioned by the artist Judy Chicago in 1970 was far more radical. Chicago, who had an established reputation in Los Angeles as a formalist painter, had already begun to invest her work with feminist concerns by 1969. That year she exhibited a series of paintings called *Pasadena Lifesavers*, in which the colours and centralized forms were intended to express symbolically both her masculine and feminine aspects. She also included a statement on the gallery wall that read: "Judy Gerowitz hereby divests herself of all names imposed upon her through male social dominance and freely chooses her own name Judy Chicago."[80] As Chicago later explained further, "I wanted to make a symbolic statement about my emerging position as a feminist. And I wanted to force viewers to see the work in relation to the fact that it was made by a woman artist."[81] Her premise came from the conflict she perceived between the fact that she was treated as a "woman" every time she stepped out her door, yet the art world could see her only as a "person" whose art had to be "neutral" in order to be acceptable. Critical of the limitations of the existing art community, Chicago declared that she "would have to commit [her]self to developing an alternative and that the meaning of the women's movement was that there was, probably for the first time in history, a chance to do just that. If my needs, values, and interests differed from male artists' who were invested in the values of the culture, then it was up to me to help develop a community that was relevant to me and other women artists."[82]

When Chicago was invited to teach at Fresno State College in California in the fall of 1970, she saw the opportunity to establish such a community. She immediately organized a class for female students only and devised a program that was the first of its kind. Realizing that many young women entered art school but few went on to professional practice, she wanted to create an environment that would encourage them in their commitment to become artists. Chicago chose fifteen strongly motivated but essentially untrained women to participate, including Suzanne Lacy, Janice Lester, Nancy Youdelman, and Faith Wilding.[83] This decision to value commitment over aesthetic prowess indicates how far Chicago felt women had to veer from the norm in order to create their own community. It also marks a conspicuous contrast to the prevailing outlook expressed by those artists who had responded to "The Artist and Politics" symposium published in *Artforum* the very month that Chicago began her course.[84] Whereas those artists generally agreed that aesthetics were inevitably compromised by political engagement or activism, Chicago created an environment wherein political commitments came first and aesthetic values were framed within a struggle for liberation.

From the outset, the Fresno program was much more closely aligned with the women's movement than with mainstream art education. Not only had it formed a community in which women artists could "start from scratch, relying on [their] own experience," but Chicago had also initiated what she called "a kind of modified consciousness-raising."[85] In this secure and permissive environment, the women began to talk about things that were never discussed in other art classes: sexuality, family and personal relationships, fear of violence and harassment, anxieties and desires of the most intimate kind. After an initial period of discussions, Chicago got them to channel these experiences into art making. Although there were no restrictions or guidelines as to media, the students spontaneously gravitated toward a role-playing approach.[86] As Chicago later explained: "One of the most important discoveries of the year was that informal performance provided the women with a way of reaching subject matter for art-making. The most powerful work of the first year of the program was the performances."[87]

At the end of the year, the students presented some of their performances as part of their studio exhibition. References to violence and rape were frequent, as were sexual fantasies. One performance, *Rivalry Play*, dealt with how women, unable to confront their "real oppressor," turn their "self-hatred" against each other. Another had a woman led onstage by a butcher (played by one of the students), who tied her to a milking machine that squirted blood into a pitcher while images and sounds of a slaughterhouse were played; the butcher then returned and poured the blood over her body. Chicago's graduate assistant, Vicki Hall, performed *Ominous Operation* in a setting with an operating table hung with gauze and lit by soft, pink lights. Dressed as a surgeon, but with an elaborate headdress of horns and twinkling lights, Hall and her satyr-costumed assistant performed a mock operation that transformed a woman into a hermaphrodite with a latex phallus.

These performances were crude but cathartic. As Chicago said in a later interview with historian Moira Roth, "performance can be fueled by rage in a way that painting and sculpture can't." By permitting the Fresno women to express previously unarticulated feelings, their performances helped them to move beyond the isolation of individual experience and to begin to recognize their oppression as a cultural group. Faith Wilding recalled: "Most people worked in Performance. None of us had done this before and we weren't aware of the tradition of Performances and Happenings. I didn't connect these Performances with art-making at all, but it was tremendously releasing. It was part psychodrama and part tapping in the dark. But it was always rooted in Feminism." For these women, performance provided a way to articulate and focus their anger into a formation of political consciousness. As Vicki Hall said, "I became a Feminist through my art. My art showed me my Feminism, which I experienced on a conscious level."[88]

After one year at Fresno, Miriam Schapiro invited Chicago to move the program to the newly formed California Institute of the Arts in Valencia (CalArts). Here the focus of their activities was the Womanhouse project, in which they created a series of installations in a derelict mansion in residential Hollywood and opened it to the public during February 1972.[89] The major theme of Womanhouse was the oppression of domesticity, which had been a key point of consternation for feminists ever since Betty Friedan published *The Feminine Mystique* in 1963. Middle-class women in this period were relatively highly educated but were discouraged from pursuing meaningful careers or participating in public life. Domestic life failed to meet their rising expectations of fulfilment, yet in a culture that provided no support for real alternatives, women continued to cling to, and judge themselves by, traditional values. Accordingly, the Womanhouse environments evoked ambivalent feelings about the conflation of domesticity and femininity. In the *Bridal Staircase*, a bedecked bride ascended to a grey and obscure future. The *Nurturant Kitchen* was entirely painted in a fleshy pink colour and covered floor to ceiling in latex breast forms. The *Menstruation Bathroom* spilled over with "feminine hygiene" paraphernalia, while in the *Nightmare Bathroom* a female figure sank into a plaster-filled tub. In *Leah's Room*, a woman sat daily applying makeup in a futile effort to stave off "the pain of aging, of losing beauty, pain of competition with other women."[90]

A series of performances by students in Chicago's Performance Workshop was also held at Womanhouse. As with the environments, the themes ranged from domestic entrapment to aspects of female sexuality. Sandra Orgel's *Ironing* and Chris Rush's *Scrubbing* drew attention to the mundane and repetitive tasks of domestic labour. In *Waiting*, Faith Wilding invoked the paralysis brought on by the social demands for female passivity (fig. 2.7). In *Birth Trilogy*, one group of women symbolically rebirthed another group into a community of women. The darker aspects of female experience were brought out in Chicago's satirical farce called *Cock and Cunt Play*. Wearing ludicrously exaggerated latex genitalia, two women played a couple whose dispute over domestic chores escalates into a violent conflict in which "Cock" accuses "Cunt" of castrating him and then beats her to death (fig. 2.8).[91] Many of these and other performances came out of the workshop's sessions on violence, brutality, entrapment, and rape, where students worked through personal experiences of abuse and assault. As Josephine Withers has noted, at the time it was a painful experience for women "to name their fears and feelings of helplessness and rage," especially in the risky arena of public performance.[92] It was this determination to take the dissolution of the boundaries of art and life beyond mere aesthetic device or conceit and transform it into a political strategy that gave these performances their visceral power.

This political determination was what distinguished the Feminist Art Program's approach to performance. Performance was taught in other courses at CalArts, and many West Coast artists were involved in performance at this time, ranging from the conceptualized body art of Bruce Nauman, John Baldessari, Terry Fox, and others to the shocking rituals of risk and violence presented by artists like Chris Burden and Paul McCarthy.[93] Although the Feminist Art Program's students' preoccupation with the conflation of art and life was shared with other performance artists of the period, important differences can be discerned in their approaches and goals. As Robyn Brentano has pointed out, whereas the desire to break down the boundaries between art and life was typically expressed in most performance works in ways that "were emblematic in nature and only rarely incorporated intensely personal material in a way that revealed the private life of the performer ... with the emergence of feminist performance, a shift occurred in which artists began to present themselves as the subject matter of their art, further eroding or problematizing the art/life dichotomy."[94]

Brentano has identified the tendency in feminist performance to draw upon and enact experiences from the artists' own lives. The women in the Feminist Art Program used performance not merely as an aesthetic

2.7 Faith Wilding. *Waiting*, 1972. Photodocumentation of performance at Womanhouse, Los Angeles, 1972. Photograph: Lloyd Hamrol.

2.8 Judy Chicago. *Cock and Cunt Play*, 1972. Photodocumentation of performance at Womanhouse, Los Angeles, 1972. Written by Judy Chicago; performed at Womanhouse by Faith Wilding and Janice Lester. Photograph: Through the Flower Archives.

end result, but also as a cathartic means to deal with traumatic experiences and to challenge the conventional roles imposed upon them. The difference in their approach was clearly demonstrated in a heated exchange that took place between Faith Wilding and Allan Kaprow, who was then teaching at CalArts. Commensurate with his idea that all ordinary things could become the material for art, he suggested to the students that even sweeping the floor could be a performance activity. At that point "Wilding jumped up to protest that half the population in the country was oppressed by household tasks and accused Kaprow of totally ignoring the feelings and history associated with such activities."[95] In contrast to Kaprow, Wilding and her colleagues saw the merging of art and life in performance not as a way to expand the aesthetic terrain of art but as a way to transform art into a tool with the potential to change life itself. The basis for Wilding's response came directly from the feminist premise that the personal is political. As Suzanne Lacy succinctly put it: "In the early days of the feminist art movement, when we were talking about the personal is political, we were saying everything that we do – from how we put our socks on to how we wash the dishes and why *are* we washing the dishes? – should be seen as political, in other words, given political importance because lived experience is the ground from which all politics come."[96]

This premise would become one of feminism's most effective strategies for negotiating a new relationship within culture. It enabled women to form an "insistent scene of their own" and provided the grounds for exploring personal experience as legitimate subject matter for art. This "scene" was crucial to building the coalitional politics that would enable feminist artists to take on the power structures both in the art world and in the larger world as a whole and thus to contribute to the struggles that would transform the political landscape of the late twentieth century.

# 3

# Cultural Feminism: The Essence of Difference

## DIFFERENCE AND ESSENCE

The feminist communities that developed in the late 1960s and early 1970s operated on the premise that once women started talking to one another about their personal experiences, they would realize the extent to which their concerns were shared by others and thus establish the basis for a politics of coalition.[1] These coalitional politics were defined by three foundational principles: that although their personal experiences may vary, all women share the experience of being subjugated as a group within patriarchy; that this subjugated status has caused women to experience their relation to society as different from that of men; and that women have never been able to participate in culture and society on their own terms. These principles led to the conclusion that women are oppressed as a group because they are women – that is, because they are unified by their sex/gender regardless of their race, class, or culture. This oppression diminishes the status of women within society, and their lack of power forces them to assume identities and roles over which they have little or no control. If the shackles of male dominance could be thrown off, women's true identity would be revealed through the discovery of a mutually comprehensible "female sensibility." Because this sensibility was seen as the common thread that linked all women, it was regarded as innate or essential to the category "woman." Moreover, the fact that women's identity and experiences were seen as fundamentally distinct from men's led early feminists to articulate a politics in which the meaning of difference itself became a ground for political struggle.

Since these early days, feminism has been profoundly vexed by the terms "essentialism" and "difference."[2] The term "essentialism," which is now often purported to subsume all feminist thought and practice from the 1970s, has acquired a particularly derogatory meaning, as will be discussed in more detail below. It is important, however, not to allow the negative associations that have accrued around the concept of essentialism to occlude a more nuanced understanding of its role within the theoretical and practical achievements of early feminism. As Sue Thornham notes, feminism's initial project tied theoretical analysis of oppression to a modern narrative of emancipation through social transformation. But, in order to achieve these goals, it was not possible to include women simply by expanding the bases of knowledge and intellectual discourse that had dominated Western thought, "for women's exclusion was not an accidental omission but a fundamental structuring principle of all patriarchal discourses." And even if women could be included in these discourses, "it could be in terms only of sameness not difference, that is, within frameworks which could discuss women only in terms of a common, male-referenced humanity ... not specifically as women."[3] In other words, if women, as they had been historically defined, had no identity or subjectivity of their own, they could not become the subjects of their own social emancipation. Recognizing this to be the case, early feminists sought to achieve the strength in numbers necessary to effect political change by focusing their attention both on identifying what made women distinctive as a social entity and on encouraging women as a class or group to share this identification.

The first step for early feminism, therefore, was to contest women's historical determination within patriarchy as nonsubjects. The key theoretical model for such thinking was Simone de Beauvoir's *The Second Sex*, first published in 1949. In this brilliant and original transposition of the ontological and ethical claims of existentialism to account for women's oppression, de Beauvoir argued that gender was a category of identity acquired by human beings as a result of the need to assert one's subjectivity by describing and prescribing roles to which the other must conform. One becomes a man by having access to the privilege and power of being able to determine one's subjectivity and role (transcendence), and one becomes a woman by relinquishing subjectivity and accepting determined roles (immanence). Observing that man has named himself the self and woman the other, de Beauvoir stated emphatically: "One is not born, but rather becomes, a woman. No biological, psychological, or economic fate determines the figure that the human female presents in society; it is civilization as a whole that produces this creature, intermediate between male and eunuch, which is described as feminine."[4] By thus redefining the ontological formation of identity and subjectivity in terms of gender, de Beauvoir made it possible for feminists to see that their place within society was constrained not by their biology, psychology, or class but by the social roles ascribed to them. This emphasis on the relationship between gender identity and social role played a crucial part in allowing women to recognize that social values were neither "naturally" determined nor neutral.

The reception of de Beauvoir's ideas among North American feminists was mixed. On the one hand, her theorization of gender relations as based on social roles rather than on nature was crucial because it allowed for the possibility of historical change. On the other hand, many North American feminists, especially radical feminists like Shulamith Firestone and Kate Millett, who called not for equal rights but for a complete historical and sexual revolution, were critical of de Beauvoir's tendency to associate subjectivity with the mind and otherness with the body.[5] For them, the roots of something as fundamental and widespread as women's oppression had to be located in the embodied and biological differences between the genders. Furthermore, although de Beauvoir had denied the existence of human nature or "essence," her tendency to treat male and female as fixed and oppositional categories became transformed in much North American feminism into a rationalization of the a priori "essence" of sexual difference.[6]

Another key voice in the articulation of feminist thinking about subjectivity has been that of another French theoretician, Luce Irigaray. Although Irigaray's impact in North America during the 1970s was limited by the delay in translation of her key works until 1985, her work is widely regarded to be of enormous significance, especially with respect to the questions of essentialism and difference that have so come to preoccupy feminist thought.[7] Irigaray's ideas on these matters will be explored in more detail below and again in chapter 6, but for now it can be pointed out that, as succinctly summarized by Naomi Schor, Irigaray's position differs crucially from de Beauvoir's in that she held the main attribute of the subject to be language not social activity. Following from this, she maintained that women could only come to subjectivity by debunking the myth of the universal subject by means of a sexually marked language, a "*parler femme*."[8] Furthermore, whereas for de Beauvoir it was the process of "othering" that positioned woman as a negative entity within patriarchy, Irigaray regarded this negative positioning as the result of the process of "saming." As Schor writes, "If othering involves attributing to the objectified other a difference that serves to legitimate her oppression, saming denies the objectified other the right to her difference, submitting the other to the laws of phallic specularity."[9]

Irigaray's insistence upon discovering the essence of difference as a way to expose and challenge the logic of saming and her famous use of embodied metaphors of femininity like "speaking lips" and "fluidity" have often resulted in strong criticisms of her work as profoundly vested in essentialist thinking. These criticisms, which must be understood in the context of the general shift toward anti-essentialist theorizing that had come to dominate feminism during the 1980s when Irigaray's texts became available in English, have, as Schor has carefully outlined, both missed the subtleties of her arguments and misunderstood the radicalness of her attack on patriarchy. Not only does Irigaray not insist upon the sameness of or among women (which would be tantamount to creating another universal), but she does not believe misogyny can be undone merely by having women acquire the power they have been denied (which would leave the phallocentric system in place). Irigaray's challenge is far more ambitious: By interjecting into patriarchy that which it has abjected, namely the feminine, she aims to reveal the violence of its logic of sameness, neutrality, and universalism.

## CULTURAL FEMINISM

Although de Beauvoir was the more immediately available model for early feminism in North America, it is also true that much feminist art from this period shared with Irigaray a desire to explore sexual difference and to theorize, from within the practice of art, how the feminine could be evoked both to provide women with a form of female *jouissance* and to challenge the myths of neutrality and universalism upon which art world aesthetics were based. Many artists sought to enhance women's self-esteem by valorizing those characteristics, experiences, and processes that had historically been associated with the degradation and devaluation of women. This can be seen, for example, in the emphasis on "vaginal iconology" in painting and sculpture as a way to counteract what Barbara Rose called the phallic form as a "fundamental idea of male supremacy."[10] This approach is especially associated with the centralized, biomorphic forms in the work of Judy Chicago and Miriam Schapiro, who claimed precedents in the work of artists like Georgia O'Keefe, Barbara Hepworth, Louise Bourgeois, and Lee Bontecou. Another strategy was to reevaluate those methods, materials, and activities traditionally associated with women's art practices, such as craft and decoration, in order to redeem these aspects of women's cultural contributions.[11] This approach, which sought to redress the canonical hierarchy that distinguishes between "high" and "low" cultural forms, was already evident in the textile-based works done in the late 1960s by Canadian artist Joyce Wieland. *Reason over Passion* (1968), for example, was named for Wieland's rendering of a political slogan introduced by Canada's new prime minister, Pierre Elliott Trudeau, as stuffed letters on a colourful quilt, which she then presented to Trudeau (fig. 3.1). For Wieland, the intent of such work was not simply to assert the legitimacy of women's traditional crafts as art, but also, as Lianne McTavish has noted, to use these materials and methods to draw attention to and humorously undermine how the gendered motto that guided Trudeau's office implicitly prioritized the masculine intellect over the feminine passions.[12]

Another key area in which early feminists focused on reevaluating women's relation to culture was the recovery of "hidden" histories. Scholars from a range of disciplines, including English literature, religious studies, history, and art history, worked to identify, reclaim, and celebrate the collective history of women, both real and mythologized.[13] One of the most famous examples of this project in the visual arts was Judy Chicago's monumental *The Dinner Party* (1973–79). This work paid tribute to thirty-nine historical women by means of elaborate, handcrafted place settings around a triangular table, with an additional 999 names inscribed on the marble floor.[14]

The celebratory and optimistic tone of Chicago's *The Dinner Party* was echoed in a growing body of literature documenting or extolling the existence of ancient matriarchal cultures that valued and honoured women.[15] Inspired by this new research, as well as by the period's widespread interest in alternative forms of religion and spirituality, a number of artists began to create performances that invoked adaptations of ancient and non-Western myths and ceremonial rituals. The emphasis on ritual, with its connotations of codified actions and behaviours within a culturally shared belief system, revealed a desire for a sense of community and history. As art critic Lucy Lippard noted, ritual had a

3.1 Joyce Wieland. *Reason over Passion*, 1968. Quilted cotton, 256.5 x 302.3 x 8 cm. National Gallery of Canada, Ottawa.

particular appeal for women because it connects the past to the present and the future.[16] These ritualized performances drew from a range of tribal, folkloric, Eastern, and ancient or mythical practices, often blended with modern associations. Images of goddesses often figured prominently in this type of performance since the association of these mythical creatures with nature, fertility, and a benevolent spirituality was a powerful, if highly romantic, source of inspiration to the burgeoning feminist movement.[17]

The first documented performance to make this association was Carolee Schneemann's *Eye Body* (1963). As noted previously, her use of snakes in this performance referred to her awareness of the serpent image as an attribute of the Great Goddess of Neolithic and Palaeolithic Europe. For Schneemann, it was both a symbol of "cosmic energy" and "the primary index unifying spirit and flesh in Goddess worship."[18] By the early 1970s, numerous other feminist artists were expressing an interest in body, nature, and female spirituality through performances that evoked ancient goddess cults. In 1975, for example, the New York artist Betsy Damon assumed the guise of a Neolithic

3.2 Betsy Damon. *The 7,000 Year Old Woman*, 1977. Photodocumentation of street performance on 21 May, New York. Photograph: Su Friedrich.

goddess in performances that explored the continuity of female energy and spirituality over the millennia. On 21 March 1977 and again on 21 May 1977, Damon appeared on the street in New York as *The 7,000 Year Old Woman,* with her hair and body painted white and lips blackened (fig. 3.2). She stood motionless in the centre of a circle marked off with sand while an assistant cloaked her with four hundred sacks of coloured flour to resemble the rows of breasts of Artemis of Ephesus. Damon then walked slowly around the circle, cutting off the bags, slashing them open and offering them to the crowd of bewildered bystanders. Having divested herself of her "shield" of invulnerability, she then returned to the centre of the circle. For Damon, such ritualized performances allowed her to reach out beyond the art community and communicate to a wider public her concern with history, fecundity, and nurturance as embodied by this ancient matriarchal archetype. She also recalled that the task of creating a female space in the streets for two hours made her feel like a guerrilla fighter and left her exhausted.[19]

The desire for performative transformation through goddess worship was also evident in a series of works by another New York artist, Mary Beth Edelson. Her *Woman Rising* (1973–74) series consisted of several parts, including performances, photographs, and painted panels of symbolic forms and images (fig. 3.3).[20] The performances were private rituals carried out in Outer Banks, North Carolina, in which Edelson "rose up" naked out of the land or water, with arms raised in the manner of ancient Cretan Snake Goddess figurines. The documentary photographs of these performances were then enhanced by painting in a mane of hair, a halo of expressionistic energy lines, and moon and circle symbols on her body. Edelson was emphatic about the unity she perceived between herself as a modern woman and the powerful female archetypes of history: "The ascending archetypal symbols of the feminine unfold today in the psyche of modern Everywoman. They encompass the multiple forms of the Great Goddess. Reaching across the centuries we take the hands of our Ancient Sisters. The Great Goddess, alive and well, is rising to announce to the patriarchs that their 5,000 years are up – Hallelujah! Here we come."[21]

Edelson continued with the goddess theme, and in 1977 she made a pilgrimage to a Neolithic cave site in Yugoslavia where a goddess was believed to reside.[22] The private rituals she performed there as part of *Grapčeva Cave* were documented in photographs, which were exhibited along with rocks and shells from the cave later that year at the Artists-in-Residence (AIR) gallery in New York. This exhibition was held in conjunction with an installation and group performance called *Proposals for: Memorial to 9,000,000 Women Burned as Witches in the Christian Era.*[23] The relationship between the two pieces was direct. The first was a tribute to the power of the goddess in ancient cultures, while the second, based on the belief that the witch was a medieval embodiment of the goddess's power "gone underground" and attacked by patriarchal society, was Edelson's answer to the question of how and when the goddess had been stamped out.

Regardless of its factual accuracy, the belief that the ancient goddess became transformed into the medieval witch is still widely held within the women's spirituality movement and is sustained by the populist appeal of films like Donna Read's *The Goddess Remembered* (1989) and *The Burning Times* (1990), both produced by the National Film Board of Canada. Such assumptions are hard to prove, to say the least. Furthermore, although scholars like Marija Gimbutus have unearthed much evidence of the existence of ancient goddess-worshiping cultures, very little is known about what these cultures were like or how real women were treated within them.[24] In truth, the function of ancient sites like Avebury, Stonehenge, or Malta remains in the realm of theoretical speculation, as is also the case with the female images and figurines found across Europe from the caves at Lascaux to the Cycladic Islands. This lack of concrete evidence has had the deleterious effect of permitting the perpetuation of unscholarly and specious speculations.

3.3 Mary Beth Edelson. *Woman Rising/Spirit*, 1973. Photodocumentation (with overdrawing) of performance in the Outer Banks, North Carolina. Courtesy of the artist.

The harnessing of such material to support a personal mythology in the performances of artists like Damon or Edelson may be seen as a benign indulgence of artistic license, but it may also be aligned with some of the most regressive tendencies the feminist movement has engendered.

Such concerns were articulated by the artist Martha Rosler, who wrote an article in 1977 that was sharply critical of this type of work for having eviscerated the social meaning of the premise that the personal is political by transforming it into a form of personal fantasy. As opposed to the "interactionist" outlook she advocated, Rosler saw such work as "essentialist" and linked it, along with the Womanhouse project, the Feminist Studio Workshop, and the Los Angeles Woman's Building, to the radical feminism of Firestone and Millett. Rosler, however, preferred the term "cultural feminism," in analogy to "cultural nationalism": "Where the latter sees race or nationality as the primary source of oppression, the former sees gender in that role ... Of course, art is a cultural phenomenon, existing in the ideological sphere, but the value of the term 'cultural feminism' is that, on the whole, the Woman's Building shares the outlook of culturally oriented movements, which stress separatism and a voluntary change in material culture and in the organization of private life."[25] For Rosler, the objective of feminism ought not to be the valorization of personal fantasies, nor the establishment of alternative institutions, nor the prioritizing of gender over class or race but rather a struggle to redress the ideological and socio-economic bases of power hierarchies across the culture and its institutions as a whole.

These early goddess-spirituality performances also raise the thorny question of the relation of women to nature. They typically alluded to the ancient goddess as Earth Mother, the omnipotent life-giver whose spirit and body were fused with the earth itself. But if such a concept made sense to cave-dwelling societies, for whom the mysteries of life were otherwise unfathomable, its appeal to women as the basis for social change in the late twentieth century seems spurious at best. Furthermore, it was highly problematic for modern women to align themselves so explicitly with nature, thus replicating the very dichotomy that had always been used to justify their subordination within patriarchy.

## BODY, NATURE, AND SPIRITUALITY

This alignment with nature was common to many early feminist performances, however, and was an implicit subtext in performances that alluded to goddess worship. Nevertheless, as shown by the contemporaneous phenomenon of earthworks, or land art, it was not just women artists who were interested at this time in the interaction between art and nature. The impetus for such work came largely from Conceptual art's critique of the object-oriented and market-based nature of the contemporary art world, which many artists hoped to bypass by working outside the gallery system. But as Lucy Lippard has shown in her book *Overlay*, this type of work, with its frequent allusions to the megalithic structures of the ancient world and to communion with nature, was also often motivated by a nostalgic antimodernism.[26] This discontent with the systems and values of the art world and with the alienation of modern society from its roots in the earth was also the impetus for many feminist performance artists, yet their interactions with nature were distinctly different in approach and attitude. For one thing, their work eschewed the grandiose scale and technological complexity characteristic of most earthwork projects at this time. In part, this was largely due to the ephemeral nature of performance itself. Yet even if some of these women artists had wanted to create large scale projects, it is highly improbable that they would have been able to garner the enormous financial and administrative support that seemed so readily at hand for their male colleagues. Such support, not incidentally, belied the presumption that earthworks were somehow able to escape the larger art world system.[27]

To be sure, such distinctions did not break down strictly along gender lines. Not all earthworks by male artists at this time required big money and big machines. In the more performative work by artists like Richard Long and Dennis Oppenheim, the body was used as a signifier of human contact with nature by the relatively simple act of tracing lines and paths within the landscape.[28] But even if the effect of such works was subtle in comparison to the gargantuan earthworks of artists like Michael Heizer, Walter De Maria, and Robert Smithson, in all cases the landscape was treated as a site outside the conventional art world that could be "rearranged" in some way through the actions of the artist.[29] By contrast, the goal of feminist performance artists' interacting with nature was not to alter the landscape by means of human intervention but to create private rituals where the female body became fused with nature in ephemeral and noninvasive ways. Their interactions with nature were based on a belief in the importance that the female element once had in the myths and spiritual traditions of prehistoric cultures, which they aimed to recover and affirm for the present.[30] Their interest in transposing aspects of ancient culture into the late twentieth century was just as anachronistic as that of their male peers but differed in its focus on a renewal of female spirituality rather than on a revitalization of contemporary art.

The fusion of body with nature in early feminist performance served to denote metaphorically their conception of the earth as a living thing, the *mater omnium* whose mysterious generative powers were present everywhere, but especially in the bodies of women. This metaphorical intent is evident in Elizabeth Sowers's *Protective Coloring*, executed on a beach in Northern California in 1973. After completely burying herself in the sand, Sowers naked body slowly emerged and knelt upon the ground like "a sandstone female figure from an Indian Temple."[31] For New York artist Donna Henes, the spiritual links between female experience and the forces of nature were embodied in hand-knotted webs that she associated with the mythology of spinning goddesses, particularly the Spider Woman of the Aboriginal tribes of the American Southwest. Henes wrote:

> webs are built from the most basic female instinct.
> are what hold the world together.
> are at once nests and traps.[32]

Henes's *Cocoon Ceremony* (1979; first performed in Brooklyn in 1978) was part of a larger cycle of work based on a trip she made around all the Great Lakes. On 21 June 1979 she plaited her hair and was rowed out to the centre of one of the smaller surrounding lakes, where she wrapped her head with yarn and then cut off her braids and left them behind to symbolize the transition to a new phase of life (fig. 3.4). The work was completed later when "energy stones" she had gathered at the Great Lakes were deposited at an Indian circle mound in Newark, Ohio.[33] Henes's work was clearly an emulative tribute to the spiritual traditions of the Indigenous people of North America, but from today's critical perspective, as informed by postcolonial discourse, it could be open to charges of cultural appropriation and exploitation.[34]

The late Ana Mendieta shared these artists' interests in myth, magic, and spirituality, but she explored them in the context of her own specific history and cultural inheritance.[35] Born in Cuba in 1948, Mendieta and her sister were sent by their parents to the United States, where they were raised in orphanages and foster homes in Iowa. As a graduate student at the University of Iowa in 1971, she travelled to Mexico as part of an archaeological project, an experience that catalyzed her life-long fascination with her Latin American heritage. Soon after, she shifted her practice from painting to performance, explaining that "my paintings were not real enough for what I wanted the images to convey, and by real I mean I wanted my images to have power, to be magic."[36] Thereafter, this magic was to be evoked by Mendieta's immersion of her body in nature in ritualistic performances that she documented in photographs or films. Her desire to meld her body with the earth was predicated on a need to redress the "tragic sense of exile" that she experienced as a result of her cultural and familial displacement:[37]

> I have been carrying on a dialogue between the landscape and the female body (based on my own silhouette). I believe this has been a direct result of my having been torn from my homeland (Cuba) during my adolescence. I am over-

3.4 Donna Henes. *Cocoon Ceremony*, 1979. Photodocumentation of performance on Lake Margarethe, Michigan. Photograph: Sarah Jenkins.

whelmed by the feeling of having been cast from the womb (nature). My art is the way I re-establish the bonds that unite me to the universe. It is a return to the maternal source. Through my earth/body sculptures I become one with the earth ... I become an extension of nature and nature becomes an extension of my body. The obsessive act of reasserting my ties with the earth is really the re-activation of primeval beliefs ... [in] an omnipresent female force, the after-image of being encompassed within the womb, is a manifestation of my thirst for being.[38]

Mendieta's reference here is to the *Silueta* and *Fetish* series that she began in 1977, in which she inscribed the outline of her body in or on the earth in private performances that drew upon pre-Columbian and Latin American nature religions, especially Santería, an Afro-Caribbean religion that blends the spiritual traditions of the African Yoruba with elements of Catholicism (fig. 3.5).[39] Substituting rocks, mud, leaves, flowers, sticks, bones, water, and sometimes red pigment for the blood, hair, and animal viscera used in Santería rituals of birth and death, Mendieta marked out her silhouette in the landscape as both the signifier and signified of her search for place and identity. In the *Fireworks Silueta* series she created wood effigies of her body, which were then set on fire, and in the *Volcano* series she dug body-shaped holes into shallow mounds, which were then ignited with gunpowder. In the documentary photographs, the gust of smoke from the exploding gunpowder creates an eerily dramatic effect as though a mysterious, magical force of energy were emanating from the earth itself.

Many viewers have regarded Mendieta's earth/body works as manifestations of the timeless connection between the female body, the female creative spirit, and the earth itself. As one author wrote, "Ana became the earth and the earth goddess became Ana. By 1980, when the series ended, Ana and the goddess were one."[40] Mendieta herself encouraged such readings of her works as evocations of a mythical "feminine" existing outside time and culture and embodying the mysterious and universal forces of nature. But as much as Mendieta's work seems to cohere with the essentialist tendencies of much early feminist art, it is complicated by two main factors. For one thing, as Miwon Kwon has observed, the fact that Mendieta's work always evoked erasure or negation of the body "is striking given that most feminist artists during the 1970s vied for visibility and self-affirming expression through figurative, literal, sometimes 'in-your-face' presence."[41] For Kwon, this continual absence, along with the character of Mendieta's photographs as souvenirs of loss, suggests that what so many critics have identified as her biographical search for origins is not the source of Mendieta's work so much as a product of it. In other words, Mendieta's earth/body sculptures are not authentications of presence or origins but rather a problematizing of the longing and desire for such authentication.

The other aspect that distinguishes Mendieta's work in the context of early feminist art is the extent to which her feminism was always tempered by her specific identification as a woman of Latin American descent. However much Mendieta shared the desire with other women at the time to reconnect with what Lucy Lippard has described as an "anthropomorphized Earth Mother," her disoriginated identity and embrace of so-called "Third World" spirituality led to a sense of alienation within the women's movement.[42] Mendieta made the critical observation that "during the mid to late sixties as women in the United States politicized themselves and came together in the Feminist Movement with the purpose to end the domination and exploitation by the white male culture, they failed to remember us. American Feminism as it stands is basically a white middle class movement."[43]

3.5 Ana Mendieta. *Alma Silueta en Fuego*, 1975. 35mm colour slide documentation of earth-work performance in Miami.

## CRITIQUES OF ESSENTIALISM

Mendieta's criticism was made in the introduction to the catalogue for an exhibition held in 1980 at AIR in New York called "Dialectics of Isolation: An Exhibition of Third World Women Artists of the US." It points acutely to one of the most troubling weaknesses of early feminism, namely its tendency to assume a unitary, homogenizing identity for the category "Woman." Although the feminist movement in North America had always claimed that it was committed to eliminating both sexism and racism, by 1980 many feminists, like the African American Howardena Pindell, who had been one of the original founders of AIR, had become disenchanted with its persistent racism. As Peggy Phelan has noted in her history of feminist art, the insistence that feminism open up its dialogue was evident not only in the AIR exhibition, but also in the publication in 1981 of the anthology *This Bridge Called My*

*Back: Writings by Radical Women of Color* and in the deep schism that occurred around 1980 within the National Organization for Women (NOW) over what many lesbians considered to be the inherent heterosexism of mainstream feminism.[44]

No such dramatic schism affected Canadian feminism, but this is not to say that it has been either monolithic or impervious to fractiousness. As with the American movement, there was division between equal-rights feminists and radical feminists right from the start, but the Canadian movement was marked by additional tensions between anglophone feminists and Québécois who linked their feminism to a struggle for an independent Quebec. Canadian feminism has also been subject to strong critiques from women of colour, many of whom have addressed the contradictions between the much-touted inclusiveness of Canada's multicultural "mosaic" and the actual disparities experienced by its waves of immigrant populations.[45]

Aboriginal women, too, have pointed out how feminism has failed to take account of the specific conditions of their struggle against a long history of subjugation to state-sanctioned dispossession and disenfranchisement. As Dian Million has written, "No people in Canada [have] been so reduced materially and discursively as Aboriginals, or so compromised politically."[46] For some Aboriginal women, like the Saskatoon artist Lori Blondeau, academic feminism is particularly guilty of this failure. At a 2001 symposium called "Locating Feminisms," sponsored by the Winnipeg group Mentoring Artists for Women's Art (MAWA), a flashily dressed woman named Betty Daybird showed up to announce that Blondeau didn't want to come and had sent Daybird in her stead. In a scurrilous parody of the standard academic format, Daybird (Blondeau) hauled in a wagon with reams of blank paper, piled it on the table and invited the audience to come up and read her "dissertation" on feminism. Her slide show documented the long journey of her search for feminism, starting out with her in a bar querying the waitresses about feminism, going off to the desert, "falling off the wagon" into several drinking binges, gambling her money away, and having to do performances along the way to earn cash. Since her search had provided few answers, she concluded that feminism had to be "inside herself." As Heather Anderson has interpreted it, this performance, which registered Blondeau's ambivalence about the relevance of feminism, was an attempt to voice frustration with the ongoing tendency of the mostly white, middle-class, and university-educated feminist community to treat her as a tokenistic other.[47]

Such conflicts, and the theoretical discourses within which they had increasingly come to be articulated throughout the 1980s and 1990s, clearly signalled that any pretence to early feminism's concept of a unified female identity was illusory and even oppressive. This concept had initially meant to serve as a strategy for building a coalition among vast numbers of women in order to give the movement the critical mass needed for a strong political impact, but it had two concomitant consequences. On the one hand, it stressed solidarity among women on the basis of what unified them as a group, giving rise to the search for an essential, shared quality or characteristic, be it nature, biology, or the elusive "feminine sensibility." On the other hand, it stressed the difference of this group from the dominant patriarchal group. But as the foregoing examples show, because this strategy for building political solidarity also had the negative effect of subsuming all women within a uniform social identity, it paradoxically isolated and alienated many women who did not identify with what was perceived as its predominantly white, middle-class, heterosexual perspective.

While the emphasis on "difference" in early feminism aimed to affirm something positive in that which had always been denigrated, the results have often been seen as naive and even contradictory. For example, connecting female identity to the natural or biological realm ended up replicating the very premise upon which the oppression of women had always been based, namely that man is superior because he controls culture, while woman is inferior because she cannot escape her bonds with nature.[48] It also subsumed the complex cultural and historical contingencies of women's oppression within a simple, monocausal explanation. Similarly, it led to the view that women's experiences were invisible and at odds with the culture's defining values and institutions because they had been obscured by the oppressive façade of patriarchy. As Vivian Gornick wrote in 1973: "For centuries the cultural record of our experience has been a record of male experience. It is the male sensibility that has apprehended and described our life. It is the maleness of experience that has been a metaphor for human existence."[49] While this statement indicates awareness that gender differences are historically and culturally inculcated and experienced, it nevertheless presupposes that if the oppressive façade could be torn away, women would be freed to discover their true and original female identity.

As feminist discourse expanded over the next two decades, however, the essentialist tendencies of its early period were subjected to critique and revision, largely as a result of the interaction between feminist and

Marxist, psychoanalytic, poststructuralist, and postcolonial theories. This intersection of intellectual thought, generally described as "feminism and postmodernism," has revised feminism's understanding of identity and subjectivity in three principal ways.

First, early feminism's attempts to explain sexism on the basis of gender alone have been repudiated as a "metanarrative" prone to the same flaws of all theories that seek to discover foundational causes to explain the "truth" of things, which in turn becomes the source of their own legitimization.[50] Such monocausal theories are seen as inherently essentializing and ahistorical, regardless of whether they are based on biological, psychoanalytical, or philosophical precepts.[51] Second, any overarching theory of the cause of sexism cannot account for the specificities of class, race, ethnicity, sexual orientation, and history that characterize the supposedly unified group designated by the category "woman." Early efforts to define a theory that could encompass all women and thus enhance sisterhood are now seen to have had the oppressive effect of eliding the very real differences among women. Awareness of diversity has led to the shift from woman to women, from feminism to feminisms, and from difference as an exclusionary group attribute to differences as a function of the relation between groups. It has forced the recognition that, as Sandra Harding says, "'We women' are both diverse and, often, in dominations [*sic*] relations – consciously or not – with each other."[52] Third, the very premise of a fixed and stable identity – such as the notion that the identity "woman" can exist prior to any other form of identity – has been challenged within contemporary critical discourse, especially as a result of the poststructuralist theories of Jacques Lacan and Jacques Derrida. Lacan's psychoanalytic theories about the impossibility of the self's being formed independently of its relation, through language, to the external social order (Symbolic Order) preclude the premise of a fixed and stable identity.[53] For his part, Derrida argued that modern philosophy since Descartes has been preoccupied with the unity of consciousness and the singularity of thought (expressed in binary oppositions such as true/false, self/other, male/female, nature/culture). He questioned such totalizing concepts by means of a method that he called deconstruction, which seeks to bring out those irreducible differences (*différances*) that are repressed or denied, especially within the signifying codes of language.[54]

This questioning of the notion of a stable, unified subject or identity has had profound consequences for feminist thought. French Feminists like Luce Irigaray, Hélène Cixous, and Julia Kristeva have used these theories to turn to their advantage the notion that women are the other.[55] Rather than a condition that must be transcended in order to attain a self-determined subjectivity, otherness can be a position of difference and critical distance from which to scrutinize the norms, values, and practices of the (patriarchal) Symbolic Order. Furthermore, the rejection of the belief that one can possess a unified, integrated self-identity that bears an essential relationship to truth or reality has allowed women to slip away from prescribed meanings and roles into what Julia Kristeva has called the heterogeneity of the subject-in-process.[56]

These theoretical debates have inevitably had their counterpart in feminist performance and art. But while artists like Adrian Piper, Martha Rosler, Eleanor Antin, Kyoko Michishita, and Mako Idemitsu, whose work will be discussed in the following chapters, had addressed questions of class, race, and ethnicity since the early 1970s, feminist art from the 1980s to the present came to propose a more emphatic and explicit engagement with what Kimberlè Williams Crenshaw has called a concept of "intersectionality."[57] As we will also see, the work of artists like Sara Diamond, Lorraine O'Grady, Lori Blondeau, and Vera Frenkel address this intersectionality in relation not only to race and ethnicity, but also to colonialism and cultural imperialism. For artists like Tanya Mars, Suzy Lake, Shawna Dempsey, Lorri Millan, Joyan Saunders, and Allyson Mitchell, the sites of intersection have been those places where normative codes of female sexuality, especially as they are perpetuated and inculcated by the powerful economies of popular culture, clash with the realities of aging and otherwise nonideal bodies as well as with those pleasures and desires that eschew what poet Adrienne Rich has called "compulsory heterosexuality."[58]

This concern with the differences between what feminism means for heterosexual and lesbian women has been particularly well developed in the context of feminist performance theatre.[59] As noted above, the question of this difference reached a crisis point around 1980 when it appeared that the American feminist organization NOW could accommodate lesbians as an identity category only by refusing to acknowledge or endorse the specific ways in which lesbian sexuality itself might differ from the heterosexual norm. The inadequacy of this position, and the anger that it generated among lesbians, is evident in the extensive range of performative theory and practice that emerged in the 1980s to counter such monolithic conceptions. As film theorist Teresa de Lauretis argued in her 1988 essay "Sexual Indifference and Lesbian Representation," lesbian forms of cultural practice assume not only that women can speak from subject positions, but also that "a woman could concurrently recognize women as subjects and as objects of female desire."[60] De Lauretis goes on to examine the premise, incomprehensible in Freudian psychoanalysis, of female homosexuality as a desire for the same that could not be reduced to the sameness of "hommo-sexuality," a term used by Luce Irigaray to signify the sexual "(in)difference" that purports women to be the same as men and to share men's desires.[61] De Lauretis's article addresses the question of what the possible conditions might be for lesbian representation so that it might move beyond a situation in which "the discourses, demands, and counter-demands that inform lesbian representation are still unwittingly caught in the paradox of socio-sexual (in)difference, often unable to think homosexuality and hommo-sexuality at once separately and together."[62]

The questions about lesbian representation that de Lauretis raised in this article are pertinent to any medium or form of representation, including art, writing, film, and theatre. In the realm of theatre, these questions resonate with particular significance in relation to the performance practices associated with solo performers like Holly Hughes, groups like the Split Britches Company, and venues like the Women's One World (WOW) Café in New York as well as in relation to the critical writing they have engendered.[63] Split Britches is a New York performance troupe formed in 1981 when its three members, Peggy Shaw, Lois Weaver, and Deborah Margolin, collaborated on their first production, *Split Britches*. When Split Britches was conceived, Shaw and Weaver had been performing with another experimental theatre group called Spiderwoman, which had been founded in 1975 by three sisters, Muriel Miguel, Gloria Miguel, and Lisa Mayo, whose father was a Kuna Indian from off the coast of Panama. With its origins as a workshop that brought together "Native and non-Native American women," Spiderwoman focused primarily on Native American themes in performances characterized by an irreverent, exuberant, and slapstick style that took aim at all expectations of "appropriate" behaviour and decorum.[64] Although Spiderwoman had always welcomed a mix of performers, the pressures of different interests contributed to the decision by Shaw and Weaver to form a separate group with a specifically lesbian focus.[65] As Sue-Ellen Case has argued, it may be more productive to regard this split as indicative of a historical moment within feminism when its normative assumptions of whiteness and middle-class values began to be challenged by women of colour and lesbians rather than as simply a breakdown of special interests.[66]

The Split Britches group developed a style and repertoire that, in Vivian Patraka's estimation, marked a clear departure "from both the universalizing rituals of cultural feminism and the documentary realism of representative women's experience, which so often was the core of earlier feminist collective performance."[67] In their collaboratively written and produced plays, including *Split Britches* (1981), *Upwardly Mobile Home* (1984), *Little Women* (1988), *Anniversary Waltz* (1989), *Belle Reprieve* (1991), *Lesbians Who Kill* (1992), *Lust and Comfort* (1995), and *Salad of the Bad Café* (2000), they used scripts that featured explicitly lesbian characters and concerns along with performance techniques – such as multilayered costume masquerades, overt sexuality, vaudevillian hyperbole, camp artifice, and Brechtian disruptions – that made room for the possibility of a new kind of representation within a new space. This new form of representation, which Case has identified as the "butch-femme aesthetic," posed an acute challenge to the woman-identified imperatives of mainstream feminism, particularly as the latter had become aligned with the antipornography movement, which pressured lesbians to assimilate into white, middle-class feminism in the 1970s by ridding themselves of their cultural roots in butch-femme role playing and working-class lesbian bar culture.[68] Case argues that it is precisely through a recuperation of these roles and this culture that a new feminist subject might emerge, and she identifies the work of Split Britches as exemplary in this regard. Her main point is that their use of camp, a discourse and set of strategies whose origins lie within the parodically exaggerated gestures and sartorial codes of homosexual culture going as far back as Oscar Wilde's trial for sodomy in 1895, allowed for a female embodiment of phallic desire that could exist by ironically manipulating "reality" with the appearances of "'pure' artifice."[69] As Case concludes, Split Britches' performances, which enact the vicissitudes of female sexuality at the semiotic level, thus represent a possible space "free from biological determinism, elitist essentialism, and the heterosexist cleavage of sexual difference."[70]

Although Split Britches and other feminist performers associated with the WOW Café have been widely acknowledged within feminist theatre studies for the challenges they bring to bear on heterosexist assumptions of the sex/gender alignment, the implications of such work have also been open to some debate. One of the main points of discussion concerns the context of the WOW Café itself, which was established in New York's East Village as a way to continue the initiatives begun with the WOW Festival in 1980. Although the WOW Café was not an exclusively lesbian milieu, it has, as Case points out, come to be primarily identified as such in its critical history.[71] For several critics, like Alisa Solomon, Kate Davy, and Jill Dolan, the WOW Café was understood as a place where lesbian sexualities were represented on stage and addressed to lesbians as the audience.[72] In summarizing such writers' critical reception of the WOW Café, Case notes that it was regarded both as a separatist space for women in general and simultaneously as a space in which camp and butch-femme role playing contradicted "the latent essentialism that separatism might empower."[73] The question that some writers have addressed about what it might mean to bring such lesbian-specific performance out of the WOW Café context and into mainstream feminist or mixed-gender audiences has also led inevitably to Lynda Hart's question, "When is a text a lesbian text?" and to its corollary: Who can or will see it as such?[74]

Following from these questions, Hart develops an intricate analysis of how making lesbians and lesbianism visible depends upon a reinscription of heterosexuality's signs. As she argues, even the reversal and parody of butch-femme roles do not offer a way beyond this impasse: "What is seen remains their *difference* from heterosexuality, and it is a difference that is 'othered,' which is to say that they inhabit a negative semantic space. Within these strategies 'lesbian' has no content outside the representation of heterosexuality."[75] Hart's proposal is to displace the politics of identity and visibility in favour of what she sees in Split Britches performances like *Beauty and the Beast* and *Anniversary Waltz* as the demonstration not of their lesbian "identities" but rather of "the construction of their desires through the history of identifications. Identity itself thus loses its meaning as a fixed construct, and sexuality is performed as a historical process that is both social and psychic."[76]

By thus invoking the premise that identity as the basis of agency or subject positions is fallacious, Hart's position, along with that of others, such as Case, Diamond, and Dolan, is aligned with the position taken by radical poststructuralists like Judith Butler, who would argue that there is no essence to identity or its presumed agency. For Butler, identity – or, rather, identification – is itself produced through performative acts that continuously reiterate the norms of the heterosexual imperative, although such performative acts may also serve as a form of "citational politics" whereby "queerness" may be performed or taken up as "the discursive basis for an opposition" to these norms.[77]

These discourses signify not only a critique of what Case has called the "latent heterosexism in feminism," but also a "move away from gender towards the representation of lesbian sex ... [at] the historical moment of the late 1980s, when the sex-radical position would finally exit the feminist discourse, to move into a new theoretical and activist alliance with gay men."[78] This desire to "exit" from feminist discourse marks a point of crisis for feminism by challenging its foundational assumption that a politics of opposition could be grounded in a subject position that could coalesce around the category "woman." Such theories have rightfully forced feminism to undergo a rigorous process of self-critique, but as Sue Thornham has noted, other feminists, while not wanting to return to a unitary concept of "woman," have expressed grave concerns about the transformative possibilities of a feminism aligned too closely with that form of postmodern theorizing that denies the possibility of stable identity categories.[79] Christine Di Stefano, for example, has argued that such theories negate the premise of gender as a category of difference that can "pose a radical challenge to the humanist Enlightenment legacy which has come under increasing feminist scrutiny as a masculinist legacy." Di Stefano also worries that the postmodern critique of identity categories and the stress on otherness tends to displace the theoretical and political strength derived from feminism's modernist insistence upon the importance of gender. In doing so, she contends, it risks undermining feminism's legitimacy as a broad-based political movement.[80] These observations raise troubling and interrelated problems within contemporary feminist theory that are germane to the investigation of the relationship between feminist theory and practice as it was manifest in performance art.

Essentially, feminism finds itself caught in a double bind.[81] On the one hand, the premise of gender as a unifying identity category, which galvanized the early feminist movement, has been challenged by postmodern critiques of coherent, originary subjectivity. These critiques have been crucial in forcing feminism to correct its essentialist tendency to lump all women together in a totalizing (and hence discriminatory to some) and transhistorical category. Still, some feminists, like Jane Flax, have expressed suspicion about the fact that the repudiation of authorial subjectivity began to be advocated, mainly by French male intellectuals, at that historical "moment when women have just begun to remember their selves and claim an agentic subjectivity."[82] Moreover, if feminists agree that there can be no coherent category "woman," this raises the acute problem of how feminism can be defined or sustained as a political practice in the interest of women's emancipation. Even Judith Butler has recognized that the loss of gender as an identity category, which is implicit in the postmodern prohibition against subject-centred inquiry, forces women to address some very troubling questions: "What constitutes the 'who,' the subject, for whom feminism seeks emancipation? If there is no subject, who is left to emancipate?"[83]

For many feminists, including Donna Haraway and Rosi Braidotti, the provisional solution is to accept the pluralistic and often contradictory aspects of women's individual and collective identities and to build from this a politics not of commonality but of affinities, alliances, and coalitions.[84] Although most feminists would certainly agree that cultural diversity and difference among women must be respected, many also worry that feminist politics might suffer if the notion of women as a unified social subject is allowed to dissolve entirely. As Linda Nicholson has noted, to evoke the ideal of endless difference can lead feminism either into political collapse or into the relativism of abstract individualism, with the perhaps unintended, but seemingly inevitable, associations of liberal pragmatism.[85] Sue Thornham has suggested that it may also result in the situation where male postmodern theory may simply appropriate "femininity" as one of its possible positions, while simultaneously erasing the work and lives of women.[86] Ultimately, warns Tania Modleski, there is the risk of ending up with "feminism without women."[87]

For Diana Fuss, who has critiqued the way that the concept "essentialism" has itself been essentialized in the theoretical literature, it is most important to distinguish between "deploying" or "activating" essentialism and "falling" or "lapsing" into essentialism. While the latter terms imply that essentialism is inherently reactionary, the former terms imply that essentialism can have strategic political value. Ultimately, she argues, we should not act "as if essentialism has an essence" but rather acknowledge that "the radicality or conservatism of essentialism depends, to a significant degree, on who is utilizing it, how it is deployed, and where its effects are concentrated."[88]

In effect, Fuss is arguing for the kind of "strategic essentialism" that Gayatri Spivak, herself a deconstructionist, advocated in her 1987 essay "Subaltern Studies."[89] Yet, for some radical poststructuralists, evoking even this compensatory form of essentialism is cause for suspicion. Lynda Hart, for example, argues that while it may be possible for political essentialisms of gender and race to resort to colour or sex to ground their strategies, lesbian and gay sexual identities "would seem to rely not on some presumably visible difference but, instead, on acts that cannot be marked."[90] Hart also cites Butler's caution that strategies are dangerously inclined to exceed their intentions.[91] Sue-Ellen Case has similarly noted that the term "strategic essentialism" reminds her "of the New Economic Policy instituted after the Revolution in the Soviet Union in 1921 that introduced 'limited capitalism,' with negative historical results." She goes on, however, to acknowledge that, "In this era of 'differences,' it is also necessary to find some notion of the 'same' that allows coalition politics and united fronts to form in resistance to the increasing attacks on women's rights, civil rights for people of color, and lesbian and gay rights."[92] Case's proposal for moving beyond the polarization of these terms that has caused such a stall in feminist thought is to "untie the notion of the seduction of the same from Freud's idea of narcissism" and to envision how notions of difference and sameness can operate in tandem rather than as oppositional categories.[93] While this may be just another way of saying that feminists must come together on the basis of affinities, alliances, and coalitions rather than of commonalities, Case's allusion to seduction reminds us of the role desire plays within feminist poetics and politics.

## FRAMING HISTORY

The problems identified in early feminism's essentialist tendencies must not be minimized, and the self-critique to which they have subsequently been subjected was necessary to the expansion of feminist discourse and politics. At the same time, we need to be attentive to how these debates have led to the stratification of the historical trajectory of feminism along so-called generational lines, with the result that bitter, internecine debates have arisen in which the attitudes and approaches of one generational "camp" are "berated" by another.[94] Although these intergenerational debates will be examined in more detail in chapter 6, what needs to be stressed at this point is the limitation to historical understanding that comes from construing and then dismissing an entire generation of thought and practice as monodimensional and categorically essentialist. In the context of art, it is true that much work from the 1970s was marked by political utopianism, biological determinism, and a naive contention that bad or false images of women could be supplanted by good or true ones, but it is also evident that the actual range of work from the period was extremely diverse in form, approach, and intent, as will be shown in the following chapters. This demonstrates that although essentialism was a distinctive tendency within the period, it was never the sole defining characteristic. When this tendency is given the substance of a generational ethos, it compromises our ability to acknowledge work that was motivated by other concerns and implies that any critical understanding of the limitations of essentialism would have been unavailable to anyone of the earlier generation.

Clearly, this was not the case, as shown by Martha Rosler's critiques of early feminist art in California, the most pointed of which was that its separatism and valorization of "woman's culture" insulated feminist art from engaging in challenges to the patriarchal order itself.[95] Rosler's observations underscore the fallacy of portraying early feminism's attitudes and strategies as monolithic. The very fact that her criticisms were levelled at a particular group demonstrates that multiple positions coexisted and that the need for political unity within early feminism did not require or demand absolute uniformity. Moreover, the substance of her criticisms indicates that available within early feminism was an understanding of gender identity and relations as arising not from natural or universal foundations but from the contingencies of history and culture.

But if Rosler presented an important critical voice within early feminist art, it was one that was overpowered at the time by the publicity that Judy Chicago generated around her sphere of activities, most notably with *The Dinner Party*.[96] Yet, despite Chicago's formidable presence and influence within early feminist art, her rather extreme position cannot be taken as characteristic of this period as a whole. For every artist like Judy Chicago, who could confidently assert a belief in female sexuality as the innate essence of female identity, there were many more for whom the matter was a big question mark. For them, the possibility of coming to speech and agency was predicated on a process of discovery akin to doing the primary research that prepares the ground for in-depth analysis. Far from asserting a totalizing celebration of a mythic feminine sensibility, the interrogative basis of this process aimed to discover how notions of subjectivity were formulated along lines of sexual difference and how this difference ramified at social, cultural, and political levels.

Although this phase of feminist work was truly a form of research, it has perhaps been misconstrued as a naive search for self-discovery because of its empirical nature and because it preceded the more theoretical investigations of subjectivity that have become associated with the postmodern tenor of discourse in the 1980s. To be sure, self-discovery was an important facet of these early investigations into subjectivity, but equally so were the acute diagnoses that women were able to make of how their cultural positioning denied them even the possibility of the coherent selfhood promised to the male subject. These investigations resulted in a dual objective for early feminism. On the one hand, there was the need to discover what female subjectivity might mean or be, and on the other, there was the need to account for how personal experiences of oppression and marginalization resulted from a culture-wide denigration of women. This latter realization points to another reason for challenging sweeping generalizations of early feminism as monodimensional or essentialist. Specifically, awareness of how gender identity and relations are contingent upon social, cultural, and historical conditions was already evident in the 1970s, contrary to the common perception that, as Miwon Kwon put it, the "antiessentialist or constructivist position [is] generally associated with the feminist practices of the 1980s."[97]

The views of many early feminists were in accordance with theatre critic Jill Dolan's recognition that "feminism begins with a keen awareness of exclusion from male cultural, social, sexual, political and intellectual discourse."[98] This fundamental understanding enabled them to grasp the extent to which their subordinate status had precluded them from formulating any sense of coherent identity. As Vivian Gornick saw it, woman's role as other rendered her an outsider, a mere chimera, an illusory projection of what the male subject defines himself not to be. As Gornick wrote further, "I am not real to the culture that has spawned me and made use of me. I am only a collection of myths. I am an existential stand-in. The idea of me is real – the temptress, the goddess, the child, the mother – but I am not real."[99] To be an outsider is to lack the means to engage in culture. It is to be alienated and silenced and to feel one's own experience to be of diminished or even negative value. The crucial question for feminists, then as now, was how to change this. As Julia Kristeva put it: "No longer wishing to be excluded or no longer content with the function which has always been demanded of us (to maintain, arrange, and perpetuate this sociosymbolic contract as mothers, wives, nurses, doctors, teachers ...), how can we reveal our place, first as it is bequeathed to us by tradition, and then as we want to transform it?"[100]

This question was pursued in various ways within the feminist movement in the 1970s. There were indeed those who searched for the "true" female identity as the essential link between all women. For many others, it led to more analytical investigations into the gender biases and inequities in social and cultural practice. Within feminist art, the pursuit of this question became the basis for performance work that was equally varied. Although existing literature on feminist performance has focused on work that dealt with the body, sexuality, and its representations, this has tended to obscure the wide range of feminist performance during this period. These performance practices were primarily subsumed in the critical writing of the day into the thematic categories of autobiography, narrative, role playing, and transformation. These thematic categories will be closely examined in the following two chapters, before returning in chapter 6 to a reconsideration of work that dealt with the body, sexuality, and representation, which will be discussed in relation to the history of theoretical and critical discourse on these topics.

# 4

# Stories to Tell: Autobiography and Narrative

## SPEECH ACTS AND FEMINIST AGENCY

In his book on linguistics, *How to Do Things with Words* (1962), J.L. Austin distinguished between two different kinds of speech: "constative" and "performative" utterances.[1] As historian Kristine Stiles has observed, this influential book was reprinted in 1975, just when the term "performance art" was gaining ascendancy over other terms used to describe live art activities since the mid-1950s.[2] This is significant, for Austin's theories articulated what was then being formulated as one of the key foundational premises of performance art. Austin referred to a constative utterance as a reliable description of a thing or event, while a performative utterance, by contrast, is a speech act that enacts something. Building on this theory, Jacques Derrida has argued that performative speech acts are open to unstable readings between intentionality and interpretation, which enables an enfolding of subject and object, speaker and listener, viewer and viewed.[3] The concept of the performative utterance has thus become seen as important to a theorizing of performance art as analogous to speech acts that do something.

This analogy between performative speech acts and performance art is particularly relevant to feminist practice. As Peggy Phelan has noted in reference both to feminist performance itself and to the writing of feminist criticism, the performative act or utterance is not a declaration of the certainty of a utopian feminist future but rather a process of rewriting and reimagining "what one can barely glimpse, can only imagine, and cannot reproduce."[4] As Phelan has more recently added, this idea of the performative opens up a new category for thinking about language and action such that "art can be understood as a specific kind of action and feminism a specific form of language. The promise of feminist art is the performative creation of new realities."[5]

The idea of the performative is thus important to feminism and feminist art both because it underscores the possibility of the performative act as an instantiation of political change and because it recognizes the extent to which feminist performance is not strictly based on visual forms but is profoundly engaged with language and discourse. The combination of language and politics as a basis for activism is well established within feminism and, indeed, has become recognized as the defining characteristic of French feminism.[6] Less well recognized is the significance of this combination for the visual arts, especially in performance, where language has figured prominently not only at the literal level of form and content, but also at the theoretical level in relation to questions concerning the role of language in structuring knowledge, subjectivity, and cultural values. Yet the relationship between language – and, by extension, art – and notions of authorship, agency, and subjectivity has raised conflicting questions for feminism. In the wake of Roland Barthes's declaration in the "The Death of the Author" that "it is language which speaks, not the author," the French feminist notion of *écriture féminine* has arisen, which proposes to circumvent the confident and empirical mastery of the phallogocentric order.[7] Inasmuch as such writing stresses plurality over unity, multiplicities rather than fixed meanings, and diffuseness against singular and instrumental certainties, it has been seen to locate the feminine as elsewhere and outside cultural discourse. As Janine Marchessault has argued, this puts women in an untenable position: "The task of inventing an entirely new language by means of negation denies women the possibility of engaging directly in the public sphere because it is seen to be completely determined by a phallic order which excludes women."[8]

By contrast, the Anglo-American approach has been to confront the existing culture directly by demanding recognition of the experiential aspects of women's culture – especially through autobiographical, documentary, and narrative iterations. As Julia Lesage sees it, the advantage of this strategy is that is has enabled women to name and describe their relation to, and exclusion from, the public sphere and to engage "in that political and artistic act that Adrienne Rich calls 'diving into the wreck.'"[9] The disadvantage is that, in addition to glossing over how the "authentic" experiences of the individual are already ideologically and culturally mediated, there is the danger, pointed out by Rita Felski, of replicating the long-standing tendency to see all women's art as self-reflective and autobiographical. As much as such forms as narrative, autobiography, and documentary were conducive to women's assertions of their own authorship and agency, Felski warns that there is no inherent correspondence between women's cultural position or point of view and a typology of aesthetic form. Rather than focusing on women's cultural practice as aiming to create a unified theory of feminist aesthetics, we must, Felski argues, consider it as a set of political strategies that address "the cultural and ideological processes shaping the effects and potential limits of production in historically specific contexts."[10]

In the case of feminist performance, the use of language-based forms served precisely as the kind of political strategy Felski advocates. The interest in autobiography, narrative, and, to a lesser extent, documentary must be seen in the context of the period's general preoccupation with conflating art and life as a way to challenge the entrenched hierarchies and categories of Modernist aesthetics. For women artists, however, the objective was not simply to contest prevailing dogma as a way to expand the aesthetic terrain of art. As we have seen, the merging of art and life in feminist performance, as a manifestation of the conviction that the personal is political, aimed to bring to attention the specific politics of gender, which, until the early 1970s, had not been conceived of in the art world as a form of politics at all. And because feminist art used personal experience to problematize the prevailing values and hierarchies of both art *and* life, it can be seen to embody the historical avant-gardes' goal "to organize a new life praxis from a basis in art."[11] The use of autobiographical and narrative practices enabled feminist artists to organize this new life praxis by asserting themselves as active and self-determined agents and by challenging dismissive assumptions that any reference to the experience of women *as* women was self-indulgent and irrelevant to art making.

It is important to acknowledge, however, that the use of narrative and language-based forms was not exclusive to feminist performance practice. Kristine Stiles has argued that in the history of performance, there was a general shift around 1970 away from the nonverbal body "actions" that had predominated in the 1960s. Stiles attributed this change largely to the advent of textual narrative in the work of Vito Acconci, who came to performance from a background in poetry.[12] But, notwithstanding the significance of his work for the development of performance in the 1970s, the implication of Stiles's observation that the prevalence of narrative modes in this period is due to Acconci's example must be qualified. For one thing, it is important to recognize that in the two years prior to 1970, Acconci's performance work rested heavily on the paradigms of Conceptual art. In that the underlying basis of Conceptual art was an examination of the conditions of aesthetic experience, with language being foremost among these conditions, Acconci's own use of language – in the form of propositions about bodily actions – was fully commensurate with Conceptual modes. What differed, as Frazer Ward has pointed out, was Acconci's implicit critique, by way of these bodily actions, of Conceptualism's refusal of materiality and physicality.[13] In other words, the use of language in Acconci's work at that time was neither new nor unique. It was only after 1970, with works like *Claim* (1971), *Seedbed* (1972), and *Trappings* (1971), that Acconci began to supplement the spare, linguistic propositions/actions typical of Conceptual art with narrative texts that drew the viewer into tense and often disturbing psychological situations.

By this time, however, the use of narrative and autobiographical forms was becoming well established within feminist practice – as, for example, in the performances done in the context of the feminist art programs at Fresno and CalArts. There is no question that Acconci's presence loomed large on the performance scene of the 1970s, but there is no reason to presume that the use of language and narrative modes in feminist performance was derived from Acconci, depended upon his precedent, and would not otherwise have been arrived at without his example. In fact, the shift in orientation that Stiles identifies around 1970 can plausibly be attributed as much to developments in feminist performance at the time as to Acconci's own work. Indeed, Lucy Lippard, who was a reliable voice of the critical milieu of the period, suggested exactly this likelihood, observing that the methods and approaches pioneered in feminist art had become widespread by the mid-1970s – even though feminist art itself was considered critically insignificant:

> Art dealing with specifically female and feminist issues became publicly visible with more difficulty than mainstream art ... This, despite the fact that the autobiographical and narrative modes now fashionable were in part inspired by women's activities, especially consciousness raising. Indeed, since much of this women's work came out of isolation and feminist enclaves, rather than

from the general "scene," and since it attempted to establish a new iconography, it was justifiably perceived as coming from an "other" point of view, and was frequently labeled retrograde for its lack of compliance with the evolutionary mainstream.[14]

Lippard's remarks provide another reason for challenging Stiles's view that the shift to narrative modes in 1970s performance was due to Acconci's influence, namely that women's approach to performance was, on the whole, distinctly different from that of Acconci and other male artists at the time. For example, when performance artists like Acconci or Chris Burden explored such concepts as power relations, risk, and vulnerability, they did so from a social position always already certain of its own power and authority and thus oblivious to what it might be like for those whose own social positions were defined by subordination and real powerlessness. These social inequities, and the ideologies that sustained them, were precisely the focus of feminist artists. Furthermore, as Mary Kelly observed, the work of feminist artists demonstrated a highly original and strategic intervention in performance practice in that it focused "on the construction not of the individual, but of the sexed subject."[15] While this focus was often on representations of the physical body, the use of narrative and autobiographical forms were of crucial importance in enabling feminist performance artists to explore how this sexed subject was constituted within social discourse.

## "WHAT AM I?": STORIES OF THE SELF

When Lucy Lippard began writing about feminist art in the early 1970s, she noted that women at the time were asking such questions as "What Am I? What Do I Want to Be?" and proposing that "I Can Be Anything I Like but First I Have to Know What I Have Been and What I Am."[16] As we have seen, these kinds of questions had been the impetus for the autobiographical and narrative-based performances of the feminist art programs and were directly inspired by the feminist model of consciousness raising. As regards the significance of this model for art practice, the artist Joyce Kozloff made an observation similar to Lippard's: "In consciousness-raising, one examines one's personal experiences to formulate one's politics. Much recent art is personal and autobiographical, and I believe that the Women's Movement has been a contributing force in giving artists permission to openly explore their inner lives in their art."[17] Consciousness raising did not simply empower individuals; it created a group politic and enfranchised a new audience. As Suzanne Lacy pointed out in 1980, this concern with audience has had important implications not just for the development of feminist art, but also for contemporary art practice in general: "Another area in which feminist theory has led the art vanguard is in the notion of audience. Today everybody talks about the audience, and so did everybody in the feminist movement in '69. However, *artists* weren't talking about it then. At first feminist performance artists brashly, even antagonistically, put the stuff out and the audience reacted in kind. After that there was a retreat into a cooler analysis: Now, what do we really want from these audiences?"[18]

This emphasis on both personal politics and audience reception was instrumental in allowing women to challenge what Francis Frascina has called the "selective tradition" of art, which was "circumscribed by a particular gendered notion of 'public' importance" and denigrated feminist art as "'unproductive,' personal or too wrapped up with the 'inner speech' of dream, desire, and fantasy."[19] By inserting such concerns into the public sphere of art, feminist artists intervened in what critic Craig Owens described as "that system of power that authorizes certain representations while blocking, prohibiting and invalidating others." Owens noted further that although women are prohibited from self-representation within this system, "woman" is ubiquitously present as the object of representation, as a sign or cipher of meanings extrinsic to herself ("Nature, Truth, the Sublime, etc.").[20] Historian Lisa Tickner had earlier made a similar observation: "She seems everywhere present in art, but she is in fact absent. She is not the expression of female experience, she is a mediating sign for the male."[21] It was precisely this absence of presence that women sought to redress through autobiography and narrative – not just through *content*, but also by foregrounding the presence of the artist as *producer* of the work. By making the artist's gender inescapably evident, such work denied the presumed neutrality of aesthetic judgment upon which rested that system of regulating power and authority described by Owens. In this sense, feminist performance and its vestigial objects (photographs, scripts, videotapes, props, etc.) can be seen as constituting what historian Henry Sayre has described as a kind of "postmodern *salon des refusés*."[22]

As Sayre goes on to suggest, autobiographical or narrative modes invoke their own history, the process or story of their making, which viewers are invited to reconstruct.[23] Indeed, personal history and memory were frequently drawn upon in early feminist performances as a vehicle for self-discovery. It was in this spirit that California artist Eleanor Antin presented her autobiographical performance *Eleanor 1954* at the Los Angeles Woman's Building in 1974 (fig. 4.1). *Eleanor 1954* was an attempt to make a connection between Antin's own history and the gallery of performance personae (the King, the Black Movie Star, the Ballerina, and the Nurse) that she had been creating at the time. *Eleanor 1954* included a video showing stills of her performance personae as well as glamorous publicity photographs of her self as an aspiring young actress. As Moira Roth recalled, Antin's narration "shifted back and forth between her past and present selves, her attitude moving from mockery to analysis to compassion toward her younger self."[24] Antin's recollections about who she was in the past thus served as a kind of touchstone for the four personae she was then in the process of formulating. As will be seen in chapter 5, Antin used the wry and ironical self-mockery seen in *Eleanor 1954* as a strategy for inhabiting but never completely becoming these personae, which thus confounds the distinctions between art and life, fiction and reality, acting and being.

In an article on Canadian feminist art and literature, theorist Linda Hutcheon has argued that women artists and writers have often used irony or parody as strategies for negotiating the duality that they experienced in their efforts both to achieve and to problematize the humanist ideal of coherent selfhood.[25] Hutcheon believes that this duality arises from a condition of marginality that has created in women what Alicia Ostriker calls a "divided self, rooted in the authorized dualities of culture."[26] The "splitting images" and "double-talking ironies" that Hutcheon identifies as feminist responses to this duality may have come to be more closely associated with the critiques of representation prevalent in the 1980s, which she explores in relation to the work of Toronto painter Joanne Tod, but she also traces them back to Joyce Wieland's work of the 1960s and 1970s. As Hutcheon notes, Wieland's work has always used wit and humour to create tension between things. She has used the traditional female crafts of quilting and embroidery to challenge and poke fun at the formalist high-art aesthetics that prevailed at the time, and with works like *Reason over Passion* (fig. 3.1), she further inflected this tension with a juxtaposition of the intellectual and affective categories set in hierarchical relationship in Pierre Elliott Trudeau's famous slogan, from which the piece takes its title. In her *O Canada* print, made in 1970 with the Nova Scotia College of Art and Design Lithography Workshop, she explicitly eroticized this tension by

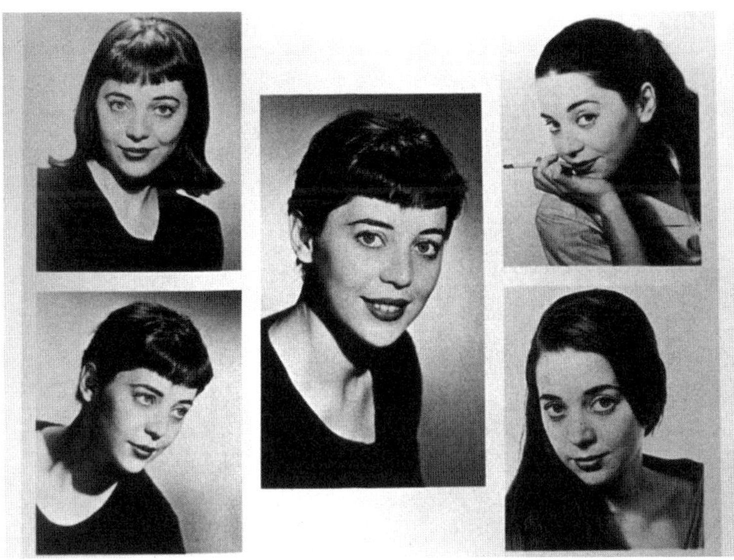

4.1 Eleanor Antin. *Eleanor 1954*, 1974. Photodocumentation of performance at the Los Angeles Woman's Building.

pressing her lipstick-covered lips to the stone in order to represent the act of mouthing the words to Canada's national anthem (fig. 4.2). This work plays ironically not only on Wieland's passionate Canadian nationalism, heightened by her time spent in New York during years of civil strife in the late 1960s, but also, as Hutcheon notes, on "the space between our senses (visual versus aural) and on our aesthetic versus realist impulses."[27] Wieland's print invoked an additional "double-talking irony" in that it injected an embodied and performative element into the rigorously linguistic and dematerialized Conceptual art practices that were then dominant at the Nova Scotia College of Art and Design and elsewhere in the art world.

Although Hutcheon's essay focuses on work from the 1970s and 1980s, it is evident that feminist art, from the early days to the present, has consistently used ironic displacements to respond to what Coral Ann Howells has called the "colonized mentality where one's self-image is split between imposed traditional patterns and authentic experience."[28] We see this not only with Antin and Wieland, but also with many other artists discussed in this book, including Martha Rosler, Martha Wilson, Lynda Benglis, Ilene Segalove, Susan Mogul, Kate Craig, Vera Frenkel,

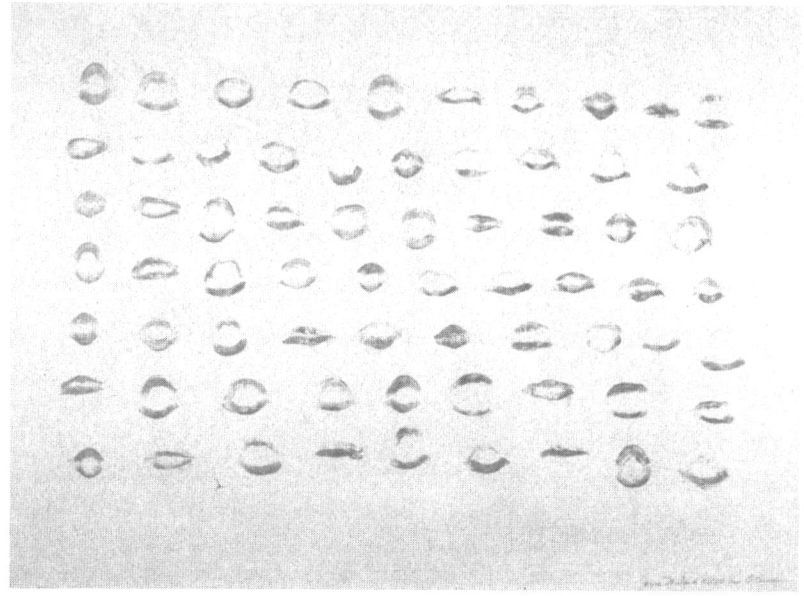

4.2 Joyce Wieland. *O Canada*, 1970. Lithographic print on white Arches paper, 70.5 x 60 cm (original in colour). Printer: Robert Rogers.

and Susan Britton from the 1970s; Tanya Mars, The Clichettes, and Wendy Geller from the 1980s; and Suzy Lake, Colette Urban, Lori Blondeau, Shawna Dempsey, and Lorri Millan from the 1990s. In all these artists' work, irony is used to perform what Hutcheon describes as the dual function of marking a *rupture* with the dominant text or code that is parodied and establishing a community of discourse that marks out a kind of interpretive *continuity*.[29]

In many feminist performances, irony surfaces in the form of bold and ribald parody, but often it has also been given a wry and deadpan inflection, as we see in one of Toronto artist Lisa Steele's early video performances, *Birthday Suit: With Scars and Defects* (1974). The video opens with the camera placed on the floor at the end a long room in Steele's apartment. Steele enters at the far end, silently undresses, and then approaches the camera to give a "show and tell" of every scar and defect her body has accumulated over the course of her twenty-seven years (fig. 4.3). The tape concludes with Steele singing "Happy Birthday" to herself. The feminist intimations of *Birthday Suit* resonate at two levels in particular. First, Steele is not passively pinned before the

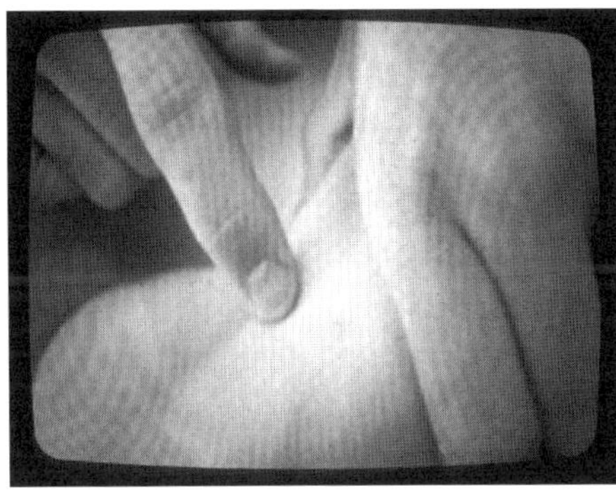

4.3 Lisa Steele. *Birthday Suit: With Scars and Defects*, 1974. Black-and-white video, 12:00 min.

objectifying camera eye; it is *she* who approaches the camera and who is in complete control of all that is seen. Second, Steele's matter-of-fact recounting of the incidents that have left their physical trace on her body moves the viewer from curiosity to sympathy and, as she carries this on for a full twelve minutes, from sympathy to astonished amusement at her long litany of mishaps, accidents, and surgeries. In contrast to the many male artists who inflicted physical punishments upon their bodies in this period as a way to provoke psychological shock and revulsion, Steele's *Birthday Suit* ironically transforms her "scars and defects" into embodied souvenirs of personal experience, memory, and the passage of time.[30]

This passage of time, which has left what Rosalind Krauss would call its "indexical marks" on Steele's body, is also marked by the long duration of *Birthday Suit*.[31] For viewers today, especially young students, who are accustomed to the quick edits and sophisticated special effects that have come to characterize both music videos and many art videos, Steele's *Birthday Suit* can also seem unbearably slow and drawn out. At the time Steele made this work, however, the crude technology of the video medium, with its reel-to-reel decks, bulky cameras, and battery packs, meant that even simple editing was an onerous and iffy affair. Like many of her colleagues who experimented with duration and performance in real time, however, Steele turned this liability into a critical strategy. As JoAnn Hanley has observed, "their long takes with repetitive or minimal action made audiences used to the fast pace of television time uncomfortable."[32] Similarly, Jan Peacock identifies the "boredom" factor as one of the primary ways in which early video set itself apart from, and in opposition to, the distracting entertainments of the broadcast medium whose technology it shared.[33] And as Anne Wagner has more recently hypothesized, when early video artists subjected their audiences to uncomfortable, sometimes abusive, and often boring displays of bodily performance, they were not only questioning whether artistic authenticity (presence) and the directness of vision could survive translation and reproduction by technological media, but also registering "the ambivalent suspicion ... that the viewer might not be there after all. She's home, glued to the TV." Yet in these works, where guarantees of pleasure have sunk "to something of an all-time low," television is the site that video art articulates, through critical refusals and negative reversals, "as a broken piece of an absent whole."[34]

The role of real-time duration and its corollary, boredom, is most often discussed in relation to early video – largely because reproduction technologies allow viewers to experience these video performances even a generation or more later. But real-time duration was also important in many "live" performances and perhaps nowhere more so than in the work of Linda Montano, for whom autobiography, memory, and the passage of time served as cathartic strategies for personal and spiritual transformation. The autobiographical element is so intrinsic to Montano's performances that she did not simply use life experiences as a source for her art, but also endeavoured to make her life itself a form of living art. Because Montano regards her life activities as art and frames them within the institutional systems of the art world, they must be acknowledged as art even though there may be nothing else to distinguish them from the activities of her everyday life.

Raised as a devout Catholic, Montano retains an abiding spirituality and ritualism in her work as an artist. She enrolled in college as an art major in 1959 but left a year later to enter the convent of the Maryknoll Sisters, intending to become a missionary nun. Although the rigorous self-discipline that she learned there would influence her performance work, she left after two years, suffering from severe anorexia nervosa. She returned to college, and by 1969 had completed two graduate degrees in art. Although trained as a sculptor, by 1971 she was working exclusively in performance and by 1973 had moved to California and begun to create performances in which art and life were linked in a direct, synthetic way.[35] Montano's first such performance was *Home Endurance* (1973), in which she remained in her house for a week, documenting all her thoughts, activities, meals, and phone calls in a journal and photographing all her visitors. Montano's intention was to concentrate on becoming peaceful and harmonious by "framing" her stillness as art making.[36]

Montano's performance continued to develop from her conviction that experiencing life as a manifestation of art leads to a heightened awareness of life and, in turn, to a heightened spiritual awareness. In *Three Day Blindfold/How to Become a Guru* (1975), she lived blindfolded for three days in the Los Angeles Woman's Building in order to alter her social habits and judgments through isolation and sensory deprivation.[37] The spiritual dimension Montano claims for her work was made even more explicit in her *Seven Years of Living Art* (1984–91). For each year of this epic performance, which was eventually extended to become *14 Years of Living Art* (1984–98), Montano devoted herself to a highly complex and individualistic interpretation of the Hindu chakras system of spiritual enlightenment, leading her both to ascetic renunciation and to religious ecstasy (fig. 4.4).[38]

Montano has claimed that her art is "about making myself more available" both to others and to a kind of therapy akin to the many forms of mysticism and self-healing that she has embraced over the years, from Catholicism to gestalt therapy, Zen, rolfing, and acupuncture.[39] Although her art activities seem self-absorbed, even solipsistic, they have been seen as a form of social work. She has received certification as a yoga therapist and hospice worker for the terminally ill, and as part of her *Seven Years of Living Art* performance, she provided Life/Art Counseling sessions one day a week at the New Museum of Contemporary Art in New York.[40] This claim seems to be contradicted, however, by Montano's statement in a 1991 interview that her goals have *not* been to effect social change but "to relax into my true nature ... as the political arena gets messier and the world gets more desperate by the moment, I try to tap into my own clarity and spiral away from my own confusion." Clearly unable to deal with the politics of the social world, Montano admitted, "I don't have a TV and I don't open a newspaper ... one of my survival modes has been: as much isolation as possible."[41] Despite her use of feminist methods, this apolitical outlook makes it difficult to reconcile her art work with the goals of feminism as a political movement rather than as a pathway to individual fulfilment. In this respect, her work may stand as an example of the danger that Martha Rosler warned against in saying that the personal ceases to be political when "the attention is narrowed down to the privatized tinkering with one's solely private life, divorced from any collective effort or public act, and simply goes on to name this personal concentration as political."[42]

Rosler's criticism notwithstanding, it may be that Montano's work, or at least some of it, proposes a different kind of political under-

4.4 Linda Montano. *Integration: Conclusion of 14 Years of Living Art, 1984–1998*, 1998. Self-portrait with photocollage by Montano of the artist as Female/Male. Photograph: Annie Sprinkle.

standing. Certainly, her renunciations of material comforts and pleasures in favour of ascetic spiritual devotions and her commitment to the therapeutic healing of others indicate a set of ethical values that stands in sharp contrast to what William Wordsworth described in his poem "The World Is Too Much with Us; Late and Soon" as the "getting and spending" mentality of modern individualism and middle-class acquisitiveness.[43] This implied critique of capitalism could be seen to align Montano's work in some ways with that of Allan Kaprow and his influences: art historian Meyer Schapiro and musician John Cage. From Schapiro, with whom Kaprow studied at Columbia University in the mid-1950s, Kaprow absorbed a Marxist understanding of art as embedded in the class-based social order of capitalism and as a theoretical model for critical resistance to its instrumental demands for labour and productivity. In turn Cage, who had absorbed Daisetz Suzuki's westernized form of Zen Buddhism, with its affirmation of paying attention to the ordinary and everyday in a way that would bring about an awareness of things otherwise overlooked, provided Kaprow with an aesthetic model for an art that was attuned to the action and conflict of the everyday world and that would provide, through the use of aleatory devices such as chance structures, a critique of a mythical individualism grounded in an interior self.[44]

But if Montano's work did imply a critique of capitalism, it was one that was predicated precisely upon the autonomy of an interior self and the premise that the single individual can resist, through force of will, the advancing secularism and commodity capitalism of postwar society. Yet this principle of liberal individualism and autonomy seems to have been radically tested in some of her works where she has committed herself to periods of enforced sociality. In *Handcuff: Linda Montano and Tom Marioni* (1973), for example, Montano and Marioni spent three days handcuffed together and "on display" to the public at Marioni's Museum of Conceptual Art in San Francisco.[45] Ten years later Montano participated with Tehching Hsieh in his *Art/Life One Year Performance, 1983–84* (1983–84). Hsieh had already completed many other one-year performances, and after six months of discussion, Montano and Hsieh agreed that they could collaborate on a performance that would require them to spend an entire year living and working together in New York while connected by an eight-foot rope, the stipulation being that they never touch.[46] Not only were such performances, which effectively recreated the conditions of penal discipline, exercises in endurance and constraint, but they also raised questions about privacy, social cooperation, and racial/gender relations (and, not incidentally, the intricately complex challenges of artistic collaboration) that may somewhat mitigate readings of Montano's work as solipsistic and depoliticized. If so, her work can be seen to accord with that of other early feminists who maintained that in order for the personal to be political, it must have ramifications at the social level.

## HOME TRUTHS: STORIES OF THE FAMILY

For many feminist artists, the strategy of connecting the personal to the political by means of narrative and autobiography was not, therefore, a means just of finding their own voices, but also of examining how language itself functioned as the dominant signifying code of the "Symbolic Order." As the artist Judith Barry wrote: "Narrative has been a part of the women's performance art tradition since women invented ritual to expiate their feelings ... Women are using narrative structure dialectically both to explore their placement within the social structure and to foster an identification with the audience. Women are beginning to speak as women in a language that represents their entry into the symbolic order and that is by definition necessarily related to the lived-experiences in which they find themselves."[47] These "lived-experiences" were beginning to be understood as decisively affected by the patriarchal conditions of all aspects of culture, both private and public. This led to another distinguishing characteristic of feminist art. Because feminist artists, unlike their male peers, were concerned with the construction of the sexed subject, they insisted upon the importance of personal, familial, and social relationships as the intrinsic conditions within which this subject is formed. Of particular significance was their examination of the role of family.

Feminist artists' exploration of family as a subject of art was a trajectory not without historical precedent. In an essay on early video by women, Ann-Sargent Wooster made a connection between feminist subject matter – "language and personal narrative, discussion of the self, sexuality, women's experience in the world, and the presence of everyday life" – and the "genre" subjects of classic art history.[48] With the emergence of the bourgeoisie as a new social force in the eighteenth century, such genre scenes became very popular in art. They also signified the collapsing of family life, domesticity, and femininity into the private sphere, which was thus separated from the public sphere of commerce, civic activity, the production of culture, and the affairs of men.[49] Although these divisions had ceased to be the subject of art in the twentieth century, their structural and ideological foundations had remained well intact into the 1960s. Initial feminist considerations of these divisions, such as Betty Friedan's *Feminine Mystique* (1963) and the Womanhouse project (1971–72), tended to focus on resistance to domestic confinement. As feminists realized that "ideology is not merely reflected, but produced in the context of the family and personal relations," the emphasis gradually shifted to an investigation of family and domestic life as the psychic and social site of identity formation.[50]

Many feminist works that dealt with the subject of the family during this period were video productions. This may be because video was particularly well disposed to capturing the narrative substance of this sub-

4.5 Lynda Benglis. *Home Tape Revised*, 1972. Black-and-white video, 25:00 min.

ject matter and to evoking the pseudo-documentary format associated with home movies. One of the earliest examples of this approach is a video by Lynda Benglis called *Home Tape Revised* (1972), which documents a visit by the artist to her family home in Louisiana (fig. 4.5). The tape opens with a scene of a man typing but then cuts to images of people whom we eventually learn are Benglis's relatives. As we see shots of her father's office, her grandmother, the family dog on a surfboard in the pool, and a car ride with Benglis's mother and sisters, we hear Benglis's voiceover describing who the people are and what they are doing. Sometimes the images are clear, and sometimes they are distorted through a technique of retaping off the monitor; in most cases, the clear images stand alone, while the voiceover narration coincides with the blurry images. In her voiceover, Benglis disrupts the narrative further by referring to the end of certain reels of tape or to sounds from outside the studio that are interfering with her recording of the audio track. The tape ends with the man at the typewriter talking aloud about writing and telling stories. Although it is never made clear who this man is or what his significance is in relation to Benglis or her family, it

4.6 Nancy Holt. *Underscan*, 1974. Black-and-white video, 8:00 min.

seems possible that his role is to signify the constructed formation of narrative and authorship, which Benglis seeks to denaturalize throughout the tape by means of technical interventions.[51]

In keeping with most of Benglis's video work during this period, *Home Tape Revised* is a self-reflexive and critical investigation of what were then believed to be the inherent properties of the video medium: "its sense of 'real' time, its supposed immediate and truthful relation to the world, and its supposedly privileged viewpoint in relation to events."[52] Benglis's distorting or "traumatizing" of the images and documentary sequences in this otherwise ordinary family portrait counteracts what Bruce Kurtz has called "the perpetual now of video time" in order to call into question the reliability of the medium and to distance herself from an emotionally involving situation with her family, most of which seems to have been mediated by the video camera.[53] Yet the circumspection and ironic distancing that characterize Benglis's approach to the formal properties of video also have their corollary here in her use of this family iconography, which introduces the element of the low-brow home movie as a disruptive intrusion into the realm of high-art video, which was dominated at the time by rigorous attention to the structural properties of the medium itself.[54]

Like Lynda Benglis, Nancy Holt worked mainly as a sculptor but also produced several videos in the 1970s that called attention to and manipulated the technical nature of the video medium. Her videos, like her sculptures, address issues of space, site, time, and perception. But whereas the sources for her sculpture came from natural phenomena, cycles, and systems, her videos incorporate memory, personal history, and the emotional connections one makes with particular places. One such place was the home of her Aunt Ethel in New Bedford, Massachusetts, which is the subject of Holt's *Underscan* (1974). This tape consists of still images taken from photographs of Ethel's home, which have been altered through the technique of underscanning, which compresses either just the sides or the whole image on the monitor (fig. 4.6). The images are accompanied by Holt's reading of letters written to her over the years by her aunt describing the details of her aunt's life, her preoccupations with her garden, her roomers, and repairs to her deteriorating house. These ordinary details reveal a subtext of aging, illness, and the certainty of death, for Ethel also tells about making funeral arrangements for a family member and herself, during which she ends up being robbed of seven hundred dollars that she had saved for the undertaker.

It may seem paradoxical that the title of Holt's tape appears to privilege technique and process over the actual contents of the tape. Given that Holt came to maturity in the milieu of post-Minimalist preoccupations with structuralist analysis, this may reflect a certain ambivalence toward the legitimacy of such personal content, but at the same time, her careful attention to telling her aunt's poignant story indicates that the subject matter per se was neither ancillary nor subordinate to technical considerations. Indeed, Holt's technique of underscanning serves as a kind of visual and structural analogy for the compression and inevitable distortion of time, memory, and personal history evoked by the old photographs and the reading of her aunt's letters. She said that she wanted to make a "portrait of someone where you never saw a person ... touching someone with them never being there. I thought about the cyclical nature of time and how it is reflected in the film and video process through editing."[55] In *Underscan* not only did Holt use technical manipulation to explore the aesthetic and formal properties of video, but by layering the distorted photographs with the reading of Ethel's letters, she also firmly located the work within a social context of family history.

The video work of Hermine Freed emanated from this same post-Minimalist ethos, and her adaptation of structuralist concerns to a feminist discourse was similar to Holt's and Benglis's. Freed often used the technical distortions and crude special effects typical of early video in works that emphasize the personal and psychological aspects of time and memory as the basis of history. As is often the case in her videos, Freed's *Family Album* (1975) utilizes images of the artist as a way to place herself in a self-reflexive relationship with the spectator (fig. 4.7). This tape incorporates a montage of old family photographs and home-movie excerpts mixed with current images recorded for the video. Freed begins by recalling family members and incidents from her past and

4.7 Hermine Freed. *Family Album*, 1975. Black-and-white video, 10:00 min.

musing about how her present identity is shaped by these memories. As the old family images are shown, Freed's narrative speculates about whether she really remembers these events or has reified them as memory based upon their photo-souvenirs. She then superimposes current images of herself and family over the old images and vice versa, describes these individuals in the past and present, and compares accounts of her relatives' memories of the past with her own.

Through these nonsequential juxtapositions of past and present, of photographic document and personal memory, Freed explores her relationship to her past. Recalling that as a child she admired older, pretty women with babies, Freed then appears with her own daughter, about age four, who holds up photographs of herself. By the end of the tape, Freed concludes that she has not been able to discover her true childhood self. She says she remains a stranger to herself, somebody who, in fact, she knows less well than anybody else. Her search for the "truth" of her identity has remained elusive, and these old family photographs provide only phantomlike traces of her own "absence of presence." It is notable that Freed made this discovery about photography, which would later be theorized by Susan Sontag and Roland Barthes, through a process of her own investigations into representational structures and visual media.[56] As with the work of Benglis and Holt, Freed's explorations of the relationship between the self and the family relied heavily on video's ability to be manipulated to create a structural syntax that echoed her subjective perceptions of time and memory as discontinuous and unfixed. Her *Family Album* seems to suggest that if our identities are formed by histories and memories as unstable as these, then what about ourselves can we really claim to know or be?

These questions of the relation between personal identity and family history were also the subject of the video *The Influences of My Mother*

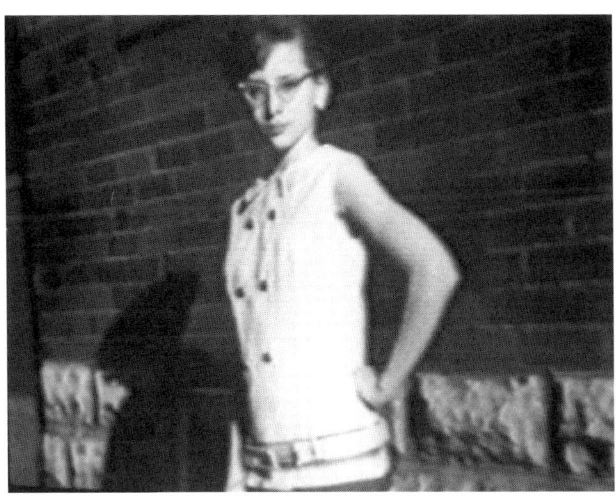

4.8 Sara Diamond. *The Influences of My Mother,* 1982. Black-and-white video, 24:00 min.

(1982), by Canadian artist Sara Diamond (fig. 4.8). As a founding member of Amelia Productions (1980), Diamond's work was grounded in the strong feminist art and video community that had been established in Vancouver as early as 1973. This community was committed to documentary practice and social activism but was also cognizant of the skeptical critiques that Martha Rosler had made of the notion of "truth" in documentary as predicated on the premise of neutrality and objectivity.[57] With *The Influences of My Mother*, Diamond aimed to expand the self-critical approach she had developed in her socio-political documentaries into what she considered "the more difficult realm of fiction or personal narrative."[58] In this video, Diamond placed the question of "truth" at the centre of an inquiry into her relationship with her mother, who died when Diamond was a young girl. In an inversion of the usual situation, where the parent constructs the child's identity, here the child constructs the parent's identity. Far from idealizing her dead mother, Diamond's six-part reconstruction creates a palimpsest of memories, photographs, documents, and mixed emotions toward the mother she hardly knew. But this is no mere sentimental journey. Diamond moves from denial of feelings for her mother, to anger at her mother's judgmental character, and finally, after recounting her mother's history as an exiled Russian Communist Jew and Canadian labour organizer, to grudging recognition of how much her own bitterness resulted from having to compete with her mother's political commitments. As Diamond searches for her own subjectivity by sifting through the past, she realizes that her perceptions of identity are as much invented as real. Released from the need to create a true or absolute identity for her mother, Diamond recognizes that what she hated about her mother as a child – her fervent political commitments and self-reliance – are the very things from which she now draws her own strength and identity. "There is no neutrality in history," she concludes at the end of the video. "We bear the realizations of our mothers' decisions."

Lisa Steele's *A Very Personal Story* (1974) recounts a similarly traumatic narrative of family crisis and personal loss (fig. 4.9). Propelled by the continuity of the narrative, which here takes on a confessional quality, Steele uses the video medium as a kind of straightforward "pen-camera" to document the retelling of the moment in real time.[59] The tape consists of a single, unedited scene in which we see Steele from the shoulders up as she sits on the floor. Her nakedness seems a metaphor for her intention to reveal all. For much of the tape she holds her hands, fingers touching, in front of her face so that they fill the screen as a kind of barrier. She begins at the end of her story: the day her mother died in 1963, when Steele was sixteen. She then recalls the beginning of this day, when everything was still normal. She vividly describes the smell of the toast cooking in the electric frying pan, setting out for school on a cold winter's day, the events of the school day, and her return home to a dark house, where she found her mother lying cold and dead. She says that she felt surprisingly unaffected by this, neither frightened nor horrified. She recalls that her first instinct was to get a blanket with which to warm and protect her mother but that she was not inclined to cover her mother's face. She says that she was aware of a great sense of loss but that it was difficult to know whether it was because of, or despite, this loss that "I felt more like myself than I had ever done before."

Despite Steele's stoic reaction to this most profound tragedy of her young life, the depth of its effect is evident in her need to return to this moment twelve years later. Although her tone is confessional, she has chosen to relate this experience to neither priest nor analyst but to a public audience who is intended to see this as art. Since 1972 Steele had been deeply involved in establishing and maintaining Interval House, a women's shelter in Toronto, and she found it very difficult to balance her commitments there with her efforts to build an art practice.[60] Her experiences at the shelter exposed her to an unimaginable private world

4.9 Lisa Steele. *A Very Personal Story*, 1974. Black-and-white video, 17:00 min.

of domestic violence, suffering, and abuse around which society constructed an impenetrable wall of silence and shame. Steele never exploited these women's experiences by incorporating them into her own art making, but she may have seen the act of bringing her own story into the public view as a way to break the silence that surrounds and represses the intimate and personal in both art and society. By proposing her own traumatic experience as an example of "the previously unseen minutiae of women's lives," Steele effectively contested the prohibition against contaminating art with the ostensibly self-indulgent and narcissistic trivialities of the private and personal.[61]

Video's potential for documenting traumatic crisis and personal loss within the family was also explored by Shigeko Kubota in *My Father* (1975). As we have seen, Kubota had been associated with Fluxus since the mid-1960s and had demonstrated a feminist awareness as early as 1965 with *Vagina Painting*. When she turned to video in the early 1970s, she showed an interest, similar to that of well-known Fluxus artist Nam June Paik, in the relationship between video and television as cultural signifier and commodity, although Kubota's approach was to use video as a diaristic medium.[62] *My Father* opens with a text display informing us that Kubota's father died on the very day that she bought a ticket to Japan to visit him (fig. 4.10). We read further that a friend called and that when Kubota told her that she was crying, the friend suggested that Kubota make a videotape of herself crying. We learn that Kubota has video footage taken in Japan two years earlier when her father had first been diagnosed with cancer. She plays this tape on the television in her apartment and sits before it crying and mourning her dead father. The earlier tape shows Kubota sitting with her sick father as they watched television together on New Year's Eve. The kitschy glamour of the Japanese pop singers on television contrasts sharply with her frail and bedridden father. The image of Kubota watching this tape on her television is intermittently superimposed with texts that reveal personal things about her father during his sickness: that the doctor didn't tell him he had cancer, that he preferred sake but settled for grape juice, and that he liked to eat chestnuts. Kubota's own expressions of grief and sorrow also appear as texts, as do her mother's descriptions of the funeral that they had for him on the same day that Kubota received the telegram announcing his death.

The disquieting effects of Kubota's tape come not only from our empathetic response to her evident sorrow, but also from the disorienting shifts in time and from the startlingly alien intrusion of the mawkish artifice of the television entertainment into her real-life tragedy. In this layered interplay between past and present, text and image, public and private, presence and absence, there is a haunting pathos in the fact that "the television emerges as the link between Kubota and her father" at this most intense moment of grief and mourning.[63]

What links this group of works, for all their diversity of approach, structure, and technique, is their insistence upon the importance and meaning of personal experiences as shaped within family structures and relations. As feminist and postcolonial theorist bell hooks has insisted, such autobiographical experiences are significant precisely because they define who and what we are. As she sees it, the experience of confronting the death of family members not only can be personally liberating, but also can invest one with the courage to resist the forces of domination and oppression. In an interview with Andrea Juno, hooks recalled sneaking in to watch her dead grandmother being taken away and thinking: "'Wow – if this is death and it can be looked

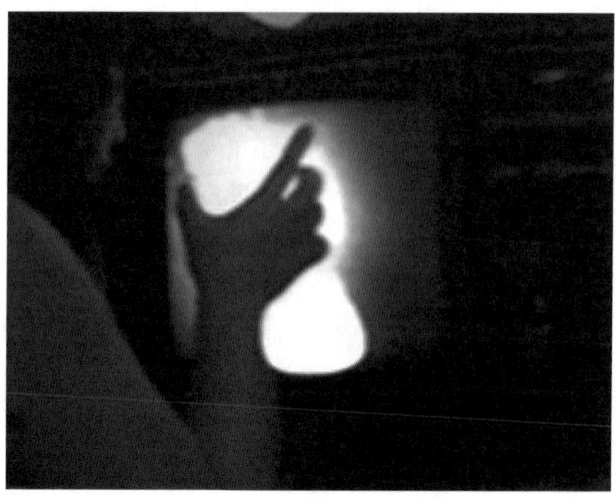

4.10 Shigeko Kubota. *My Father*, 1975. Black-and-white video, 15:24 min.

at and faced, then I can do *anything* I want to in life! Nothing is going to be more profound than this moment!' And I see this as a *moment in time that shaped who I became* ... that allowed me to be the rebellious child I was – daring and risk-taking in the midst of my parents' attempts to control me."[64] Like the work of these artists, much of hooks's work is what she describes as "confessional" in nature. She is unequivocal about how the use of personal material can play an important role in disrupting the enforced separation between the private and the public and showing how it is connected to a politics of domination: "I know that in a way we're never going to end the forms of domination if we're not willing to challenge the notion of *public* and *private* ... if we're not willing to break down the walls that say 'There should always be this separation between domestic space/intimate space and the world outside.'"[65]

## THE PRIVATE AND THE PUBLIC

The need to break down the barriers between private and public that hooks identifies had in fact already been addressed in a number of feminist performance and video works from the 1970s. Taking the intimacy of the family as a starting point, these works considered how the ideological values inscribed there have political connotations for gendered, classed, and raced relations of power and domination. These works, not surprisingly, often articulated a very critical assessment of family structures and relationships. One of the earliest such examples is a video produced by Kyoko Michishita called *Being Women in Japan: Liberation within My Family* (1973–74). Michishita was trained as a writer and studied journalism at the University of Wisconsin, where she also became involved in the women's movement in the early 1970s. Around this time she also began to make videos, adopting a method and style more aligned with *cinema verité* than with the structuralist manipulations that dominated North American video art at the time.

*Being Women in Japan* documents the recovery of Michishita's sister from brain surgery, which hospitalized her for four months (fig. 4.11). Michishita's interest was not only in the personal struggle of her sister to regain her health, but also in how this crisis caused a major rupture in the daily life of her sister's family. Much of the footage is of interviews with family members at the hospital (translated into English in a voiceover by Michishita). She asks her young nieces and nephews how they feel about their mother's long absence and how they cope with

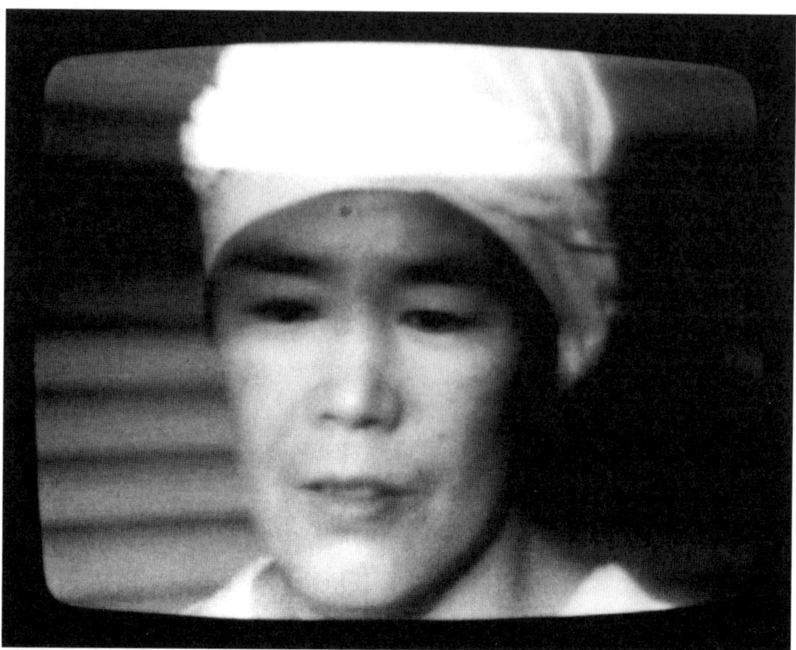

4.11 Kyoko Michishita. *Being Women in Japan: Liberation within My Family*, 1973–74. Black-and-white video, 30:00 min.

domestic details such as meals, housekeeping, laundry, and help with schoolwork. It becomes clear from these interviews that, as Ann-Sargent Wooster put it, "her sister is more needed than respected in the family and that her function is defined by food preparation and the maintenance of the routines of domestic life – with little acknowledgement of her individual identity."[66]

Michishita also talks with her sister and their mother about their perceptions of women's abilities and feelings compared to those of men. Both the mother and sister feel that it is a question of individual rather than gender-based differences, but Michishita reminds them that Japanese women must always be obedient to a man – whether father, husband, or son – and cannot, in fact, do as they wish or fulfil their individual capabilities. Michishita's tape thus serves both as a document of her sister's recovery of her life to the point when she finally returns home and, through the conversations she initiates, as a catalyst for her sister's changing awareness of herself and of her right to be recognized as something more than a domestic servant and mother.

In the mid-1970s the American artist Ilene Segalove also produced a number of videotapes examining women's traditional roles within family life. These works address the materialistic preoccupations and lifestyle of her family with a subtle and deadpan irony. These videos have feminist significance not only because they put the unseen minutiae of women's domestic lives in the public eye, but also because, as Segalove remarked, they were done at a time when "just to put your hands on the equipment [was] a feminist act."[67] Grouped together as *The Mom Tapes* (1973–76), these short vignettes have a technical virtuosity resulting from Segalove's desire to emulate the look and feel of television, which she saw as the centre of her family life growing up in the affluent neighbourhood of Beverly Hills. Intrigued by the way that television blurred the distinction between fantasy and reality, Segalove wanted to put her own family, especially her mother, on the TV screen.

*The Mom Tapes* reflect upon Segalove's social upbringing and her relationship with her mother, who acts as "straight man" in these slightly sardonic depictions of the "emptiness, loneliness, and dependence on material possessions that characterize the life she documents."[68] In *Advice from Mom*, Segalove follows Mom around the house with the camera, asking her advice on where to buy a range of items, from steaks to shoes to furniture. In another segment, Segalove flaunts Mom's advice by walking through the very underpass that we hear Mom's voice cautioning her never to use because criminals might be lurking there; she then shows the tape that she made in the underpass to Mom on their living room TV. In *The Red Slippers*, we hear Mom telling the story of how she picked up a pair of red shoes for Ilene on a recent trip to the Orient, while we see the shoes hanging from two huge nails on the wall of Segalove's apartment. "With you, everything is art," sighs Mom.

In *Professional Retirement Home*, Segalove's mother takes us on a tour of their luxurious, rambling modern Californian home, which she says is now too big since the children have moved out (fig. 4.12). She points out the finer features of the house, but admits that "It's hard to keep such a big house clean." "I sure do a lot of walking here," she says, as we follow her around the pathways and patios connecting the numerous levels and wings. But even though it is so big and she has to walk so much, Mom loves the house and could not imagine moving into a condominium. Her solution is to invite "a few nice couples" to come and live there, turning it into a "professional retirement home." Although Segalove's tapes reveal a genuine affection for her mother, she shows her as a woman trapped within an insular and self-absorbed

4.12 Ilene Segalove. *Professional Retirement Home*, 1975. Black-and-white video, 8:00 min.

world and fed on the bourgeois lifestyle fantasies of consumption and privilege promulgated by American television and marketing. Segalove's ambivalent feelings toward her family seem to echo, and even be a dimension of, the relationship she explores between video as art and television as popular culture.

During the 1970s, Martha Rosler also produced a body of work that addressed the conditions of bourgeois family life. These works insistently demonstrated her conviction that art must be a critical force within the everyday life of our culture. Rosler began as an abstract painter in the 1960s, but her outrage at the war in Vietnam provoked her to begin to do what she has described as "agitational works."[69] Early examples included several photomontage series that used strategies of disjunction and defamiliarization to create socially critical images. In the series *Body Beautiful, or Beauty Knows No Pain*, begun in 1965, Rosler juxtaposed lingerie advertisements with body parts from *Playboy* magazine in cut-and-paste collages to reveal both the objectification and the commodification of the female body. In the series *Bringing the War Home: House Beautiful* (1969–72), Rosler created a shattering intrusion of Vietnam's belligerents and victims into the serene enclaves of suburban domesticity by seamlessly splicing photographs from *House Beautiful* and *Life* magazines.[70]

During this period, Rosler also read Michael Fried's 1967 essay "Art and Objecthood." As discussed in chapter 1, Fried attacked Minimalist sculpture in this essay, regarding it as a threat to Modernism because it confused the transcendental "presentness" of art with the mundane "presence" of things. Since Minimalism insisted upon the literalness of the here-and-now experience, Fried deemed it to be "theatrical" and thus the negation of art.[71] Rosler concluded that "he was right, but on the wrong side of the question."[72] For her, the experiential immediacy of theatricality was precisely the strategy needed to make art that could forge a new and more active relationship with her audience. In Rosler's view, "we should all be activated as subjects of a culture that intended to make us all audience spectators rather than citizen participants."[73]

Rosler's determination to activate her audience's awareness of the political dimensions of everyday life was further honed by her growing involvement with the feminist movement in the early 1970s. As Rosler's work demonstrates, however, she was always attentive to how gender intersected with other forms of power and domination, including those of class, race, and cultural imperialism. *Service: A Trilogy on Colonization* (1973–74), for example, was a mail-art project consisting of three postcard novels about the multiple ways that women are colonized as service providers in our culture. The first, *McTowers Maid,* was about a woman who organized the workers in a fast-food chain; the second, *Tijuana Maid,* was about a Mexican woman working as a maid in a middle-class home in San Diego; and the third, *A Budding Gourmet,* was about a middle-class housewife who takes a gourmet cooking course for self-fulfilment. This trilogy was the first of Rosler's several works examining food as a central issue in women's lives. She said that "food is the art of womanhood ... It is an art product, but one that is made for the delectation of others and which disappears ... I also saw food in relationship to class differentiation."[74] As *Service: A Trilogy on Colonization* makes clear, Rosler also saw food as a tool of cultural oppression.

In 1974 Rosler reprised the *Budding Gourmet,* one of the three stories from *Service: A Trilogy on Colonization,* as a video (fig. 4.13). The tape opens with Rosler, playing the *haute bourgeoise* housewife epitomized by Segalove's mother, sitting at a table while leafing through cookbooks and food magazines. Close-ups from these sources are spliced

4.13 Martha Rosler. *A Budding Gourmet*, 1974. Black-and-white video, 17:45 min.

4.14 Martha Rosler. *Semiotics of the Kitchen*, 1975. Black-and-white video, 6:00 min.

with photographs of gourmet food shops and people labouring in the Third World. Oblivious to these images, the budding gourmet delivers her monologue about food and cooking, all the while accompanied by soft, classical music. "I wish to become a gourmet," she says, and then explains the importance of good cooking in order to enjoy life fully because people eat for pleasure, unlike animals (or poor people, as we might infer from the images). Following the formula of magazines such as *Gourmet* and *Bon Appétit*, she links gourmet food to travelling and eating in foreign countries. She bows to the great tradition of European cuisine, however, reading recipes developed by George Auguste Escoffier, chef to the European elite at the turn of the twentieth century. She also describes how epicureanism is linked to manners, etiquette, and breeding, which, she avers, allows food connoisseurs to be more sensitive to different cultural traditions.

Rosler's deadpan irony makes her critical intentions unmistakable. As both Amy Taubin and Laura Cottingham have pointed out, Rosler's voice serves as one of her most potent critical devices. With her distinctively Jewish Brooklyn accent and her dispassionate but precise intonation and phrasing, Rosler's voice draws us in yet distances us, coaxing us "to reflect on information with critical intelligence rather than easy emotion."[75] As she recounts the budding gourmet's aspiring fantasies, the preparation and consumption of food are unmistakably marked as signifiers of class privilege and a means of rationalizing cultural imperialism. The connections Rosler implied here between ideological formations of gender, class, and race clearly discount the tendency to categorize all 1970s feminist art as essentialist. Moreover, by examining women's roles within the context of "ideal" family values, Rosler exposes the extent to which women, too, are complicit in fostering and sanctioning forms of privilege and exploitation.

But if Rosler's investigation of the politics of food did not shy away from implicating women within the bourgeois ideology of the family, she also used food as a sign of feminist rebellion. In her video *Semiotics of the Kitchen* (1975), Rosler said that she was concerned with the notion of the "'language speaking the subject,' and with the transformation of the woman herself into a sign in a system of signs that represents a system of food production, a system of harnessed subjectivity."[76] In this parody of a cooking demonstration, a deadpan Rosler dons an apron and begins an alphabetical tour of familiar kitchen implements (fig. 4.14). She announces the name of each item and mimics its function with increasing and disarming aggression: "bowl ... chopper ... dish," and so on. As Jan Peacock has written, "When she reaches the word 'icepick,' and then plunges one into a wooden cutting board with broad and repeated stabs, one begins to see where the alphabet leaves off and where the 'semiotic' is heading." As she reaches the last six letters of the alphabet, she abandons all references to the kitchen and instead uses a knife and fork to slash these letters into the air like a samurai warrior. At the end of Rosler's "coolly furious piece of homicidal comedy," she looks at the camera and shrugs.[77] With this simple gesture, she assures the viewer that she is "not a victim in the sense of someone crushed. She's still there at the end, stuck to the spot, no further brutalized than at the beginning."[78]

Like bell hooks, Rosler has always insisted that the forces of domination and oppression as played out in the private sphere are inseparable from our more conventional understanding of their impact in the public sphere. As Rosler put it, "We accept the clash of public and private as natural, yet their separation is historical, and the antagonism of the two spheres, which have in fact developed in tandem, is an ideological fiction – a potent one. I want to explore the relationships between individual consciousness, family life, and culture under capitalism."[79]

The exploration of these relationships has continued to be an important dimension of feminist art into the 1980s and 1990s. The work of Tonia Di Risio, for example, uses performative video to examine how feminine identities are both constructed and resisted within familial relationships as they traverse generational transitions and/or ethnic-cultural divides. Born in Canada to a postwar Italian immigrant family, Di Risio has grown up and been "constructed" as a Canadian who experiences her Italian heritage mainly through the stories, foods, religious artifacts, domestic crafts, and social rituals that link her to her female ancestors and the past. Di Risio's videos, therefore, attempt to form a juncture between ethnicity and cultural hybridization. In *Parlare* (1996) Di Risio juxtaposed her stumbling and inadequate efforts to speak her "mother tongue" on a video monitor with a massive array of photographs signifying the feminine Italian heritage in the form of banal and bureaucratic passport portraits along with more intimate and homey details of decorative "feminine" motifs and patterns in mosaic, lacework, and ceramics. In *Progresso* (1998) these decorative lacy motifs form a projected carpet on the floor between two video monitors through which Di Risio and her grandmother attempt to communicate by enunciating heavily accented paired adjectives in their respective "foreign" languages, which, like the Italian feminine "bella" and the gender-neutral English "beautiful," never quite seem to mesh (fig. 4.15).

More recently, Di Risio has been constructing dollhouses from kits, which she modifies by adding architectural and decorative details typical of the Italianate-Canadian homes built by immigrant families in Toronto in the 1950s and 1960s as a way to indicate their new middle-class prosperity and to signal their Italianness to Canadians and other immigrants. The "dolls" that inhabit these homes are miniature photographic cutouts of Di Risio, her mother, and her grandmother dressed for housework and doing domestic chores. The dollhouses are sometimes shown on their own, as in *Homemade: A Showcase of Fine Family Homes* (2002), but Di Risio has also created animated videos, such as *Good Housekeeping* (2001), in which the Tonia doll scrubs and cleans under the strict direction of the mother and grandmother dolls, while the audio track plays Italian and English words about dirt and cleaning (fig. 4.16). Clearly, the Tonia doll does not live up to her family's expectations, but by affectionately poking fun at her mother and grandmother, and at herself, Di Risio reveals the conflicts that are embodied in her simultaneous desire both to become a modern, self-determined Canadian woman by escaping the gendered expectations upheld by her

4.15 Tonia Di Risio. *Progresso*, 1998. Photodocumentation of installation with colour video, 44:51 min., at the Art Gallery of Nova Scotia, Halifax. Photograph: Robert Zingone.

traditional immigrant family and to acknowledge the extent to which her identity and sense of place is grounded in this family history.[80]

In the work of Halifax artist Gillian Collyer, the experience of domestic life as the intersection between familial and social relations is seen through a more foreboding lens, one that suggests something of the oppressive forces that hooks and Rosler spoke about in the separation of the private and public spheres. Throughout the 1990s, Collyer produced a series of works that addressed the embodied and coded signifiers of femininity and masculinity by means of needlework, embroidery, and found clothing.[81] In her performance-based exhibition of the work called *hand-held* (2000), Collyer shifted her focus to the psychic tensions that lurk within the familiar objects of domestic life (fig. 4.17).[82] For the duration of this exhibition, Collyer, wearing a surgical gown and mask, sat at a high table and methodically wrapped small kitchen implements, ranging from mundane cutlery to highly arcane culinary tools, with hand-spun grey yarn. The wrapping was meticulous, carefully following the contours of each object but allowing for little metal points, knobs, and rivets to poke out here and there. Once wrapped, these objects were displayed on eight medical trays on wheeled stands (fig. 4.18). The contrast between the intimacy associated with these little domestic

4.16 Tonia Di Risio. *Good Housekeeping*, 2001. Colour video, 4:55 min.

tools and the clinical effect of the performance setting was the psychic axis point around which the work turned. In one way, these hand-held objects represent the world of home and family, of food and nurturance, of love and security. But made strange – and strangely menacing – by this skin of wrapped wool and by their display on surgical trays, their ominous potential to do violence was disturbingly revealed. For Collyer these objects, and the hands that hold them, are ambivalent. They can dispense love but also inflict harm. In this way, they convey the ambivalence of family life and its dynamics of power and, potentially, victimization.

*Hand-held*, however, was a refusal of victimization. These objects, and the wrapping of them, functioned as the kind of transitional phenomena theorized by D.W. Winnicott as crucial to the child's process of separation from the mother.[83] Like Collyer's *hand-held* objects, the child's transitional object is intensely charged: It brings comfort in the face of anxiety. For Collyer the act of binding up the sharp metal points and blades of these ostensibly benign kitchen tools was a way both to contain their threatening power and to metaphorically cover over shameful family secrets. But the wrapping can also signify a compulsive reordering of the world, a kind of serious play whereby painful

4.17 Gillian Collyer. *hand-held*, 2000. Photodocumentation of performance and installation at the Art Gallery of Nova Scotia, Halifax. Photograph: John Hillis.

4.18 Gillian Collyer. Detail of *hand-held*, 2000. Performance and installation at the Art Gallery of Nova Scotia, Halifax. Photograph: John Hillis.

memories are confronted, enfolded, and swathed in the healing bandages of Collyer's fuzzy, homespun wool. *Hand-held* emanated from deep within a psychic space of personal trauma and repression, but it moved these experiences out into the spaces of the social. In so doing, Collyer challenges our ideas about domestic life. Like Rosler, Collyer sees the nuclear family as historically determined within capitalism and sees the separation between private and public as an ideological fiction that sustains its hierarchical structure of power and powerlessness. *Hand-held* worked to break down this separation, to transform its isolating borders into a porous "skin" that allows the individual and the social, the private and the public, to flow and merge into a state of mutual accountability.

This feminist concern for family life and domesticity as a crucial point where individual and social experience intersect is also evident in recent performance work by another Canadian artist, Margaret Dragu, who has always merged her art and her political and artistic activism within the context of everyday life. Although deeply committed to feminism, Dragu, like Rosler, has always chafed at its tendencies to sever issues of gender from those of class and race. While working as a stripper in Toronto in the early 1980s to supplement her meagre income as a performance artist, Dragu was actively involved in the formation of a short-lived strippers' union, the Canadian Association for Burlesque Entertainers (CABE). Even though many feminist spokeswomen for anti-censorship and sex workers' rights supported this initiative, some other feminists attempted to entice Dragu away from such "exploitative" sex work by hiring her as a cleaning lady. The irony of this was not lost on Dragu, either at the time or later, when she became a mother and saw the connection between the low-paid and unpaid work that women continue to do in our society:

> As a mother, I am among the lowest paid (and unpaid) workers in our society. Domestic work is invisible. That is why illegal immigrants are nannies for the middle and upper classes. No one is watching ... When CABE was formed ... the only neophyte union I could relate to was the domestic workers' union from Ottawa, which was busy exposing members of parliament who hired illegal aliens to be their nannies and cleaning ladies. After all, I was a stripper, a cleaning lady, and a woman. I liked the domestic workers' union's understanding of class and race issues. There are a lot of similarities between strippers and cleaning ladies. And mothers. Perhaps this is because my politics and art come from the kitchen.[84]

4.19 Margaret Dragu. *Cleaning and Loving (It)*, 2000. Photodocumentation of street performance, 16 July, Toronto. Presented by Fado Performance Inc. Photograph: Debbie O'Rourke.

On 16 July 2000, Dragu again took her characteristic melding of art, politics, and community service to the street in a performance in Toronto called *Cleaning and Loving (It)*. This performance came at the end of a two-week artist's residency with Fado Performance Inc., during which Dragu enacted a series of kitchen-cleaning performances around Toronto. The public part of the performance began with Dragu scrubbing the steps of the Ontario Legislature building at Queen's Park and then wended its way as a parade through the downtown, with participants enthusiastically sweeping sidewalks and cleaning grime from bus shelters, mail boxes, and buildings (fig. 4.19). Following, however coincidentally, on the heels of the violent confrontation between riot police and antipoverty activists on those very Legislature steps a month earlier, the poignant implications of cleaning up the bloody residue resounded loudly, at least for those in the art community who came to participate in her performance and perhaps also for the bystanders around Queen's Park, who, if they were Toronto residents, would have surely known about this highly public and publicized mêlée.[85] Although Dragu's performance was not a direct response to the antipoverty protest, it nonetheless alluded clearly to the erosion of civil values and the dismantling of the networks of social caring that had also raised the ire of the antipoverty activists.

Although the work by Di Risio, Collyer, and Dragu was done decades after "second-wave" feminism first began to identify the complex issues arising from the sexual division of labour and its concomitant hierarchical separation of the public and private spheres, it attests to the intransigence of many social factors that still adversely affect women's lives, especially as a result of reduced social spending by governments in the past two decades. Feminist activism has challenged many aspects of contemporary society, but as Roberta Hamilton has pointed out, "the restructuring of economy, political life, and family that would be necessary to support these changes in practice have proved elusive," mainly because most public policy has failed to address the private conditions of family life.[86] Although the majority of women with children under age three are now in the workforce (61 per cent in 1999 according to Statistics Canada), the workplace continues to operate on the assumption that there are no conflicts between parenting and work.[87] The responsibility for childcare is largely left up to women, who have adopted different strategies for dealing with work and family. Some affluent families hire full-time caregivers or nannies, but while this may serve the needs of high-status career women, it also points to the discrepancy between feminism's egalitarian ideals and the reality for many women. Sedef Arat-Koc has pointed out, echoing Dragu's own observations, that because most of these caregivers come from Third World countries, the relationship between female employers and their domestic workers "emphasizes, most clearly, the class, racial/ethnic and citizenship differences among women at the expense of their gender unity."[88] The lack of structural accommodations to women's participation in the public sphere has led many to take up part-time work, but this tends to lead to jobs, not careers. Although successive Canadian federal governments have been promising publicly funded daycare since 1986, this has yet to be implemented. Until the state takes some responsibility for addressing the competing demands of work and parenting, the economic inequalities between women and men will be sustained into the future.[89] Not only will this continue to leave women with the larger burden for negotiating the conflicts between public and private life, but it will also keep them vulnerable to the forms of violence that are all too often perpetrated and hidden in the privacy of the home and thus all too easily disavowed by public-policy makers and legislators fixated on tax cuts and so-called fiscal restraint.

As the work discussed in this chapter abundantly demonstrates, identifying and analyzing the nexus of connections between the personal and the political, the private and the public, has always been a central concern for feminism. Although it may not be possible to identify how feminist performance art has contributed directly to policy change and political action, its strategies of autobiography and narrative have given expression at the aesthetic level to feminism's broad demands for cultural and social change while also producing innovative aesthetic forms. As the critic Arlene Raven wrote, "personal narrative entered women's visual vocabulary as expression and public disclosure of the great rush of speech which women exchanged privately when they broke their silent isolation within home, studio or workplace to gather for consciousness-raising conversations. These expressions eventually took many creative forms within visual arts – visual 'speech,' inventive linguistics, diaristic and imaginative narratives, words with and as images."[90] Such feminist practices have had a significant impact upon mainstream art by bringing to light issues generally submerged or even denigrated within the dominant cultural discourse and by exposing the fallacy of the Kantian notions of disinterest and universalism that had underpinned Modernist aesthetics. Moreover, by grounding their references to personal experience within the context of the social world, feminist artists have demonstrated how it is possible to sustain the avant-garde goal of organizing "a new life praxis from a basis in art."[91]

# 5

# Roles and Transformations

## PERFORMATIVITY: "WHAT DO I WANT TO BE?"

The exploration of autobiographical and narrative material provided feminist artists with a voice and a place from which to speak about their particular experiences as women. But if one of the questions that autobiographical and narrative modes addressed was "What am I?" its corollary was "What do I want to be?" As a question that implied the possibility of both personal and social change, it led many artists to engage with the ideas about subjectivity and otherness that Simone de Beauvoir had so forcefully articulated in *The Second Sex*. We recall that de Beauvoir had concluded that, in defining himself as the subject, man relegated woman to the position of object, or other. She argued that woman has been confined to this position of immanence because of the limits, definitions, and roles imposed on her within patriarchal society. De Beauvoir acknowledged that there are no easy ways for women to escape this immanence, but she insisted that if women are to overcome the forces of circumstance, the process must begin with their recognition and assertion of their right to self-determination.[1]

The impact of de Beauvoir's emphasis on the forces of social circumstance and the imposition of roles and restrictions for women is evident in feminist performance that examined the relationship between identity, roles, and transformations. Two main trajectories can be discerned within this broader theme. One consists of the work of artists who asserted their subjectivity through their capacity to be agents of their own identities, which they could transform at will. The other consists of work in which performance was used both to challenge notions of fixed identity and to expose the oppressive assumptions and fallacies upon which such notions were based. In both cases, the concept of "performativity" is central. This concept emerged in the late 1980s from a basis in postmodern philosophy and, especially through the writings of Judith Butler, has come to have decisive consequences for theories of both gender and performance.[2]

Butler's concept of performativity is itself based on de Beauvoir's feminist revision of existential, phenomenological, and psychoanalytic critiques of Cartesian thought as articulated in the work of Jean-Paul Sartre, Jacques Lacan, and Maurice Merleau-Ponty.[3] René Descartes formulated a dualistic conception of subjectivity in which consciousness (*cogito*) is disembodied, transcendent, and opposed to the brute materiality of the body. In this conception, which has dominated Western thought since the Enlightenment, the subject "I" is constituted through knowledge derived from the disembodied and objectifying "eye" of vision.[4] By contrast, these mid-twentieth century critics of Cartesianism postulated theories of subjectivity as embodied, intersubjective, and contingent upon self/other relations.[5]

De Beauvoir's exposure of the sex-blind models of her colleagues' critiques of Cartesian subjectivity revealed that the (male) subject's promise of disembodied transcendence is not only illusory, but in fact dependent upon a condition of phenomenological interdependence whereby woman is "doom[ed] to immanence since her transcendence is to be overshadowed and forever transcended by another ego (*conscience*) which is essential and sovereign."[6] As Butler succinctly put it, women are perceived to "occupy their bodies as their essential and enslaving identities."[7] But in keeping with de Beauvoir's categorical assertion that "One is not born, but rather becomes, a woman," Butler, too, concluded that there is no essential femininity (or masculinity).[8] Rather, we "perform" our subjectivities by means of stylized and repeated acts of speech and gesture that create the illusion of an abiding (gendered) self. For Butler, there is no inherent correlation between sex and gender. Our ideas about gender and sexuality converge to construe an ontological fallacy of biological sex as the essence of gender, but this fallacy is itself a "regulatory fiction" or "essence fabrication."[9]

Although Butler's concept of gender performativity postdates the period of early feminism, it nonetheless has important ramifications for early feminist performance art that explored social roles and identity transformations. Since, as de Beauvoir stated, prevailing conceptions of subjectivity worked to "stabilize [woman] as object," the manipulation of roles and the enactment of self-transformation in performance seemed to offer the possibility of resisting such imposed and stabilizing determinations.[10] As Elin Diamond has pointed out, however, Butler rejects discussions of performativity in relation to theatre (and, presumably, performance art) because they imply the existence of a performer "who ontologically precedes and then fabricates gender effects."[11] For Butler, this is impossible because no identity can exist before, outside, or beyond the gendered acts that perform it.[12]

This point brings us to the distinction that needs to be made between Butler's theory of performativity and performance as a cultural form. Although performance encompasses performativity, Butler distinguishes between the two because performance is a "bounded act" predicated on the conscious application of the performer's "will" or "choice" as a humanist subject, while performativity "consists in a reiteration of norms which precede, constrain, and exceed the performer."[13] While this is a useful distinction, Diamond and others have suggested that Butler oversimplifies the complexity of performance. Geraldine Harris, for example, has argued that the performer who activates such will or choice in the "bounded act" of a performance can indeed establish a critical distance from performativity, although this can only happen "when the difference *and* the interdependence of performativity and performance are both remarked and preserved, not where they appear as identical." As she goes on to explain, this can occur when the bounded or framed act of performance as mimetic practice is used to point to or make intelligible how the performativity of sex/gender depends on having the appearance and effect of being "real."[14] What Harris describes is similar to the use of Brechtian "alienation effects" discussed below, whereby the feminist performer in art or in theatre can simultaneously inhabit herself (as woman/character) and stand beside herself (as actor/agent) in order to show or mimic how the reiteration of stylized acts produces gender, rather than the other way around.

For her part, Diamond acknowledges that "'performativity' is not an 'act' but a 'reiteration' or 'citation.'" Yet she questions Butler's rejection of performance as cultural form in discussions of performativity: "[W]hy should we restrict its iterative sites to theory and to the theorist's acts of seeing? Theatre, too, is theory ... [and performance] is the site in which performativity materializes in concentrated form, where the 'concealed or dissimulated conventions' of which acts are mere repetitions might be investigated and reimagined."[15] At the heart of this distinction between performance and performativity lies the question of subjectivity and agency. Because Butler's theory of the performativity of sex/gender purports to explode the very idea of gender as a category of identity, it seems conducive to feminist performance that used roles and transformations to expose the fallacy of fixed identity. At the same time, however, the radical implication of Butler's position that gender is a "regulatory fiction" seems antithetical to early feminism's objectives of seeking subjectivity and self-determination. This does not discount Butler's relevance, however, for as Rebecca Schneider has argued, "her theories employ an important notion of agency: that thinking a world makes a world."[16] In other words, while there may be no essence of gender identity available to be "expressed" outwardly, the enactment of transformations and role playing enables a self-determined and reciprocal play between the limiting binaries of subject and object positions that feminists and others have sought to expose and undermine in and through performance.

## PERSONA TRANSFORMATIONS

Feminist performance that used role playing and transformations often relied on the creation of personae or characters. As historian Moira Roth observed, "some of these creations were lifelike and closely linked to autobiographical sources while others, distanced from the artist's personality and everyday life, were clearly framed as artistic inventions."[17] This admitted the performance of identity as multifaceted, unfixed, and open to determination. Furthermore, because this strategy highlighted the artifice of performance as play, as representation, it was predicated not on a naive assertion of the ontological "presence" of the body/self, but rather on an understanding of that body/self (or selves) as fully mediated within the Symbolic Order of language and culture.[18] In this sense, feminist performances using personae and characters were more in keeping with the acting strategies of Brecht's epic theatre than with the Stanislavsky tradition of "method acting," epitomized in its American manifestation by Marlon Brando as Stanley in the movie *A Streetcar Named Desire*, where the credibility of the fiction requires the actor to be completely effaced by the character or role being played.[19] By contrast, Brecht wanted the actor to maintain a distance from the character so as to avoid empathy, which he felt suppresses critical reason. As Elin Diamond has argued, through the use of "alienation effects," the Brechtian "performer-subject disappears neither into a representation of the character *nor* into a representation of the actor: each remains processual, contingent, incomplete."[20] As Rebecca Schneider put it, this double agency enabled the feminist performance artist to wield her own "alienation effect *as a 'woman'*" and, in Alisa Solomon's terms, "to make those quotation marks around 'woman' visible," thus widening the distance between signified and signifier and calling attention to the gap.[21]

For the American artist Eleanor Antin, this gap in signification and the question of the mutability of identity had been ongoing concerns since the mid-1960s. Her *Blood of a Poet Box* (1965) was a work in the Fluxus mode that gathered 100 microscope slides of poets' blood in an ironic play on the idea of creative genius since the blood smears revealed nothing of the "essence" of the individual poets' identities, and her *California Lives* (1969) and *Portraits of Eight New York Women* (1970) consisted of assemblages of artifacts of consumer and domestic culture meant to evoke the professional and personal attributes of real and fictitious individuals in rebus-like "portraits."[22] By the early 1970s, Antin had turned her interest in identity formation onto herself by creating a gallery of specific, yet typological, characters. In a statement that she wrote to accompany her *Eleanor 1954* performance at the Los Angeles Woman's Building in 1974, she explained how her personae were derived from her early aspirations as an actress: "I decided to try and find her, that old Eleanor of 20 years before, that desperate romantic, who became an actress out of a kind of perverse honesty brought on by her suspicion that she hadn't any self of her own and might as well call a spade a spade by borrowing other people's."[23] While Antin's invention of performance personae relates to her early acting ambitions, each one was derived from a complex hybrid of autobiography and fiction that she referred to as a "mythological machine ... capable of calling up and defining my self. I finally settled upon a quadripolar system, sort of a magnetic field of 4 polar charged images – the Ballerina, the King, the Black Movie Star and the Nurse."[24]

Antin's male role as King was formed in response to her question "If I were a man, what sort of man would I be?" and to her realization that, once dressed as a bearded man, she closely resembled Van Dyke's portrait of the English king, Charles I (fig. 5.1).[25] In this historical figure she discovered "a kind of phenomenological core stunningly and intensely related to me, of a small, Hamlet-like man, alternatively power mad and depressed, alienated from the world by a stubborn romanticism – the romantic ruler of an absolute void."[26] Like all Antin's characters, the King was able to slip between the art world and the real

5.1 Eleanor Antin. *The King of Solana Beach*, 1975. Photodocumentation of street performance at Solana Beach, California.

world with ease. Although he appeared in photographs, videotapes, and performances in art galleries, his main interaction was with his "subjects" at Solana Beach in California, where he conversed with beer-swilling surfers about the war in Vietnam and with senior citizens displaced by real-estate developers.[27]

Antin was just as easily able to slip between roles. From deposed and exiled king, she moved to inhabit another character on the margins of society, the Nurse. Antin's initial interest in the Nurse character came from her questions about the clichéd and subservient role of nurses in contemporary and popular culture – "a jaunty blend of servant and geisha, sharing features with many other women's service professions like secretaries, airline stewardesses and wives."[28] Her video *The Adventures of a Nurse* (1976) was a satirical soap opera starring Antin as Little Nurse Eleanor along with a cast of paper dolls (fig. 5.2). But realizing that the levity with which she played Nurse Eleanor did not address her intent to acknowledge the dignity of the profession created by

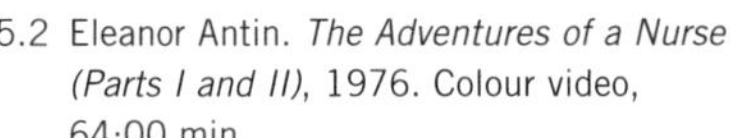

5.2 Eleanor Antin. *The Adventures of a Nurse (Parts I and II)*, 1976. Colour video, 64:00 min.

5.3 Eleanor Antin. *The Ballerina and the Bum*, 1974. Black-and-white video, 53:00 min.

Florence Nightingale, she reinvented herself as Eleanor Nightingale, who aided the sick and wounded in *The Angel of Mercy* (1977), an elaborate reenactment of the Crimean War documented as a video.

Antin's Ballerina emerged simultaneously with the King and Nurse and similarly explored the gaps and connections between identity and appearance. After studying ballet for several months, she began to have herself photographed in order to see "what kind of ballerina I was becoming."[29] Realizing that she could convincingly portray a Russian-style ballerina, she assumed this persona and prepared for her New York premier in *The Ballerina Goes to the Big Apple*, performed along with *Eleanor 1954* at the Woman's Building in 1974. Later that year, Antin revealed her talents for Chaplinesque parody in the video *The Ballerina and the Bum*, in which these two characters meet in a train yard and discuss life, hopes, and dreams while waiting for their boxcar to depart for New York (fig. 5.3). By 1975 the Ballerina was performing on stage in *The Little Match Girl Ballet*, and by 1979 she had finally made it to New York. By then, however, she had transformed into the great Black Ballerina, Eleanora Antinova, star of Diaghilev's Ballet Russes.[30]

Antin had already developed a black persona, the Black Movie Star, whose role differed from the others in that Antin's intention was not to *be*, but to *act*. But when a photograph of the Black Movie Star was published in the magazine *Chrysalis*, feminist author Michelle Cliff wrote to the editor attacking Antin for "Blaxploitation." In response, Antin replied:

> As for my being a Black Movie Star, it is the nature of movie stars to play roles, to act ... My blackness is the existential center of my work, calling up the theatrical structure of reality by placing the role of the actor – she who is "other" than herself – up front. Blacks are "the other," as women are "the other," as, for that matter, artists and kings are "the other" ... But we blacks do not experience ourselves as "the other," as we kings do not experience ourselves as "the other." Thus there is a continuous struggle between the world and the self over the nature of reality.[31]

This short-lived character has never been fully addressed in the literature on Antin. In his essay for Antin's 1999 retrospective exhibition, Howard Fox simply refers to the Black Movie Star as "an outsider, an oddity, a highly visible interloper, someone who doesn't quite belong."[32] In her essay for the same catalogue, Lisa Bloom positions Antin as one of the few artists during the 1970s whose work addressed racial and ethnic differences, yet she does not analyze the Black Movie Star persona. She acknowledges that Antin's Black Ballerina ran decidedly against the grain of the "whiteness" of the entire culture of the ballet, but for Bloom, Antin's construction of herself as Eleanora Antinova serves mainly as an analogy for her Jewish ethnicity: "By representing herself as black, rather than what she is – white and Jewish – Antin seems ... to point out that Jewish stereotypes and discrimination against Eastern European Jews earlier in the century are ideologically akin to such treatment of blacks."[33]

As with all Antin's characters, autobiography was the starting point, but Antin also saw autobiography as malleable, mobile, and active: "Autobiography in its fundamental sense is the self getting a grip on itself ... [It] can be considered a particular type of transformation in which the subject chooses a specific, as yet unarticulated image and proceeds to progressively define [herself] ... The usual aids to self-definition – sex, age, talent, time, and space – are merely tyrannical limitations upon my freedom of choice."[34] The autobiographical origins of Antin's characters bound them to herself, but she never wholly became them, nor they her. The credibility of her transformations was always subtly undermined by their evident artifice, thus ensuring that the gap between herself and her personae always remained to signify her subjectivity not as being but as the *agency* of being.

This foregrounding of imposture was a structural device utilized extensively in feminist performance to draw attention to the complex relationships between subjectivity and social positioning. In an essay for an exhibition on the history of performance art, Robyn Brentano made this perceptive observation:

> As many performers confronted the gaps and differences between their subjective perceptions, dreams, and fantasies and the realities of a gender-biased world, they began to develop fictional personae and to work in quasi-narrative forms to negotiate the divide and challenge stereotypes of women. Concern with showing the contingencies of identity and representation of women led to a kind of doubly-aspected performance in which the artist was both herself and other. In many works, the performer conveyed both an air of authenticity and the falseness of her inscribed identity. Performance used disruptive strategies to reveal the multiplicity of selves required of women in daily life.[35]

In other words, the authenticity and the falseness of these performance personae were held in tense counterpoint as a way to disrupt the fictive naturalism associated with characterization and to confound distinctions between art and life, fiction and reality, acting and being. The use of this Brechtian device reveals the growing perception among women that femininity was simultaneously a role that women played and an identity or position that determined how they experienced the world.

Sometimes these invented personae, like Lynn Hershman's Roberta Breitmore, took on a self-propelling existence similar to Antin's. Initially conceived as a kind of living portrait, by 1975 the Roberta Breitmore persona had begun to assume a life of her own, with a driver's license, bank account, therapist, and welfare file. Hershman documented her existence in photographs, films, drawings, and live performances as well as in a detailed diary of her thoughts and experiences (fig. 5.4).[36] Historian Josephine Withers has described the Breitmore character as a metaportrait, an archetype of the "Everywoman," a view that seems commensurate with the essentialist tendencies of much early feminist art.[37] Yet Martha Rosler, who was critical of such tendencies in general and was bothered by what she saw as Hershman's preoccupation with Bre-

5.4 Lynn Hershman. *Roberta Breitmore's Construction Chart*, 1973. Third generation "C" print, 45.1 x 60.2 cm (original in colour).

itmore's alienation and loneliness, recognized the inherent subversiveness of her pursuit of an identity cobbled together within "the interstices of orderly society."[38] Indeed, in contrast to the normal outcome of the process of individuation, Hershman declared, "When Roberta becomes 'real' enough, it is likely she will commit suicide."[39] This moment occurred in 1978, and Breitmore was put to rest by means of a ritualistic burial in Italy.

The work of both Hershman and Antin exemplified the interest among women performance artists at this time in personal transformation as a way to problematize notions of identity as fixed and singular. Although it was very characteristic of feminist performance in California, where there was a well-established community of feminist artists, it recurred elsewhere and in different contexts.[40] In Vancouver, for example, the artist Kate Craig invented a fictive persona, Lady (Barbara) Brute, in 1970, but this character did not emerge within a feminist art context; indeed, none existed there at the time (fig. 5.5). Instead, Craig was part of a group of young Vancouver artists who were interested in Dada absurdity, puns, and pranks and who had a Warholian fascination with mass culture.[41] The group was strongly oriented to performative activities, and during the period 1969–70, each member invented an alias. Although they often operated independently of each other, Eric Metcalfe's Dr Brute and Craig's Lady Brute were consorts of a kind, and both used the leopard spot as the symbol of their fictive personae. But where Metcalfe was content with a leopard-covered saxophone and a tuxedo with leopard lapels, Craig collected a vast inventory of leopard paraphernalia and clothing, which she wore in her appearances around Vancouver as Lady Brute, doing normal things like riding the bus, visiting the park, or going shopping.

The Brutes' fascination with the leopard pattern lay in its associations with camouflage, sexuality, and kitsch, which converged with their interests in glamour, power, and the banality of mass culture.[42] Leopard skin is particularly associated with female sexuality, suggesting wildness, exoticism, and feline sensuality. As such, it has acquired a favoured place in the repertoire of fetishism.[43] Yet Craig's own view of Lady Brute and her fetishistic trappings was ambivalent. Unlike Metcalfe, who identified wholly with Dr Brute, Craig saw Lady Brute as a mask to be put on or removed at will: "I never felt I *was* Lady Brute. One of the wonderful things about Lady Brute was that there was a stand-in at every corner. If I wore the leopard skin, it was only to become a part of this incredible culture of women who adopted that costume ... It was a way of exaggerating something that already existed in the culture."[44] The leopard gear thus served as a device by which Craig could be publicly disruptive of middle-class propriety, problematize the relationship between self and image, and, as Grant Arnold has noted, "identify with a specifically female culture for whom images of glamour operate simultaneously as a form of social bondage and a potential source of power."[45]

5.5 Kate Craig. *Lady (Barbara) Brute*, 1973. Photograph: Rodney Werden for FILE *Megazine*'s issue "Nude Egos in a Nude Era."

Eventually Craig became aware that Lady Brute had been too invested in the fantasies of her male peers, and accordingly, she retired her in a performance that was documented in a video called *Skins: Lady Brute Presents Her Leopard Skin Wardrobe* (1975). This coalescing of Craig's feminist consciousness, signified more by the abandonment than by the invention of Lady Brute, coincided with her deepening involvement in the running of Western Front, which had been founded two years earlier by Craig and seven other artists. Western Front was part of a network of artist-run centres that emerged in Canada in the early 1970s under new funding policies of the Canada Council for the Arts.[46] These centres were crucial to the formation of contemporary art practice in Canada, where there was no history either of an indigenous avant-garde or of significant patronage for contemporary art.[47] Women participated actively in these centres but still had to fight for rights and recognition. Craig's unlikely tactic was to collect an array of pink garments, called *The Pink Poem* (1977–80), which she wore during the course of everyday interactions with her male colleagues: "I read that psychiatric and penal institutions often painted their walls pink because it was believed this gentle colour calmed people. In those days we women were trying to achieve certain goals in institutions dominated by men. My strategy was to wear pink clothing in order to calm them while making demands that may have caused them anxiety."[48]

Craig's experience alludes to some of the particular circumstances that have to be accounted for in understanding the history of feminist art in Canada. Prior to the establishment of the artist-run communities in the 1970s, many Canadian artists who were engaged in contemporary practice had to leave Canada for either Paris (e.g., Paul-Émile Borduas, Jean-Paul Riopelle) or New York (e.g., Joyce Wieland, Michael Snow). The artist-run network helped reverse this tendency by providing a community of discourse and limited financial support, although these centres had to be continuously vigilant in justifying their existence. This milieu presented Canadian feminist artists with a complex problem, for they had to work with their male colleagues just to establish the basic resources and legitimacy of the artist-run network while also struggling against them in order to insist that their feminist concerns be acknowledged.

It was precisely this dual concern that Vera Frenkel addressed in *The Secret Life of Cornelia Lumsden: A Remarkable Story* (1979–86). This cycle of work used stories, installations, and videos to create the life of Cornelia Lumsden, a fictive Canadian author who wrote a famous book in 1934 called *The Alleged Grace of Fat People*. Lumsden was said to have gone missing on the eve of the Second World War and to be living in poverty in Paris. In the 1979 video *Her Room in Paris*, Lumsden herself never appears, but she is discussed by four characters, all played by Frenkel: the Friend, the Rival, the Expert on her life and work, and the Commentator for the Canadian Broadcasting Corporation (CBC) news (fig. 5.6). Frenkel thought of this "as a very Canadian and a very feminist work." Not only was the famous missing novelist a woman, an oddity itself at the time, but the idea of her living in exile was also very Canadian "because in this country, the role of the artist is such a vexed question." So complete was the creation of the Lumsden fiction that she passed for real in *Lost Canadian*, an installation done for the Canadian Pavilion at Expo '86 in Vancouver. This work included a bank of forty-eight video monitors along a long corridor that told the Lumsden story through narrative and image sequences as part of "Au pied de la lettre," an exhibition of famous Canadians like Glenn Gould and Marshall McLuhan. Frenkel explained: "The Expo piece was about why there was no place for [Lumsden] in this country. I am not Lumsden, and she is not me. But I did create her. And I found an extraordinary resonance with her experience not only among artists but among people who understand the price paid for creating a disaffected public. This work had those kinds of implications."[49] Frenkel thus identified closely with her invented persona and was interested in blurring the boundaries between fiction and reality to see how each was constructed. Nevertheless, she saw the Lumsden character more as a metaphor for social relations than for personal experience, one that could give voice to Frenkel's acute awareness of the intertwined difficulties both of surviving as a Canadian artist and of gaining international visibility for Canadian culture.

5.6 Vera Frenkel. *The Secret Life of Cornelia Lumsden: A Remarkable Story*, 1979–86. Part I, *Her Room in Paris*, 1979. Photodocumentation of installation (partial view) with 60:00 min. looped colour video narrative and props at Fine Arts on Markham, Toronto, 1979. Photograph: Helena Wilson.

## SOCIAL ROLES

This focus in feminist performance on social roles and the ideological structures that determine femininity was far more prevalent than blanket characterizations of early feminist art as essentialist would lead us to believe. The limitations of this crude assessment are especially evident when we consider how sophisticated the strategies of feminist artists had to be just to get gender on the table as a legitimate question for art practice. The art world at the time was preoccupied by aesthetic concerns that precluded any such considerations. Even the most vanguard art forms like Minimalism and Conceptualism required compliance with the dominant, ostensibly gender-neutral, aesthetic values. Even Conceptual art was so circumscribed by self-reflexive propositions about art and its limits that it was unable to engage with the political turmoil then permeating American society. As Blake Stimson put it, "ultimately, most conceptual art confined itself to the laboratory of the art world."[50] Moreover, its critique of modernist individualism militated against the very subject-centred inquiry that formed the basis of new modes of political understanding emerging at this precise moment through the agencies of the feminist and civil rights movements.[51] As Lucy Lippard said in her catalogue essay for the 1995 exhibition "Reconsidering the Object of Art," Conceptual artists might have paid "lip service" to the significance of these emergent movements, but their hostility to the idea that women could make good, or, in the critical language of the day, "serious," art is evident in the dearth of women associated with Conceptual art. Indeed, only nine women were among the fifty-five artists included in this major exhibition of Conceptual art.[52]

This is a small percentage, but it shows that although these aesthetic waters were well patrolled by their male inhabitants, it was not impossible for women to negotiate them and, in some cases, to adapt the critical methodologies of Conceptual art to a specifically social and/or feminist agenda. Part of this agenda was to expose the fallacy of aesthetic autonomy and gender neutrality in art, and part was to dislocate these dominant aesthetic premises by investigating the contentious relationships between subjectivity, identity, and social role that these premises sought to obscure. One of the works in this exhibition, for example, was Eleanor Antin's *Carving: A Traditional Sculpture* (1972). This work documents the daily effects of a thirty-six-day dieting regime in which Antin reduced her weight by ten pounds (fig. 5.7). It referred,

5.7 Eleanor Antin. *Carving: A Traditional Sculpture*, 1972. Installation view. 148 black-and-white photographs, 17.8 x 12.7 cm each, with text.

with tongue-in-cheek, not only to the traditional method of sculptural carving at a time when such practice seemed almost obsolete, but also to the way that women feel compelled to alter and improve their bodies in order to achieve the prescriptive ideals of feminine beauty. Moreover, by documenting the entire process in a series of 144 clinical-looking black-and-white photographs, Antin seemed to mock both Conceptual art's fetishizing of documentation and the way that the beauty, fitness, and cosmetic-surgery industries favour the formulaic cliché of the before-and-after photographs, which miraculously occlude the disciplined renunciation, labour, and often painful healing required by the "self-improvement" makeover.

This merging of Conceptual and performative practice also became evident around 1970 in the work of Adrian Piper, who was another one of the women included in "Reconsidering the Object of Art." Piper's early work so thoroughly embodied the ideals of Conceptual art that by 1969 she had already begun to gain international recognition in

Conceptual art circles even though she was still a student.[53] Although her work since that time has changed dramatically, mainly through her critique of the prohibition against subject-centred inquiry inherent in Conceptual art, Piper still considers herself a Conceptual artist.[54] The turning point came in 1970 when a series of events occurred that, along with her awareness of the women's movement, changed her entire outlook on art: the invasion of Cambodia, the brutal attacks against antiwar protesters at Kent State and Jackson State Universities, and the student uprising at City College, where she had just begun undergraduate studies in philosophy.[55] Piper's initial response was to revise the work that she had planned for the "Information" show at the Museum of Modern Art and to replace her submission to the "Conceptual Art and Conceptual Aspects" show at the New York Cultural Center with the following statement: "The work originally intended for this space has been withdrawn ... I submit its absence as evidence of the inability of art expression to have meaningful existence under conditions other than those of peace, equality, truth and freedom."[56]

Reflecting on her "position as an artist, a woman, and a black," Piper now found herself unable to express her growing social concerns "in *any* aesthetic language I had at my disposal."[57] Her need to take account of what was going on around her led to her dissatisfaction with art that referred back to what she called "conditions of separateness, order, exclusivity, and the stability of easily-accepted functional identities which no longer exist."[58] Instead, she became interested in eliminating the art object or conceptual proposition as discrete form, "as a kind of Kantian 'thing in itself,' with its isolated internal relationships, and self-determining esthetic standards."[59] Her solution was to bypass the art object or conceptual documentation as mediation between the artist's creative process and the viewer's interpretive reaction by using performance to confront the viewer directly with Piper's own unpredictable and uncontrollable presence.

Piper's first such performance took place unannounced in April 1970 at Max's Kansas City, a popular hangout for the New York art crowd. Wearing a blindfold, earplugs, nose plug, and gloves, Piper walked around the crowded bar for an hour, speaking to no one. While this insulated her from the "art consciousness" of the day, her self-objectification also turned her into a spectacle; yet, paradoxically, this enabled her to function as a subjective agency capable of affecting change in others. She referred to this subjective agency as a catalytic force that concentrated the entire artistic experience into a moment of confronta-

5.8 Adrian Piper. *Catalysis IV*, 1970. Photodocumentation of street performance, New York. Photograph: Rosemary Mayer.

tion in which "the work has no meaning of independent existence outside of its function as a medium of change; i.e. it exists only as a catalytic agent between myself and the viewer."[60]

By the fall of 1970, these ideas had become the basis for Piper's *Catalysis* performances. These took place in ordinary public settings because she wanted to avoid any association with an art context, which she felt would "*prepare* the viewer to be catalyzed," thereby eliciting a predetermined set of responses and making actual catalysis impossible.[61] In these performances, Piper carried out normal, everyday activities but with alterations to her appearance that ranged from the bizarre to the grotesque. In *Catalysis I* she rode the subway at rush hour and went browsing in a book store wearing clothes that had soaked for a week in a putrid mixture of vinegar, eggs, milk, and cod liver oil. In *Catalysis III* she painted her clothes, attached a "WET PAINT" sign, and went shopping for gloves at Macy's department store, while in *Catalysis IV* she walked and rode the bus around Manhattan with a towel stuffed into her mouth and trailing down her front (fig. 5.8). In *Catalysis V* she signed out books at New York's Donnell Library with a concealed tape-recorder playing prerecorded belches at full volume. What interested Piper in the *Catalysis* series was not only "letting art lurk in the midst of things," but also being both the subject and object of an art capable of provoking an active and undetermined response.[62] Although some reactions were hostile, Piper found that if she addressed people in ordinary ways, such as asking for the time or apologizing for bumping into someone, she could elicit a normal response. This was enlightening to her because it showed that she could transcend "the differences I was presenting to them by making that kind of contact."[63]

Piper's study of philosophy enabled her to articulate her artistic concerns more precisely as an investigation of subject-object relations between "1) myself as solipsistic object inhering in the reflective consciousness of an external audience or subject; and 2) my own self-consciousness of me as an object, as the object of my self-consciousness."[64] In *Food for the Spirit* (1971) Piper documented the physical and metaphysical changes that she underwent during a period of fasting and isolation while reading Immanuel Kant's *Critique of Pure Reason*. In response to her anxiety that she was disappearing into a state of Kantian self-transcendence, she periodically photographed herself, both clothed and nude, in front of a mirror while reading passages from the *Critique* into a tape recorder. By thus documenting herself as the embodied object of her philosophical enquiry, Piper simultaneously made explicit her own particularized subjectivity as a black woman.[65] As Maurice Berger has noted, this marked a decisive shift away from the aesthetic privileging of the mind over the body and of the intellectual over the corporeal that had thus far predominated in Conceptual art.[66]

Although *Food for the Spirit* was a private performance, Piper's disavowal of artistic autonomy soon led her to return to the problematics of the external world and to what would become an ongoing preoccupation with the social negotiation of racial identity. Drawing upon the "methodological individualism" that she had discovered in the *Catalysis* series, she began *The Mythic Being* series (1972–75).[67] Wearing an Afro wig, dark glasses, and a moustache, she assumed the guise of an abrasive, hostile, working-class, inner-city black or Latino youth (fig. 5.9). As her alter ego, *The Mythic Being* enabled Piper to "change not only gender but class, and [to acquire] the overt racial characteristics she lacked."[68] But although *The Mythic Being* series addressed her social awareness that the civil rights movement had failed to overcome the class subordination of blacks, it also encompassed many autobiographical elements. The speech bubbles that accompany the photographic panels of *The Mythic Being* were drawn from Piper's journal entries, which revealed her obsessions about "the failure of friendship,

5.9 Adrian Piper. *The Mythic Being: Getting Back*, 1975. Photodocumentation of street performance, Cambridge, MA.

of dialogue; self-interest, mistrust, and mutual indifference; dishonesties, evasions, polite surfaces, deflected contact."[69] Appearing among the art gallery ads in the *Village Voice* or seen mugging one of Piper's friends on the street in Cambridge, Massachusetts (where Piper was then a graduate student in philosophy at Harvard), *The Mythic Being* was an image of Third World hostility and alienation, an "antagonistic Other [that] represented the alien in all of us."[70]

This merging of personal and social politics is central to all Piper's work and is grounded in her engagement with Kantian philosophy. She wants to reconcile Kant's moral theories – which posit the self as dependent upon a rationally consistent and coherent view of the world that enables experience to be assimilated into a priori categories – with her own awareness of how people respond to difference (e.g., race, gender, class) by making what she calls "pseudorational defenses":

> Through the work I try to construct a concrete, immediate, and personal relationship between me and the viewer that locates us in an indexical present that is itself embedded in the network of political cause and effect. In this way my work differs from what I call "global" political art that attempts to educate its viewers about issues that bear no direct and obvious relationship to their lives. My purpose is to transform the viewer psychologically, by presenting him or her with an unavoidable concrete reality that cuts through the defensive rationalizations by which we insulate ourselves against the facts of our political responsibility.[71]

Piper's strategy for addressing racism is thus not merely to identify its individualized effects, but also to locate the process of transformation directly in the viewer or public in order to make them cognizant of their own responsibility for the social operations of oppression. Nor is it her intent to celebrate difference. Indeed, she repudiates those poststructuralists who denigrate Kant's values of universality because, in doing so, "they ignore much of what we all have in common as human beings, the cognitive capacities we actually share."[72] But as staunchly as Piper defends the validity of the modernist concepts of rationality and objectivity for women and people of colour, which she feels are denied them by poststructuralism, her own propositions about how identity is negotiated within performative acts is not entirely incompatible with poststructuralist readings of her work that stress the instability of identity and subject positions.[73]

Martha Wilson is another artist whose work emerged within the context of Conceptual art by struggling to reconcile its critical strategies and priorities with her emerging feminist concerns. Wilson was exposed to Conceptual art at the Nova Scotia College of Art and Design (NSCAD) in 1969 when she and her partner, Richards Jarden, came to Halifax from Ohio.[74] While Jarden studied at NSCAD, Wilson completed her master's degree in English literature at Dalhousie University. After dropping out of the doctorate program over a dispute with her supervisor, she began teaching English at NSCAD. The conceptual orientation at NSCAD opened new possibilities for Wilson, who said that "It was an unbelievable revelation that visual art could consist of language."[75] By 1971 Wilson was producing works that were typical in form and structure of Conceptual art's linguistic mode but that differed in dealing not with abstract aesthetic concepts but with propositions about identity and cultural relationships:

*Unknown Piece*: A woman under ether has a child in a large hospital. When she comes to, she is permitted to select the child she thinks is hers from among the babies in the nursery.

*Cultural Piece*: A WASP couple and a non-English-speaking ethnic couple have babies and trade them. The children may be told the identity of their parents if they ask.

Despite her enthusiasm for Conceptual art, Wilson's title for this series – the *Chauvinistic Pieces* – alludes to the alienation that she felt from a community that she sought to be part of but that excluded her both as a woman and as an interloper with no credentials as an artist.[76]

Ironically, Wilson's increased proximity to the centre of art production – and socialization – seems to have reinforced her sense of her marginal and, at best, supporting role as the English-grammar teacher. As an artist, she remained firmly fixed in the "blind spot" of her male peers.[77] But, in a move deftly calculated to make a spectacle of her own invisibility, Wilson began to produce works pairing textual propositions with photographs that made the gendered implications of these pieces unmistakable. In *Breast Forms Permutated* (1972), nine different pairs of breasts (conical, spherical, pendulous, etc.) are arranged in a modernist grid, with the theoretically "perfect set" in the centre (fig. 5.10). Although *Breast Forms* may be seen as a perverse parody of the

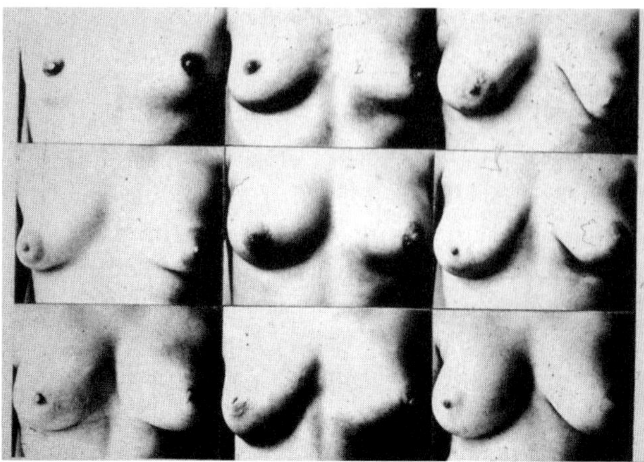

5.10 Martha Wilson. *Breast Forms Permutated*, 1972. Postcard with photographs (recto) and text (verso), 12.5 x 17.6 cm.

oppressive effects of women's compulsion to measure their social and individual worth according to body image, it also operates as a critique of visibility itself in its ridiculing of what Amelia Jones has called the "Western fixation on the female body as object of a masculine 'gaze.'"[78] As feminists have argued, the scopic regimes of representation are problematic not simply because they position women as passive, sexual objects "given-to-be-seen," but also because, as Rebecca Schneider writes, "our cultural ways of knowing [have been] traditionally wrapped up with visuality, with vision set forth as proprietary, transcendent of tactility, omnisciently disinterested, and essentially separate from the object which it apprehends."[79] However, for Wilson the emerging artist, the question of visuality was fraught not only with the problem of how women are positioned within representation, but also with the problem of how to pose questions about visuality and representation within an artistic milieu defined by what Benjamin Buchloh has described as Conceptual art's denigration of aesthetic pleasure and concomitant "rigorous elimination of visuality."[80]

Wilson responded to this dilemma by augmenting her textual propositions with enactments of her own body/self, which not only scuttled the Conceptualists' prohibition against visuality, but also transformed visuality itself – through the "rhetoric of the pose" – into an aggressively performative action.[81] Each of these works was composed of textual propositions and photographic documents of performative actions that

5.11 Martha Wilson. *Posturing: Drag*, 1972. Photodocumentation of performance in the artist's studio, Halifax. Photograph: Douglas Waterman.

explored gender constructs as fluid and potentially transformative. In *Posturing: Drag* (1972) Wilson performed a double sex transformation by posing as a man impersonating a woman and wrote in the accompanying text that "Form determines feeling, so that if I pose in a role I can experience a foreign emotion" (fig. 5.11). Wilson's doubled layer of dissembling unleashes the tensions of sexual ambiguity and thus recalls Judith Butler's argument that performative acts invoking sexual ambiguity confuse the binary framework of gender to reveal "the very notion of an essential sex, a true or abiding masculinity or femininity" as a regulatory fiction.[82] In *Captivating a Man* (1972) Wilson posed as a man enhanced by makeup in a "reversal of the means by which a woman captivates a man: the man is made attractive by the woman. In heterosexual reversal, the power of makeup turns back on itself; captivation is emasculation" (fig. 5.12). Wilson's drag persona closely resembles Man Ray's famous photograph of Marcel Duchamp as Rose Sélavy, surely

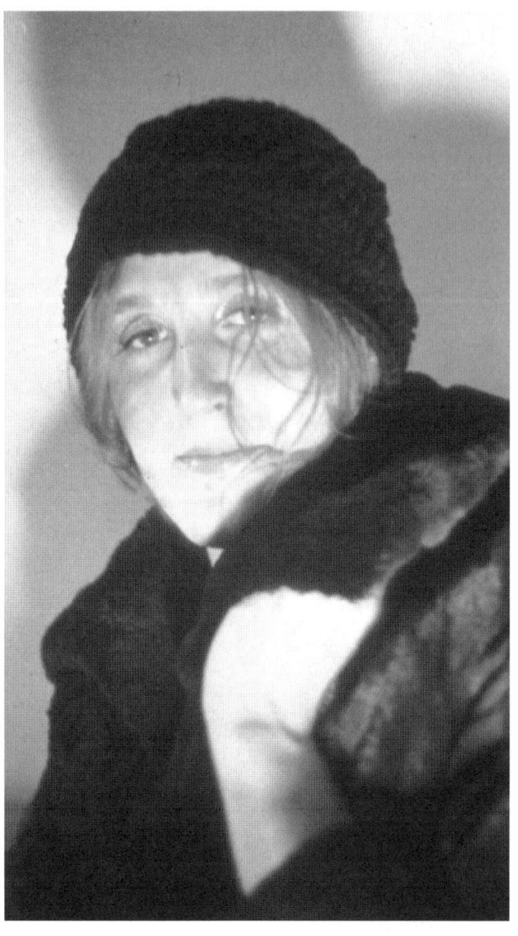

5.12 Martha Wilson. *Captivating a Man*, 1972. Photodocumentation of performance in the artist's studio, Halifax.

no coincidence given the stature of Duchamp within NSCAD's Conceptual community. This allusion to Duchamp as the father-genitor of Conceptual art suggests that Wilson intended her transformation to question both gender and artistic identity in a way similar to how Amelia Jones described Duchamp's "self-feminization" of the "author-function" as a disruption to the "masculine authority of modernist authorship."[83]

This question of the relationship between authorship and gender was central to Wilson's explorations of identity and subjectivity. Although works like *Painted Lady* (1972), in which Wilson transformed herself into a paradigm of hyperbolic femininity, have given rise to interpretations of her work as preoccupied with how beauty myths objectify and

5.13 Martha Wilson. *Painted Lady*, 1972. Photodocumentation of performance in the artist's studio, Halifax. Photograph: Richards Jarden.

oppress women, a closer reading suggests that her work was engaged with more complex questions (fig. 5.13).[84] For example, in the catalogue to the 1996 exhibition that used Judy Chicago's *The Dinner Party* as the centrepiece of a reconsideration of 1970s feminist art, Wilson's work is summed up as an interrogation of "the ways in which beauty myths and the male-dominated public sphere objectify women and diminish their sense of themselves as subjects."[85] But, to take a more nuanced approach, Wilson's stylized exaggerations can also be seen as key strategies for gaining visibility as an *artist* without becoming objectified as a *woman*. As the explanatory text for *Painted Lady* indicates, the disappearance of Wilson's own features behind the stylized mask produces an "absence of preconditions" that is empowering, not objectifying: "A range of possible expression, of unaccustomed attitudes, can fill this vacuum; absence of self is the free space in which expression plays. Thus the obstacle, the painted surface, is ironically the means of expression." Although Wilson focused in these works on the fictive appearances and perceptions of the objectified self, these mutable effects were always counteracted by her own assertions of agency and subjectivity. Wilson's play with representations led her to the conclusion that "artmaking is an identity-making process ... I could generate a new self out of the absence that was left when my boyfriends' ideas, my teachers', and my parents' ideas were subtracted."[86] By manipulating the binary framework and naturalizing narratives of gender identity, Wilson revealed how they also obscure and authenticate the masculinist assumptions of artistic identity.

Wilson's provocative allusions to the deeply entwined relationship between gendered subjectivity and artistic agency were ignored or denigrated by her male peers. She was told by one faculty member that "serious art is only made in black and white, and women don't make it anyway," and during one of his visits to NSCAD, even Vito Acconci dismissed her work as "self-indulgent and irrelevant."[87] Discouraged by the dismissive attitude that she encountered at NSCAD, Wilson left for New York in 1974, where she continued to do role-based performance and also founded Franklin Furnace as a centre for time-based art. She left behind a legacy of videotapes, which began to be unearthed in the mid-1980s by female students who were becoming aware of the growing international presence of feminist art and who began to demand changes in the faculty and curriculum.[88]

One of these students was Susan Britton, whose work encompassed the creation of characters who propelled the elaborate narratives of performance-based videotapes. Her video *Susan* (1976) illustrates precisely what Brentano referred to as the "doubly-aspected" nature of feminist performance in that it conveyed both the authenticity and falseness of an inscribed identity.[89] Drawing from autobiographical facts and fictional inventions, Britton constructed a *cinema verité* portrait of a prostitute named Susan (fig. 5.14). As the camera follows her around town, a first-person voiceover tries to dispel conventional notions of the prostitute as a degenerate creature of the night by talking about how she misses her family in Winnipeg and enjoys spending Sunday afternoons in the Public Gardens, although she also conjures up an alien underworld of pimps, johns, and encounters with police.

As with Britton's later videos, *Susan* reveals an interest in the kind of generic characters generated by the mass media. As Jan Peacock has observed, "Susan's breezy walk through the Public Gardens owes as much to the opening sequence of the *Mary Tyler Moore Show* as it does to the film portrait genre." She also notes that Britton/Susan adopts an easy intimacy with the camera, drawing us into a familiar dynamic that "leaves us in the same unresolved place that television leaves us in, but which it pretends not to: equipped with only partial, conventionalized, and superficial information, we are no closer to knowing who 'Susan' is."[90] In this way, Britton calls to mind how oppressive female stereotypes are produced and legitimated within the clichéd language and

5.14 Susan Britton. *Susan*, 1976. Black-and-white video, 10:30 min.

images of popular culture. Still, while the one-dimensionality of her character ironically echoes the devices used in the culture industry, Britton's ability to invest the work with a more incisive critique is limited by her use of parody as a simple inversion of its cultural referent.

Parody, however, can serve as a more penetrating mode of critique. In her study *A Theory of Parody*, Linda Hutcheon notes that parody has been traditionally denigrated because it is derivative in nature and depends upon already existing forms to fulfil itself. In a culture that places value only on the "original," parody is seen as parasitic. But it is precisely this quality that can make parody critically effective because it undermines the Romantic fallacy of originality, thus forcing "a reassessment of the process of textual production." By inserting itself into existing cultural texts and forms, parody exposes the power relationships between those social agents who possess the "original" and the others who possess the parodic alternative.[91] For Rosi Braidotti, parody can be empowering for feminism when it mimics situations or experiences not by flat repetition but rather by "open[ing] up in-between spaces where new forms of political subjectivity can be explored." In other words, it is not the parody itself that destroys phallocentric structures "but rather the power vacuum that parodic politics may be able to engender."[92]

5.15 The Clichettes (Louise Garfield, Janice Hladki, and Johanna Householder). *Having My Baby*, 1986. Photograph: David Hlynsky.

5.16 The Clichettes (Louise Garfield, Janice Hladki, and Johanna Householder). *Go to Hell*, 1985. Photograph: David Hlynsky.

Hutcheon and Braidotti clearly articulate why parody's subversive potential has been so compelling for feminist artists. This potential was fully implemented by the Toronto performance group called The Clichettes (Louise Garfield, Johanna Householder, and Janice Hladki). The Clichettes made their debut at the Tele-Performance Festival in 1978, an event themed in response to television as content and technology. Dressed in kitsch-punk outfits, The Clichettes (with Elizabeth Chitty) lip-synced to Leslie Gore's "You Don't Own Me" while posturing aggressively and pounding their fists on the floor in a full-frontal feminist assault. Their main inspiration came from the Hummer Sisters (founded in Toronto in 1976 by Deanne Taylor and Marien Lewis), who specialized in political and social satire in the form of exuberant song and dialogue. The Clichettes soon elaborated their routines by means of narrative frameworks, often co-written with author Marni Jackson. In *Half Human, Half Heartache* (1980), they played three aliens who land on Earth and undergo emotional heartache while practising how to become human girls, whom they can only imitate through lip-syncing. As Householder explained, "Lip-sync ... happens to be, in itself, a good metaphor for the cultural imperialism experienced by women."[93] The Clichettes applied their satirical techniques in several performances in the 1980s as "mock-males" in various guises, one of which had them cruising the audience in shiny suits and white patent-leather shoes while lip-syncing to Paul Anka's "Having My Baby" (fig. 5.15). In another of their outrageously defiant performances, they lip-synced to Motorhead's "Go to Hell" while strutting their heavy-metal stuff in naked male-torso outfits and making obscene gestures to the audience with their tongues and guitars (fig. 5.16).[94]

The Clichette's raucous style appropriated popular-culture forms, and as Clive Robertson pointed out, because their travesty of celebrity entertainments was not detached and ironical, it enabled them to be critical without alienating their audience.[95] In her book on laughter as a strategy of feminist art, Jo Anna Isaak explains that laughter can be a metaphor for transformation and that by offering libidinal gratification, it can "provide an analytic for understanding the relationships between the social and the symbolic while allowing us to imagine these relationships differently." For laughter to have this effect, the viewer must recognize that he or she shares the repressions that are represented: "What is requested is not a private depoliticized *jouissance* but sensuous solidarity. Laughter is first and foremost a communal response."[96]

After tracing the history of the relationship between women and laughter as a rebellious force from the medieval carnivals of Mardi Gras, through Rabelais's satires, and into the present, Isaak argues that feminist incursions into popular culture have demonstrated that it can indeed be a locus from which to generate the kind of politically engaged critique traditionally deemed possible only within the realms of high culture and the avant-garde.[97]

These incursions were taken back to their Rabelaisian source in the early work of Canadian performance artist Tanya Mars. In 1974 Mars conjoined Elizabethan and modern gender determinations in wearable sculptures called *Codpieces: Phallic Paraphernalia.* At the time, Mars was one of the founding members of Powerhouse, a women's art gallery in Montreal, and as Nell Tenhaaf writes, the exhibition of the *Codpieces* put the gallery on the map in its still-fringe neighbourhood along an upper part of Montreal's St Laurent Boulevard and in the Canadian artist-run community in general.[98] These codpieces, made of found objects that included an oil can, a polystyrene meat tray, a chess set, and a gas mask, were scandalously modelled by six naked men at the *vernissage.* In the mid-1980s, Mars reiterated this relationship between embodiment, sartorial style, and identity in a trilogy of parodic performances representing archetypes of female power.

*Pure Virtue* (1984) tells the story through skits, dialogue, and vignettes of Queen Elizabeth I, the Virgin Queen who took the throne of England at age twenty-five in 1558 (fig. 5.17). Elizabeth's power and authority to rule were always qualified by her gender, and she wore her chastity like a badge that set her apart from other women. Although Elizabeth is a historical figure remote from contemporary society, she served as a metaphor for how women's relationship to power is still much defined – either restricted or advanced – by their sexuality. At the centre of *Pure Virtue* is the question of virginity, which, suggests Gary Kibbons, is perhaps anachronistic, but in representing the suppression of desire demanded of women, it alludes to the conflicted relationships between desire and power along gender lines. Unlike Elizabeth, who came to power only through lack of a proper male heir, women today have negotiated power through "systematic political and cultural work undertaken ... in open conflict with patriarchal relations."[99] Still, this acquisition of power often carries difficult consequences for heterosexual relations, and as the Queen lifts her magnificent skirts to reveal how the loss of chastity may be concealed – an intricate procedure requiring

5.17 Tanya Mars. *Pure Virtue*, 1984. Performance at the Rivoli, Toronto. Costume: Elinor Rose Galbraith. Photograph: David Hlynsky.

leaches and a raw chicken – we are humorously reminded of the high cost it often entails for women.

In *Pure Sin* (1986) Mars took on the role of Mae West, the mouthy Hollywood goddess whose bawdy sexual power and defiant refusal to submit to conventions of demure femininity were legendary (fig. 5.18). Like Elizabeth, West was a woman of superlative dimensions, which Mars again signified through elaborate costuming. In flamboyant dress and blonde bouffant wig, Mars as West is the bodacious sex queen, who lassos, herds, and seduces her entourage of boy toys. As Dot Tuer has noted, Mars's emulation of West's hyperbolic femininity does not assert the "truth" of the feminine, nor does it allow us to mistake the feminine, as Derrida warned, "for a woman's femininity, for sexuality, or any of those other essentializing fetishes."[100] Still, Mars, like many women, is suspicious of the patriarchal ease with which woman is announced as the void, the nonidentity who occupies the postmodern rhetorical function of *différance*. Her riposte was *Pure Nonsense* (1987), in which she explored the fetishistic fantasies of castration

5.18 Tanya Mars. *Pure Sin*, 1986. Performance at A Space, Toronto. Costume: Elinor Rose Galbraith. Photograph: David Hlynsky.

anxiety through the eyes of Alice in Wonderland. As the embodiment of the power of imaginative creativity, Alice foiled the assumptions of the psychic "loss" women suffer through lack of a penis. After being awakened from a dreamy idyll and abruptly informed by Freud that she has lost her penis, Alice, aghast, set off to find it, querying the inhabitants of Wonderland, who vex her with absurd answers to the riddle "Why does a Venus not have a penis?" Refusing to submit to their Oedipal fantasies of sexual difference, Alice was nonetheless mightily relieved in the end when she lifted her ruffled crinolines to discover an impressive rubber penis (fig. 5.19). And with this comic gesture, the girl-child Alice deflated the whole apparatus of phallocratic mastery and subordination.

5.19 Tanya Mars. *Pure Nonsense*, 1987. Publicity poster for performance at the Music Gallery, Toronto. Costume: Elinor Rose Galbraith. Poster design: John Ormsby (original in colour). Photograph: David Hlynsky.

5.20 Suzy Lake. *Forever Young*, 2000. Centre panel of triptych of laminated photographic prints, 210 x 107 cm each (originals in colour).

Mars's performance style in her trilogy on women and power can be characterized as burlesque in that it veers from mock seriousness to ribald vulgarity – but always with a cutting edge. This trafficking between the worlds of popular entertainment and feminist political critique has also been a strategy used by Canadian artist Suzy Lake. In the early 1970s, Lake produced photo-based work that addressed feminist considerations of identity formation, appearance, and voice. In *On Stage* (1972–75) Lake adopted the looks and gestures taught in professional modelling, and in *Co-ed Magazine* (1973), she assumed the girlish looks of 1960s debutantes in casually posed images, although they were made freakish by the application of mummer's white-face over Lake's features. In the photo-silkscreen *A Genuine Simulation of ...* (1974), Lake again painted over her own face to create a stylized and excessive *maquillage*. As Lee Rodney has noted, these devices treat Lake's own portraits as "painted surfaces," the grounds for a representation not of her *self* but of the masquerade of femininity that women have learned to imitate.[101] Rodney cites Luce Irigaray's theoretical formulation of mimesis as a way to make this process visible and bring about critical resistance. Irigaray writes:

> One must assume the feminine role deliberately. Which means already to convert a form of subordination into an affirmation, and thus begin to thwart it ... To play with mimesis is thus, for a woman, to try to recover the place of her exploitation by discourse, without allowing herself to be simply reduced to it. It means to resubmit herself – in as much as she is on the side of the "perceptible," of "matter" – to "ideas," in particular to ideas about herself, that are elaborated in/by a masculine logic, but so as to make "visible," by an effect of playful repetition, what was supposed to remain invisible: recovering a possible operation of the feminine in language.[102]

In 1998, during the height of Spice Girl mania and lip-sync contests, Lake returned to the performative basis of her early work by playing the role of Scary Spice in a group performance that brought down the house at an arts fundraiser in Toronto. Lake subsequently reprised the role in a series of photographic self-portraits.[103] Caustically entitled *Forever Young*, they portray the middle-aged Lake as the pop-star idol of the bubblegum set. She has all the right trappings: big frizzy hair, trashy jewellery, belly shirt, leopard print leggings, and chunky platform boots (fig. 5.20). But she is mutton dressed as lamb. In a culture that pushes aging women to the outer limits of (in)visibility, while turning youth culture into a prolific and lucrative industry, Lake's defiant gesture is indeed satire of a rare order. Her middle-aged pop star is funny not just because she is so incongruous, so outré, but also because her style-over-substance posturing is self-mocking. As such, it avoids the detached cynicism that ironic parody can engender when it serves as a mockery of others. By contrast, Lake's performance is a variation on camp parody, which relies upon a strong identification with a situation while comically appreciating its contradictions.[104] We don't laugh *at* Lake's desperate desire for the sex appeal of eternal youth but *with* her ability to skewer the culture that inculcates such ludicrous fantasies. Lake's self-mockery enacts the power of humour to be both defiant and offensively subversive.

Colette Urban is another Canadian artist who has used laughter and the absurd possibilities of costume as feminist strategies. Urban's costumes and props are often made from what the Surrealists called *objets trouvailles*: the cast-offs and detritus of a technological, capitalist society that nonetheless carry the possibility of "convulsing" the viewer through their psychic, symbolic, and social associations. Urban's performances often use such objects to invoke the gendered spaces and experiences of domesticity and childhood where identity takes shape, which she then unsettles and makes strange. In *a song to sing, a tale to tell, a point to make* (1989), the performance began with a male voice reading from the outdated how-to manual *Hundreds of Things a Girl Can Make* (1945), while Urban emerged wearing a girlish dress and sticklike arm extensions covered in long white gloves (fig. 5.21). In contrast to the supercharged confidence of the "Wonder Woman" lyrics heard from a record player, Urban awkwardly manipulated a gravel-filled globe with her prosthetic arms until the performance ended with the hopeful notes of the song "Somewhere Over the Rainbow." Curator Barbara Fischer writes that "Identity in this performance is a position wrested from somewhere between a disastrous inability and an impossible perfection; Colette Urban is strangely empowered, or enacts power obliquely, as she turns and rattles the world globe."[105]

Urban's allusions to the fragility and tension inherent in negotiating subjectivity in a social context are meant to trigger unexpected responses on the part of her viewers, who are often recruited as participants. In *Consumer Cyclone* (1993), for example, Urban toured a shopping mall wearing a costume laden with a dishevelled array of clothing and cosmetic paraphernalia used to construct and maintain feminine beauty

*Above*

5.21 Colette Urban. *a song to sing, a tale to tell, a point to make*, 1989. Performance at Western Front, Vancouver. Photograph: Elisabeth Feryn.

*Left*

5.22 Colette Urban. *Consumer Cyclone*, 1993. Performance at shopping malls in Montreal and Quebec City. Photograph: Elisabeth Feryn.

(fig. 5.22). By repeatedly shouting the phrases "Regardez-moi. Regardez-toi. Look at me. Look at you" through a toy megaphone, Urban activated the spectatorial reification of the mall as consumer fantasy, revolving as it does around the commodity status of bodies and images, especially female ones. As the object on which these fantasies had literally materialized and to which they had stuck, Urban aimed to provoke a subjective response on the part of the shoppers and, if only momentarily, to disrupt the flow of their capitalist reverie with her self-reflexive declamations.

Like Colette Urban, Quebec artist Sylvie Tourangeau uses objects in performances that embody the possibilities of transformation and change. Tourangeau initially collaborated with her brother, Jean, in such performances as *Sans titre* (1977) and *Les Tourangeau à La Chambre blanche* (1978), which featured Jean's poetic disquisitions as the point of departure for both quotidian and aesthetic (e.g., dance) actions emanating from a single text. In their performances, Sylvie began to take on a more explicitly gendered role, one that ultimately set her in aggressive conflict with Jean as the male speaker, as in *Les Meilleurs mots sont de lui* (1979) and *Sylvie a eu peur a ...* (1980), in which Sylvie played the female protagonist who struggled to disrupt her brother's recitations of patriarchal, canonical, and theoretical texts.[106]

In 1980 Sylvie Tourangeau began to work independently of her brother in works that adapted the Québécois predilection for textual poetics in performance to a consideration of the relation between words, such as the verbs *chercher*, *savoir*, and *apprendre*, and of the gestures and movements that they might evoke, as in *Ouvrir* (1980). In *Le Corps des possibles* (1981; with Nicole Blouin), words were eschewed altogether in favour of a response by the performers to their perception of the energy that flowed between them, the audience, and the architectural space of the performance itself. During the 1980s Tourangeau began to place herself in a state of self-interrogation in relation to her audience in works such as *En déroute ... je vole toujours* (1982), which revealed how ordinary actions and the manipulation of objects could evoke a multiplicity of meanings. For Tourangeau, performance is implicitly a processional art form that gives rise to "a polyvalent, destabilizing process of simultaneously confronting certainty and ambivalence."[107] By 1987 her commitment to the transformational possibilities of performance was embodied in her role as Mlle Chang/Changement, the trickster-heroine of a fictitious Chinese mythology in the performance *Via Memoria* (fig. 5.23).

5.23 Sylvie Tourangeau. *Via Memoria*, 1987. Photodocumentation of performance at Espace Go, Montreal. Photograph: Martin Labbé.

Since then, Tourangeau's performances, such as *Une autre vie* (1994), *Trois actions pour une distanciation* (1996), and *Ça tient qu'à très peu de choses* (1996), have been primarily preoccupied with how objects, as material artifacts and signifiers of social meaning, can transpose, embody, and prolong the evanescent performative experience.[108] The objects that Tourangeau has used in her performances since the late 1980s, which include things as mundane as rubber boots and raincoats and as exotic as Buddha statues or futuristic headdresses, were assembled together as fragmentary traces in *Objet(s) de présence* (1998). This changing exhibition installation composed of artifact-souvenirs evoked the shifting ground between reality and memory, sound and silence, shadow and light, being and becoming. Here Tourangeau explored the object as the emotive and associative embodiment of that which is fugitive and lost in the process of performance. Above all, she sought to engage the question of presence and absence, as summated in the script written on the wall above the silhouette of a woman's body lying on a chaise-lounge: "*Mais ... où est la présence?*"[109]

The questions of presence and absence, in both their literal and figurative aspects, and the capacity of performative acts to elicit self-determined change have been pivotal to an ambitious and extensive range of feminist performances that dealt in one way or another with role playing or transformation. Considerations of subjectivity and agency have been paramount in this body of work, but the recurring use of Brechtian strategies to mark the distance between artist and role indicates that these performances did not make merely naive, utopian, or essentialist claims to coherent subjectivity. Rather, on a theoretical level, such performances revealed and disputed the limiting binaries of subject and object positions while also, on a pragmatic level, performing what Lucy Lippard called an "exorcism" of the oppressive, authoritative assumptions and expectations of imposed female roles.[110] In this sense, even those performances that explored the possibilities of roles and transformations from the position of "the personal" can be seen as political enactments no less than those that focused more explicitly on the social effects of women's historical subjugation. As a whole, these performances engendered an aesthetic practice whose ultimate goal was to transform life itself.

# 6

# Embodiment and Representation

## BODIES OF DIFFERENCE

The history of feminist performance has often been viewed as primarily occupied with the female body and its representation. For example, in her 1997 book *The Explicit Body in Performance*, Rebecca Schneider explains that she has coined the phrase "explicit body" as a way to explore "the explosive literality at the heart of much feminist performance art and performative actions."[1] Amelia Jones's 1998 book *Body Art: Performing the Subject* does not exclusively concentrate on female artists, but she argues that work by feminist and "otherwise nonnormative artists who particularize their bodies/selves" is central to her thesis that the significance of body art is its ability "to expose and challenge the masculinism embedded in the assumption of 'disinterestedness' behind conventional art history and criticism."[2] While I have argued that the history of feminist performance cannot be encompassed solely within the parameters of a focus on "the body," it is undeniable that the body has been an imperative and pervasive concern in feminist performance from early days to the present. Over this period of time, a wealth of theoretical and critical writing on the body and its politics has developed, which can be brought to bear profitably on the historical investigation of feminist performance art undertaken in this study. This chapter will begin by addressing why the body is important to feminist discourse and by summarizing the key theoretical positions regarding its potential as a site of critical resistance before moving into a detailed analysis of how and what the body and its representations have come to signify within the histories of feminist performance and the writing about it.

The anthropologist Mary Douglas has shown that the body operates symbolically within the social rules and rituals of all cultures for the primary purpose of "the ordering of a social hierarchy."[3] Taking this as the departure point for her succinct overview of writing on the history of the body in Western culture, Janet Wolff cites a range of studies that have examined efforts to bring the body under social control by suppressing bodily appetites and desires in order to serve the ideologies of bourgeois capitalism and its need for a "reliable, docile, regular workforce, [and] its dependence on the self-regulation of its subjects."[4] But if all bodies in all cultures come under forms of social control, feminism asks what role the regulation of bodies has had in positioning women as subordinate to men within a hierarchy of sexual difference. This question was first addressed by Simone de Beauvoir, who, we recall, concluded that man has named himself the self and woman the other, thus promising himself the transcendence of the mind, while consigning woman to the immanence of the body. Man imagines himself free of such immanence because "he thinks of his body as a direct and normal connection with the world, which he believes he apprehends objectively." De Beauvoir conceded that the "facts" of biology might make it more difficult for a woman to become a self but noted that these "facts" did not preclude this self-becoming since "there is no true living reality except as manifested by the conscious individual through activities and in the bosom of society."[5]

De Beauvoir's prescient declaration that woman is made, not born, has been foundational to feminist thought, yet her notions of sexual difference and political strategy have not gone unchallenged. For post-structural feminists, de Beauvoir's faith in dialectical resolution as an emancipatory strategy is troubling. De Beauvoir believed that since the difference women embody was as yet *unrepresented* – except as defective other – the task of feminism was to bring this entity into representation through ideology critique and thus lay claim to a subjectivity on par with that of men.[6] By contrast, Luce Irigaray has argued that women's "otherness" is not just as-yet-unrepresented, but also *unrepresentable* within the existing framework. Because woman is defined in a negative relation to patriarchy as waste or excess, no simple reversal of the order of things is possible. Thus the goal of equality is illusory because it can be achieved only by assimilating women into the masculine regimes of thought and practice. In the long run, history would repeat itself, she writes, and "revert to sameness: to phallocratism. It would leave room neither for women's sexuality, nor for women's imaginary, nor for women's language to take (their) place."[7] Irigaray urges women not to erase or disembody sexual difference but to assert its specificity and to redefine it as a positive entity.

These two streams of thought have produced a polemical clash between those who, like de Beauvoir, struggle for equality by identifying and eradicating the ways that sexual difference has been used as a pejorative sign of the "feminine" and those who, like Irigaray, uphold sexual difference as a political strategy for envisioning new modes of language, knowledge, and embodied experience. Although these two traditions have sometimes been regarded as mutually exclusive, Rosi Braidotti has argued that we should see them "as complementary and part of a continuous historical evolution."[8] She advocates that feminists should struggle both to change the historical asymmetry of the sexes *and* to question the categories that this asymmetry has produced and that feminism proposes to deconstruct. Braidotti shares the skepticism of theorists like Teresa de Lauretis, Monique Wittig, Judith Butler, and Donna Haraway that the category of gender is itself a regulatory fiction that both normalizes sexual difference and obscures other kinds of differences among women.[9] But, like Denise Riley, Braidotti proposes that feminists should think and act from the proposition of "as if." As Riley put it, "it is compatible to suggest that 'women' don't exist – while maintaining a politics of 'as if they existed' – since the world behaves as if they unambiguously did."[10] In Braidotti's view, we can acknowledge that the primary site of subjective location is the body – not as a natural entity but as the site of intersection between the biological, the social, the material, and the symbolic. The parodic, paradoxical, and conditional mode of "as if" allows women to reject the presumed universalism of the subject while still accepting the signifier *woman* as the subject of discourse without having either to define what that is or to exclude the differences among women.[11]

These insights are useful for considerations of how women artists have used their bodies in performance and representation as well as for considerations of the debates that have arisen regarding such practices. At the core of these debates is the question of whether women's bodies, so heavily marked by preexisting meanings of sexual hierarchy and objectification, can be the site of feminist political intervention without being reappropriated into these dominant meanings.[12] These debates, which will be discussed in more detail below, have now come to be framed within a generational model in which 1970s feminists' supposedly naive and "essentialist" ideas about the body and sexuality were displaced by the "anti-essentialist" discourse analysis of 1980s feminists, who in turn have been criticized by "third-generation" feminists for failing to address the primacy of the "real" physical body and for thus causing the denigration and subsequent neglect of early feminist art.[13] Although this process of feminist self-critique is necessary and valuable, the use of generational periodizing as the basis for polemical dispute is problematic. For one thing, while it is certainly appropriate and timely for feminists today to redress the inaccurate characterization of early feminist art as reductively essentialist, this should not come at the cost of belittling the important contributions made to feminist discourse during the 1980s as now "calcified into an orthodoxy," as Susan Kandel puts it.[14] For another thing, we should we be skeptical of historical readings that diminish the legitimacy of earlier critical perspectives by privileging our own as more correct or accurate. As Griselda Pollock urges, we need to allow feminism to exist as a "space for momentary conjunctions and creative conflict" that neither flattens out its historical process nor obscures our own positions within it.[15]

## BODY WARS

"Your Body Is a Battleground" declaimed Barbara Kruger in one of her art-advertisements of the 1980s. Since the early 1970s, feminists had waged a struggle for control over their own bodies in legal, political, medical, and cultural domains. As Lisa Tickner has noted, women had only to look around in the realms of both art and popular culture to see that they were everywhere but nowhere, except as the mediating sign for the male.[16] For all their ubiquitous presence, the endless parade of women's bodies signified nothing but the fantasies of representation, fantasies that, in de Lauretis's words, rendered women "unrepresentable except as representation."[17] Pushing their own bodies and selves into this terrain of absence and "lack," feminist performance artists produced an unexpected – and sometimes threatening – clash between literal bodies and the symbolic meanings that they convey.

This was no easy task. From the late 1960s into the early 1970s, body art, a development from both Minimalism and Conceptualism, was thoroughly dominated by male artists.[18] As discussed in chapter 2, this contradicts the frequently expressed view that performance appealed to women in this period because it was a new and open field that had not already been staked and claimed by male artists. In fact, Lucy Lippard's groundbreaking essay "The Pains and Pleasures of Rebirth: European and American Women's Body Art" makes it clear that women had good reason at the time to perceive the field of body art as hostile terrain. She wrote that "from 1967 to 1971 when Bruce Nauman was 'Thighing,' Vito Acconci was masturbating, Dennis Oppenheim was sunbathing and burning, and Barry Le Va was slamming into walls," it seemed highly unlikely that body art would "appeal to vulnerable women artists just emerging from isolation," especially since they faced the danger that their intentions would be misunderstood: "A woman using her own face and body has a right to do what she will with them, but it is a subtle abyss that separates men's use of women for sexual titillation from women's use of women to expose that insult." Lippard also noted that although there is an element of exhibitionism in all body art, a woman who used her body was in a situation of double jeopardy, particularly if she was physically attractive. She risked not only having her image reappropriated as an object of male sexual desire, but also eliciting accusations of narcissism and self-indulgence. Lippard wryly stated that "Because women are considered sex objects, it is taken for granted that any woman who presents her nude body in public is doing so because she thinks she is beautiful. She is a narcissist, and Acconci, with his less romantic image and pimply back, is an artist."[19]

Lippard alluded to the danger that women might inadvertently collude in their own objectification and to the particular conundrum arising from the fact that a woman's sexuality was seen not only as inseparable from her activities as an artist, but also as the basis for regarding these activities as incompatible with the achievement of "great" or "serious" art. For feminist artists in the early 1970s, then, the challenge was both to undermine long-standing prohibitions, prejudices, and exploitative attitudes toward female sexuality and to confront their implications for women *as artists*. Their struggle was both artistic and political. Consequently, feminist artists played a crucial role in formulating a new kind of art practice that was able to achieve a degree of social resonance to which most artists of the late 1960s and early 1970s could make only rhetorical claims.

## TRANSGRESSIONS AND TABOOS

One way that feminist artists formulated their resistance to how female bodies and sexualities had been determined and disciplined within patriarchal culture was to transgress taboos and defiantly flaunt the connotations of the corporeal body as "abject." As Julia Kristeva defined it, the abject is what the subject must expel in order to be an "I." It is the alien within us, but it is also associated with those borders of the body where the inside meets the outside, with the fluids discharged from orifices, and with matter out of place. It also has two meanings. *To abject* is to undergo the operation of expelling the alien within, while *to be abject* is to be a nonsubject, to be enslaved, in de Beauvoir's terms, by the immanence of the body.[20] For feminist performance artists, the task was to reveal and resist the operations of cultural repression by which the female body and the feminine had been aligned with the abject.

Given that menstruation has been one of the most rigidly enforced taboos around female sexuality, it is perhaps inevitable that, as Lisa Tickner said, it *invited* feminist artists to violate the taboo.[21] One such example was the video *What a Woman Made* (1973), by Mako Idemitsu, a Japanese artist living in the US at the time.[22] The tape begins with a fuzzy image gradually coming into focus, revealing a tampon gracefully leaching a trail of menstrual blood into a pristine toilet bowl (fig. 6.1). Just as we realize what this image represents, an authoritative male voice interjects, reading excerpts from the Japanese bestseller *How to Raise Girl Children*, written by the former babysitter to the royal family. This misogynistic text barely conceals a revulsion that conflates physiology and personality in an utterly degrading assessment of the innate nature of Japanese women. They are described as pieces of property to be safeguarded until marriage, as lacking talent, and as indecisive and unable to solve problems by themselves. They are expected to be passive, obedient, and, above all, pleasant at all times. By thus layering this aesthetic image with a text that codifies the litany of defects and negative characteristics imputed to female "nature," Idemitsu reveals the impossibility of simply detaching and reclaiming a "positive" female biological imperative from the cultural prescriptions that determine and constrain its meanings.

In other works from this period, the transgression of social codes was enacted through parodic refusals that recall Irigaray's theory of mimicry as a strategy to "un-read" the texts of phallogocentric discourse by

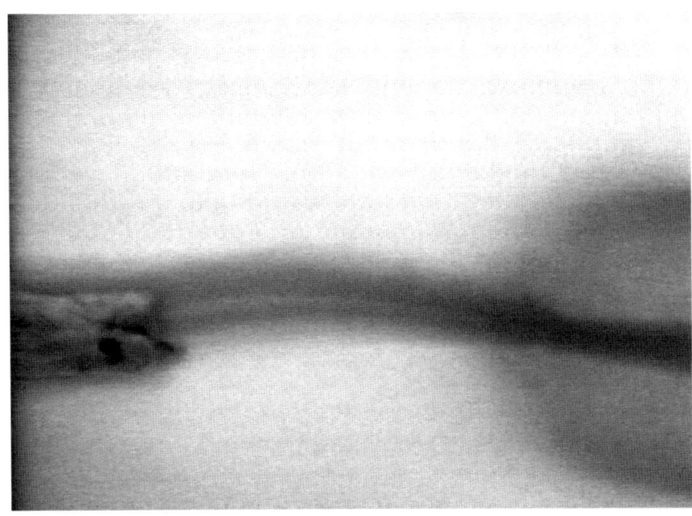

6.1 Mako Idemitsu. *What a Woman Made*, 1973. Black-and-white video, 11:00 min.

reading back into them to reveal what they do to and say about the "feminine."[23] In her video *Take Off* (1974), California artist Susan Mogul wittily enacts an "un-reading" of Vito Acconci's *Undertone* (1972).[24] *Undertone* exemplified Acconci's work from this period, which used structural premises to traverse public and private boundaries by means of bodily manipulations, inappropriate disclosures, and predatory aggressions. Acconci enters the frame and sits at the far end of a table, like a victim of an interrogation. With head lowered and arms concealed, he tells us that there is a girl under the table rubbing his groin and so on. At intervals he looks up to address the viewer directly, saying things like, "I need to know you are there listening to me, tense and on edge, forcing me to keep talking to you, screening out my lies, pushing me against the wall to keep me from deceiving you." In *Undertone* Acconci eroticizes the relationship between performer and viewer, forcing the viewer to complete the scene and become inseparable from the fantasy itself. Mogul's *Take Off* repeats the set-up of *Undertone*, but she tells us that there is nobody under the table rubbing her legs and groin; instead, she has a vibrator under the table, which she then pulls out to show the viewer (fig. 6.2). Jettisoning Acconci's intensely confrontational demands upon the viewer as witness to his fantasy, Mogul matter-of-factly describes the vibrator, where she got it, what kind it is, and how many

6.2 Susan Mogul. *Take Off*, 1974. Black-and-white video, 10:00 min.

batteries it takes. She then repeats these two actions, pleasuring herself with the vibrator under the table and making banal comments to the viewer, such as her observation that the cost of batteries is a small price to pay for sexual satisfaction.

On one level, Mogul's *Take Off* is a straightforward mockery in which Acconci's overburdened claims to psychosexual power are deflated by her insouciant mimicry of masturbating with a battery-operated sex-aid. On another level, her playful nonchalance perhaps alluded to the fact that despite the explicitly sexual undertones of so much of Acconci's work, the art world seemed thoroughly oblivious to the way that it reiterated hierarchies of sexual difference. The sexualized engagement of Acconci's work has recently been addressed by Amelia Jones, who argues that in fluctuating between obsessive assertions of his "normative masculinity" and attempts to "feminize" his body (hiding his penis, plucking out chest hair, pulling on his nipples in works like *Conversions* and *Openings*), Acconci not only unveils what is normally hidden – that the body of the artist/genius is male – but also "*performs* himself as open-ended and contingent on spectatorial desire, pointing up the incoherence of masculinity itself."[25] Jones is careful to admit that Acconci's work enables, but does not ensure, such a reading. Certainly, critics at the time recognized that Acconci investigated relations of power and domination in often explicitly sexual ways, but they seemed insensible to why this might be problematic for women.[26] Acconci himself has acknowledged – in retrospect – that even though he "hate[s] maleness ... and male domination," his work was "really sexist," a point that he then rationalizes by saying that assumptions of the sex/gender basis of power relations are so "culturally imbedded" that he readily fell into them.[27]

6.3 Lynda Benglis. *Female Sensibility*, 1974. Colour video, 14:00 min.

The asymmetrical way that sexually explicit art by male and female artists was perceived at this time is also made evident in the work of Lynda Benglis. Benglis's video *Female Sensibility* (1974) functioned, as did her other videos from this period, to tease out the tensions between technical process and content (fig. 6.3). This tape opens with a close-up of two women's heavily made-up faces. Slowly and deliberately, they nuzzle their faces together and then begin to kiss and caress one another. The audio consists of a montage of radio programming, including a talk-show host razzing callers about male-female relationships, country-and-western music, a discussion about parapsychology, and advertisements for keeping America beautiful. The contrast between the barrage of random samplings of commercial media culture and this charged display of female (homo)eroticism creates a disconcerting disjunction between public and private that forces the viewer into an unequivocal confrontation with the role of voyeur. Although the desire and discomfort elicited in the viewer is reminiscent of Acconci's work, what distinguishes Benglis's tape is how it explicitly frames the dynamics of viewing within the politics of sex and gender so as to refute the ostensible neutrality of both the production and reception of art.

At one point in the video, Benglis's voice cuts in, talking on the phone about an upcoming exhibition of her work for which she is planning an announcement featuring a photograph of herself. At the time, Benglis was living in California, where, as Lucy Lippard has noted, "an honored macho tradition is the exhibition announcement showing a photograph of the artist – usually featuring a cigar, cowboy boots, a truck, or a dog – rather than his work."[28] In a parody of this macho tradition, Benglis produced a series of four publicity photographs, the most scandalous of which appeared as a full-page colour advertisement in the November 1974 issue of *Artforum*. Naked and slicked up like a bodybuilder, Benglis assumes an aggressive, hand-on-hip pose, sporting nothing but sunglasses and a gigantic latex dildo (fig. 6.4). Benglis's photograph sparked a wild controversy in the art media, which accused her of narcissism, pornography, and penis envy. A group of irate *Artforum* editors condemned her ad as "an object of extreme vulgarity ... brutalizing ourselves and ... our readers."[29] Although the critic Robert Pincus-Witten wrote favourably about Benglis's work in general, he felt that the photographs were trite, especially in comparison to what he saw as Acconci's more meaningful engagement with sexuality (like other male critics, he ignores Acconci's *sexism*): "Benglis' sexual photographs are not to be confused with Vito Acconci's performances on erotic themes ... Superficially, Benglis' work reveals the tasteful, the glossy, and the narcissistic, while Acconci's secret sexual systems are more populist, and tend toward the squalid, the exorcistic, and the puritanical."[30]

Benglis said that she wanted to create a "media statement ... to end all statements, the ultimate mockery of the pinup and the macho."[31] The macho exemplar that Benglis is widely assumed to have had in mind was Robert Morris's exhibition announcement that had appeared in the April 1974 issue of *Artforum*.[32] Naked from the waist up, wearing a German Second World War helmet, aviator sunglasses, wrist cuffs, and studded dog collar, Morris flexes his bulky biceps while grasping a massive chain draped around his neck. Whether or not his image, with its violent and militaristic overtones, was itself a parody of machismo, as Amelia Jones suggests, it caused not a ripple in the art press, unlike the excoriation that Benglis received. Feminists at the time, however, recognized her work as a defiantly transgressive gesture and the reaction to it as clear evidence of the art world's gender bias and blindness.[33] It thus revealed a growing awareness among feminists of how the Modernist myths of aesthetic neutrality, autonomy, and disinterested judgment of "quality," which Jones investigates so thoroughly, were used as convenient devices to downgrade the work of women artists and to justify their exclusion from professional recognition.[34]

In ways that are similar to Benglis's assertion of embodied sexual difference within the discourse of body/object relations that preoccupied artists like Morris in the 1970s, the work of Janine Antoni in the 1990s has blurred the lines between sculpture and performance by producing objects and installations that are not so much representations of the body as enactments of it.[35] In works like *Chocolate Gnaw* and *Lard Gnaw* (1992), Antoni emulated the monolithic geometries of Minimalist

6.4 Lynda Benglis. Two-page artist's "centrefold" in *Artforum* 13, no. 3 (November 1974): 4–5 (original in colour).

sculpture by casting huge cubes of chocolate and lard and then eroding their Platonic wholeness by gnawing away the edges of the cubes. In *Lick and Lather* (1993) Antoni again used her body to produce sculpture, this time by having casts of herself made in chocolate and soap in the form of classical busts, which she then resculpted by licking away at the surfaces. For Antoni, such works provoked questions about the relationship between portraiture and self-representation in art, about the permanence of the monument versus the ephemeralness of her materials, and about the tension between the publicness of honorific sculpture and the private rituals of eating and bathing.[36]

In *Loving Care* (1993) Antoni again took up a dialogue with the history of art in a performance that alluded to a well-known work by the Fluxus artist Nam June Paik called *Zen for Head* (1962), in which Paik in turn had made reference to Jackson Pollock's drip paintings by dipping his tie into a bucket of paint and dragging it along a roll of paper laid out on the floor. For her part, Antoni dipped her hair into Loving Care hair dye and "painted" or "mopped" the floor of the Anthony D'Offay Gallery in London with broad, sweeping strokes (fig. 6.5). Antoni's work engages with the history of sculpture, however broadly defined, not so much to parody its conventions and traditions as to rethink the relation of the body to the object in ways that foreground the gendered associations of embodiment. Inasmuch as her work entails both a ruining of heroic traditions and a simultaneous evocation of pleasurable and abject sensations, it can be seen as an enactment of the canny kind of mimicry that Irigaray espoused, where mimesis, as Naomi Schor has written, "comes to signify difference as positivity, a joyful reappropriation of the attributes of the other."[37]

Antoni's use of chocolate alludes to the relationship between women and food that many feminist artists have explored. As Rosemary Betterton has argued, this relationship is one that evokes the powerful tensions between desire and repression that are inscribed upon the bodies of women.[38] It encompasses the symbolic taboos that we associate with food, the transgression of which risks abjection, as well as anxieties about uncontrollable appetites, the release of which elicits the threat of what film theorist Barbara Creed has called the "monstrous-feminine."[39] As Susan Bordo has shown in her study of bodily ideals in twentieth-century society, these anxieties are both symptomatic and productive of the ways that female bodies are brought under control, such that food and dieting have become central signifiers of the conflicting needs for control and release in consumer capitalism.[40] This intersection between female anxieties, cultural ideals, social control, and commodity capitalism was explicitly addressed in a video by Tanya Mars called *Mz. Frankenstein* (1993), which was presented in the form of an infomercial for a machine called the Relax-a-cizor, marketed by a US manufacturer to thousands of women for home use in the 1950s. Demonstrated by Mars as Dr Frances Stein, the Relax-a-cizor promises an effort-free way to achieve beauty by getting rid of ugly fat, but in truth, the complex efforts to attach the various straps and pads to Mars's ample body, and the resulting overtones of sadomasochistic bondage, appeared neither relaxing nor effortless. Mars's video takes satirical aim both at our social obsession with physical perfection and at the spurious claims of those profiteers who seek simultaneously to inculcate and exploit the bodily anxieties aroused by such normative ideals.

In *Brains on Toast: The Inexact Science of Gender* (1992; fig. 6.6), Canadian artist Joyan Saunders similarly explored pseudo-scientific and mechanistic claims to the ability to regulate female sexuality and desirability. Saunders's video, however, examines more precisely how such normative ideals cannot contain the particularities of lesbian sexuality. Using vignettes structured around the categories of "brains, hormones, reproduction, and private parts," Saunders's video features a humorous lesson by a butch dyke on how to walk, sit, and stand so as to take up more space and appear more imposing (i.e., more masculine) as well as an encounter between two lesbians whose erotic play, which includes bondage and deep body-piercing, is graphically and unflinchingly portrayed.

As Lynda Hart has pointed out, such portrayals confront not only the pulp-novel traditions of the 1950s and 1960s that characterized

6.5 Janine Antoni. *Loving Care,* 1993. Photodocumentation of performance at Anthony D'Offay Gallery, London. Photograph: Prudence Cuming Associates Ltd, London.

lesbians as pathological and deviant, but also the more immediate schism caused within the feminist movement by the inability of straight feminists to recognize and accept any forms of lesbian sexuality that did not replicate normative heterosexuality; in other words, the inability to accept that lesbian women might seek from one another something different from what heterosexual women sought from their partners.[41] As Jill Dolan has summarized it, the feminist movement could accept someone saying "I am a lesbian" as an indication of an identity position, but because sex acts are what mark gay and lesbian bodies as different, saying "I practice lesbian sex" would "initiate a discourse that might displace the emphasis on life-styles and relationships and break open the sanctimonious strictures of politically correct lesbian identifications."[42] By transgressing heterosexist taboos in her video, Saunders broke open these strictures to reveal what cannot be contained within a monolithic concept of feminine sexuality.

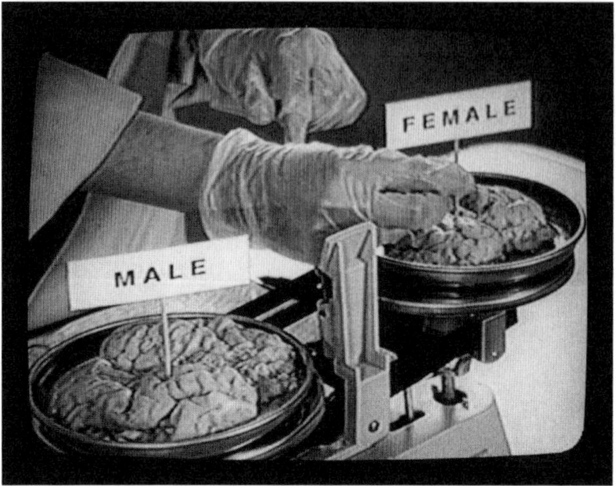


6.6 Joyan Saunders. *Brains on Toast: The Inexact Science of Gender*, 1992. Colour video, 26:30 min.

**RE-VISIONING**

The rift within feminism over its difficulty in reconciling difference and sameness has been particularly divisive, but feminists have also found themselves in conflict over the question of pleasure and its relation to criticality within feminist art. To return momentarily to Benglis's video *Female Sensibility* as an example of pleasurable female eroticism, it should be noted that both Susan Krane and Amelia Jones have read it as an expression of a "distinctly erotic narcissism."[43] As we have seen, feminist performance artists who displayed their bodies were often accused of narcissism. But while it is undeniable that charges of narcissism against women's art carried a special invective, Christopher Lasch's 1978 book *The Culture of Narcissism* shows that it was a critical term used loosely and widely in the 1970s to "cover all forms of 'vanity,' 'self-admiration,' 'self-satisfaction,' and 'self-glorification.'"[44] It was, then, a convenient term of disparagement imputing to an artist's work a lack of engagement with social and political discourse. When levelled at women's art, narcissism was therefore a multipurpose put-down implying that it was shallow, undeveloped, vain, and/or self-absorbed. The real point was a refusal to recognize that the subject of women *as* subjects could have any significance whatsoever to the "public importance" of art.

Over the years, many feminists have "re-read" narcissism in positive terms as a potential site of political resistance. Freud actually emerges here as an ally, for he did not see female narcissism as necessarily negative since narcissistic women acquire "a certain self-contentment which compensates them for the social restrictions that are imposed upon them in their choice of [the male as love] object."[45] For feminists who examined the relation of the feminine to the realm of visual representation, this self-sufficiency of the narcissist was important because, as Mary Jacobus wrote, "for once Freud defines *woman* not in terms of lack but in terms of something she has: primary narcissism replaces the missing phallus."[46] For Jo Anna Isaak, the real potential comes from the connection Freud later made between narcissism and humour.[47] Freud explained this connection by writing that "humour has something liberating about it; but it also has something of grandeur and elevation … The grandeur in it clearly lies in the triumph of narcissism, the victorious assertion of the ego's invulnerability. The ego refuses to be distressed by the provocations of reality, to let itself be compelled to suffer. It insists that it cannot be affected by the traumas of the external world; it shows, in fact, that such traumas are no more than occasions for it to gain pleasure."[48]

For Amelia Jones, what is most significant about female narcissism is its ability to evoke pleasure and desire. As Jones reads the work of Benglis, Hannah Wilke, and other feminist artists, they stage their bodies not to deny the objectification of female subjects but to solicit the viewer's desire to possess the female body as object. By "literalizing this desire" within a narcissistic scenario, the distance between self and other, artist and viewer, is collapsed, thus threatening "Western phallocentric subjectivity, which insists upon the oppositional staging of an other (who lacks) to legitimate the self (who ostensibly has)." Jones argues further that this also undermines the traditional mode of artistic interpretation whereby the viewer assumes a position of authoritative mastery from a point of critical distance.[49] But this reading of the relationship between viewers and female artists' bodies on display as intersubjectively engaged is very different from – and, indeed, in explicit opposition to – theories of representation and spectatorship that were initiated in the writings of John Berger and Laura Mulvey in the early 1970s and later elaborated by numerous writers on art and cinema.[50] As Janet Wolff summarized it, "The devastating implication of this work in general appears to be that women's bodies (particularly the nude, though not just that) cannot be portrayed other than through the regimes of representation which produce them as objects for the male gaze, and as the projection of male desires."[51]

From Jones's perspective, this body of discourse, which dominated in the 1980s, has had negative consequences for our understanding of how feminist artists in the 1970s used their bodies because it portrays them as naively believing that they could escape such objectification. But as I have argued, such generational critiques are often oversimplified and exaggerated. For example, Jones writes that because of their "Marxian distrust of art forms that elicit pleasure, that seduce rather than repel viewers," British feminist proponents of this discourse, including Mulvey, Lisa Tickner, Griselda Pollock, and Mary Kelly, "turned definitively away from the body." Kelly is described as "unbending" and "prescriptive" in her insistence "that *any* artwork including the artist's body is *necessarily* reactionary," while Pollock is said to presume arrogantly that the strategy of "Brechtian distanciation" that she advocates is the only one that is "effectively (or properly?) feminist." Jones views their position as rigid because they assume "that spectators will necessarily react or participate in a predictable way" and thus reiterate "one of the most damaging impulses of modernist criticism: the definitive evaluation of works of art in terms of an externally conceived, hierarchical system of value (in this case, replacing Greenberg's aesthetic categories with Brechtian ones)." Jones acknowledges the value of their critiques at the time but says that their "wholesale dismissal" of "the strategic force of body art projects in the late 1960s and 1970s" has blinded them to "the contingency of all meanings and values of cultural products on the social and political contexts of reception as well as on the particular desires of the interpreter in question (here, Pollock and Kelly themselves)."[52]

Jones is correct that the anti-essentialist discourse associated with these feminists has had negative ramifications for the critical fortunes of early feminist art. And certainly we should be suspicious about why feminist art began to receive mainstream recognition only in the 1980s when artists like Cindy Sherman and Barbara Kruger, whose media-based work focused in coolly distant ways on how women are positioned within the regimes of representation, began to be written about by male critics like Hal Foster and Craig Owens, who applauded such work as evidence of 1980s feminism as "an instance of postmodernism."[53] At the same time, Jones's totalizing condemnation of 1980s feminist discourse in fact repeats the same "wholesale dismissal" of which the latter is supposedly guilty, thus greatly diminishing the relevance of her own critique.

The problem with this kind of critique is not just that its argumentation is tendentious or that its allegiances are partisan (e.g., American versus British) but rather that it gives the impression that feminist artists and intellectuals were capable of pursuing only certain kinds of questions or strategies at certain times. On the contrary, just as feminist artists in the 1970s were concerned as much with the "regimes of representation" as they were with their literal bodies, neither was there a turning away from the body and/or its representations in the 1980s. In lieu of fixing this history within the framework of a generational teleology, I would argue instead for a consideration of feminist artists' strategies and techniques, which emanate, as does most feminist discourse, from the two traditions outlined earlier, namely de Beauvoir's "ideology critique" of social and material conditions and Irigaray's "mimetic repetition" of the semiotic and symbolic bases of power and knowledge. And while these strategies and techniques have shifted from time to time, place to place, and artist to artist, I concur with Rosi Braidotti that they should be viewed not as oppositional but "as complementary and part of a continuous historical evolution."[54]

## MAKEUP, MIRRORS, AND MASQUERADE

When Teresa de Lauretis wrote that "woman is unrepresentable except as representation," she meant that women are forcibly confronted with their double alienation from subjectivity in representation because they can appear in the "phallic order of patriarchal culture" only as already signified. She insisted, however, that women *can* represent themselves from within the chinks, cracks, blind spots, and marginal spaces of hegemonic discourses – that is, from within what she called the "space-off" of film theory, the space that is "erased, or, better, recontained and sealed into the image," which includes both the camera (the point of perspective) and the spectator (the point of reception and interpretation).[55] In Lucy Lippard's terms, for women in the early 1970s, these "space-offs" included the camera and video monitor, which "have indeed become the mirrors into which for centuries women have peered anxiously before going out to confront the world."[56]

The scrutiny of these reflective spaces, and of women's self-surveillance within them, was often conveyed in works using cosmetics. One of the earliest was *Leah's Room* at Womanhouse (1972). And in a video from the same year called *Representational Painting*, Eleanor Antin underwent a transformation involving a facial, makeup job, and fashion change meant to show how "a woman paints herself to represent herself to the world."[57] If, as Lippard observed, "to make yourself up is literally to create, or re-create, yourself," then the act of making up is indeed a form of representation, a fictional construction.[58] Yet the purpose of makeup, at least in Western culture, is to use artifice to create the illusion of its absence so that beauty appears as "natural." Especially in the early days of the feminist movement, women's anxiety was palpable about whether they ought to reject this artifice outright. Even though Martha Wilson had been using cosmetics in performances in which she took on the guise of both a hyperbolic femininity and its drag counterpart, when she first met New York artist Jacki Apple, with whom she collaborated in 1973 in a performance called *Transformance (Claudia)*, she was shocked by Apple's "real-life" appearance: "She looked professional all over, eye makeup to high heels. I thought artists weren't supposed to look like that. A sexist belief, something inherited from Gertrude Stein, a woman has to be un-pretty to be taken as seriously as a man."[59]

Realizing that prettiness, as a signifier of sexual difference, was an impediment to being perceived as a subject (that is, to being taken "as seriously as a man"), Wilson produced a series of works from 1973 to 1974 that explored the conundrums of female desire and desirability. In *Images of My Perfection/Images of My Deformity* (1973), Wilson catalogued parts of her body according to what she regarded as their degree of attractiveness or unattractiveness. Presented with all the formal rigour of Conceptual art, the lists and photographs document the basis upon which value or its lack is inscribed on women's bodies. In *Makeover* (1974) she shifted her attention to the face, that most public locus of both identity and the prescriptive ideals of feminine beauty, although in this case the outcome was a lurid, clownish mask. The makeover process was elaborated further in a set of paired photographs entitled *I Make Up the Image of My Perfection/I Make Up the Image of My Deformity* (1974). In these photographs, and in her video of the same title, makeup – the quintessential tool of feminine perfectibility – is used to mimic femininity itself and to re-present it as a façade of tenuous and conflicted fragments (fig. 6.7).

Wilson's play with representation enacted what some feminists have theorized as the potential of mimicry and masquerade to problematize

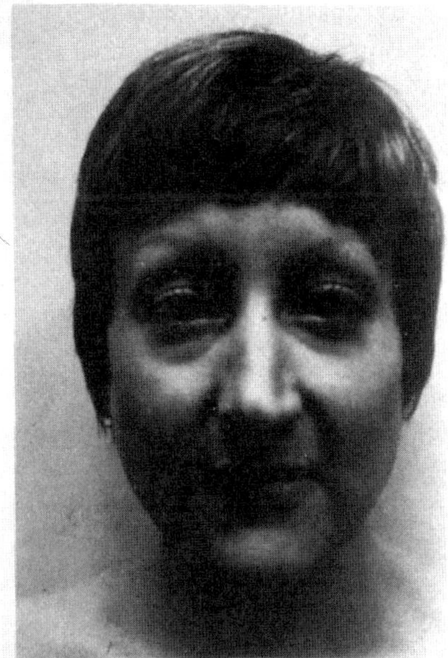
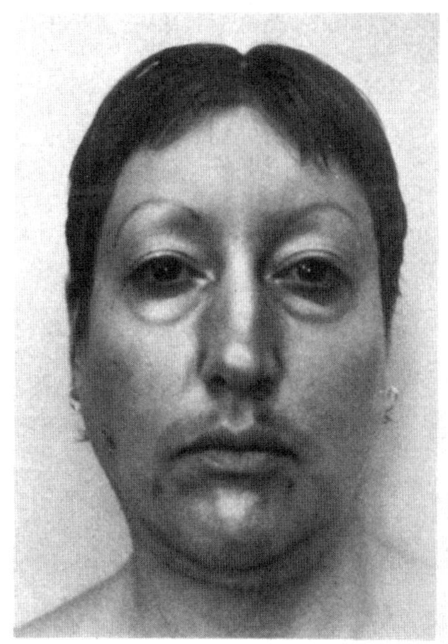

6.7 Martha Wilson. *I Make Up the Image of My Perfection/I Make Up the Image of My Deformity*, 1974. Photodocumentation of performance in the artist's studio, Halifax.

the relation of femininity to itself in representation. As Laura Mulvey argued in her analysis of conventional, Hollywood-type cinema, the rigid structures of spectatorship present women as the given-to-be-seen, as passively locked within the active and objectifying gaze of the male protagonist. This, said Mulvey, presents a dilemma for the female spectator. Identification with the hero entails a certain "masculinization" or psychological transvestism, while identification with the female character requires her to adopt a passive position characterized by a closeness or proximity between herself and the feminine object on display.[60]

In her article on "Film and the Masquerade," Mary Ann Doane argued that women could resist this closeness through the strategy of female masquerade. Doing so would allow a woman to "produce herself as an excess of femininity," to don a hyperbolic mask that flaunts femininity by holding it at a distance, thus resisting the patriarchal positioning of femininity "as closeness, as presence-to-itself, as precisely, imagistic."[61] Irigaray holds a different view, however, arguing that the female masquerade actually exacerbates a woman's double alienation because, in positioning her as an "object of consumption or of desire by masculine 'subjects,'" it reifies her as a nonsubject alienated from language.[62] For Irigaray, mimicry is a more subversive strategy because it allows women to pass from "imposed mimesis" – in which the female is positioned as mirror to the male, reflecting and confirming the truth of his centrality – into a female miming that has no recognizable referent.[63] Building upon her earlier study of the critical possibilities made available through an intertextual reading of Brechtian and feminist theory, Elin Diamond has made a perceptive connection between Brecht's repudiation of imitative or naturalist theatre and Irigaray's concept of mimicry.[64] Just as Brecht's alienation effects work to make ideology visible, Irigaray's mimicry shatters the illusions of the equivalence between mimesis and truth by "showing the show" through which such truth-claims are staged, thus revealing the "divisive effects of the patriarchal Self in a body that is not the Same."[65]

## SHOWING THE SHOW

This "showing the show" enabled feminist performance artists to mimic their cultural positioning as mirror to the sameness, or "hommo-sexuality," of the patriarchal subject and, by shattering the truth-claims of this subject, to treat what Braidotti calls "the myth of Woman" as a now "empty stage where feminist women can experiment with their own subjective becoming."[66] In other words, feminist performance artists could strategically traverse subject and object positions, an insight made, as we recall, by Lippard in 1976: "When women use their own bodies in their art work, they are using their *selves*; a significant psychological factor converts these bodies or faces from object to subject."[67] Yet as Jacques Lacan pointed out, to (mis)represent or mimic representations of femininity in the patriarchal order is a treacherous game because "images and symbols *for* the woman cannot be isolated from images and symbols *of* the woman. It is representation … the representation of feminine sexuality … which conditions how it comes into play."[68]

The pitfalls that Lacan warns about are exemplified in the work of Hannah Wilke and in its controversial reception. Wilke's diverse body of work encompasses sculpture, performance, video, film, photography, posters, and book works, and it is characterized by autobiographical references and a complex layering of imagistic and linguistic metaphors. Wilke's own female sexuality is always central: "Since 1960, I have been

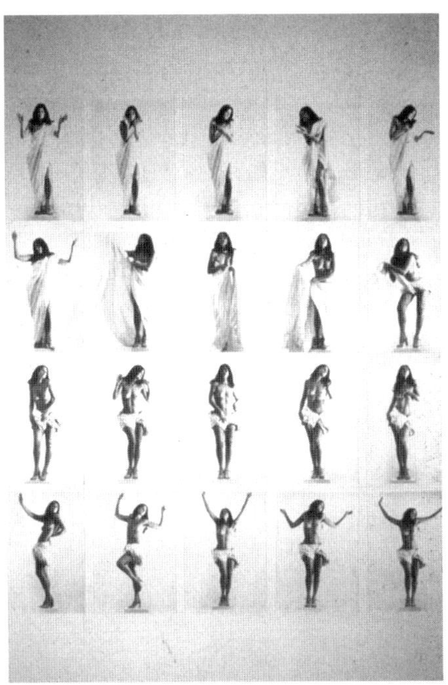

6.8 Hannah Wilke. *Hannah Wilke Super-T-Art*, 1974. 20 black-and-white photographs, 1.02 x 81 cm overall; 25 x 18 cm each. Photograph: D. James Dee.

concerned with the creation of a formal imagery that is specifically female ... Its content has always been related to my own body and feelings, reflecting pleasure as well as pain, the ambiguity and complexity of emotions."[69] In her work, Wilke's decidedly beautiful face and body were often "scarred" by small labial motifs (made from chewing gum) intended to convey metaphorically the psychic and physical wounds suffered by women under patriarchy. In one performance, *Hannah Wilke Super-T-Art* (1974), Wilke posed as both Christ and Venus, suggesting that she was both victim and giver of pleasure; indeed, her self-designation was "Sugargiver" (fig. 6.8).[70]

Although it seems clear that Wilke was not merely a gratuitous exhibitionist, many feminists have been troubled by the question of whether viewers were able to make the distinction in her work between, in Lacan's terms, images and symbols *for* the woman and images and symbols *of* the woman. As Lippard noted, "her own confusion of her roles as beautiful woman and artist, as flirt and feminist, has resulted at times in politically ambiguous manifestations that have exposed her to criticism on a personal as well as on an artistic level."[71]

Acknowledging that Wilke's work was ambiguous about whether it was resisting or acquiescing to the codes of female objectification, Amelia Jones suggests that what most bothered feminists was its perpetuation of the stereotype of women as narcissists.[72] But, in fact, it is not true that feminists could not appreciate the value of "defiant narcissism," for this is exactly the grounds upon which Lippard applauded Benglis's *Artforum* image. In contrast to Benglis, however, Wilke's art did not seem to make a feminist stance explicit and thus left too much open to interpretation.[73] As Judith Barry and Sandy Flitterman put it, "she does not make her own position clear; is her art work enticing critique or titillating enticement?"[74] As Jones reads it, however, this ambiguity and confusion was precisely the point. Strategically posing as a narcissist enabled Wilke to "wrench open conventional alignments of the female body with a debased and quintessentially objectified self-love." Moreover, she says, because Wilke's seductive narcissism drew viewers into a relationship of desire with Wilke herself, it worked to undermine the Modernist fallacy of distanced and objective interpretation.[75]

Jones's reinterpretation of Wilke's work opens up the possibility of reading it in multiple ways. Nonetheless, it must be noted that since attitudes toward narcissism in general and female narcissism in particular were so negative at this time, it is hard to imagine that if Wilke's work really was a positive, feminist recuperation of narcissism, it would have been recognized as such. This negative view of narcissism was especially evident in writing on video. In his 1976 article "Video Art, the Imaginary and the Parole Vide," Stuart Marshall argued that the tendency of video artists to use the camera/monitor as a mirror indicated a preoccupation with what Lacan had identified as the "mirror stage" of development.[76] In the mirror stage, the child first recognizes itself as an independent and cohesive being (ego), but this is only a misrecognition of unity, for the child really becomes two: the self who sees and the self who is seen in the mirror image. This oscillation between self and self-as-other is only resolved as the child proceeds through the Oedipal crisis and enters, through language, the social matrix of the "Symbolic Order."[77]

As Marshall saw it, video that was preoccupied by self-reflection was trapped, like the child in the mirror phase, in the regressive, pre-Oedipal, and therefore presocial stage of development. Of the four artists that Marshall focused on, three were women: Joan Jonas, Lynda

Benglis, and Hermine Freed. Significantly, he did not note that Lacan specifically associated the mirror stage with female identity because the female's incomplete resolution of the Oedipal crisis positions her perpetually outside the Symbolic Order as the objectified other.[78] Ignoring the possibility that these artists' work might be read as initiating an engagement with these problems of sexual difference and subjectivity from a feminist perspective, he commends Vito Acconci as the only one of the four who addresses the subject/object positions in voyeurism in a positive, self-critical way. By contrast, the three women are dismissed as embodying a regressive narcissism manifest in their indulgent, uncritical exhibitionist display.[79]

In the same year, Rosalind Krauss published the article "Video: The Aesthetics of Narcissism," in which she made the point that video is distinctive because unlike most art forms that must be seen in terms of their physical conditions, video must be seen in terms of psychological conditions, specifically narcissism. Krauss argued that the very nature of the video medium, with its mirror reflection and feedback, locked artists into a preoccupation with self-regard that is narcissistic because it signifies "the unchanging condition of perpetual frustration." She disparaged video's tendency to collapse subject and object, which made it difficult to maintain critical distance, and she related narcissism in video art to "the problem of narcissism within the wider context of our culture" and to the way that the art world had been "deeply and disastrously affected by its relation to mass media." In the end, she concluded that video can escape its narcissism only by assaulting the medium or exploiting it in order to criticize it from within.[80] As an important critical voice of the period, Krauss clearly demonstrates in this article the general opprobrium in which narcissism was held at this time, both in art and in society.

Although Krauss referred to two women artists, Lynda Benglis and Joan Jonas, she, like Marshall, remained oblivious to how they were positioned differently, as women, in relation to subjectivity, and she certainly did not acknowledge the possibility that they might be using narcissistic self-reflection as a specifically feminist kind of critical strategy. Like Benglis, Jonas explored the formal and technical properties of the video medium in an effort both to materialize her own body and psyche and to engage viewers in a consciousness of their own ways of looking. In *Mirror Check* (1970), for example, Jonas stands naked before an audience and examines parts of her body with a hand mirror.

6.9 Joan Jonas. *Organic Honey's Visual Telepathy*, 1972. Black-and-white video, 17:24 min

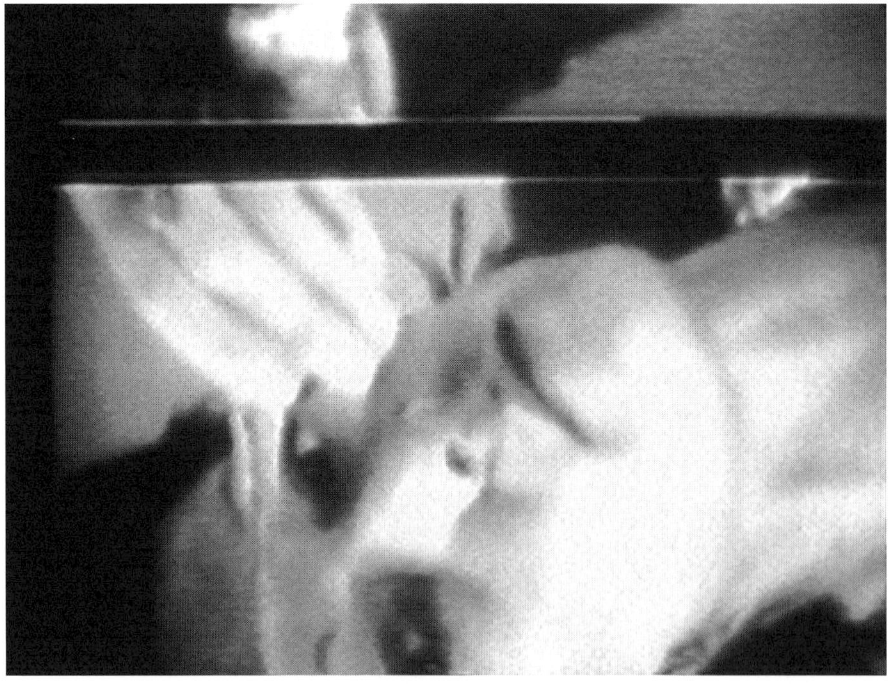

6.10 Joan Jonas. *Vertical Roll*, 1972. Black-and-white video, 19:38 min.

Jonas wrote that "From the beginning the mirror provided me with a metaphor for my investigations as well as a device to alter space, to fragment it, and to reflect the audience, bringing them into the space of the performance. These events were rituals for an audience that was included by this reflexion."[81] This suggests that although *Mirror Check* might seem to epitomize Krauss's critique of video as narcissistic, Jonas's self-display was derived less from a "condition of perpetual frustration" than from a concern to investigate structures of spectatorship. This concern was given a more explicitly feminist inflection in Jonas's work over the next few years.

In *Organic Honey's Visual Telepathy* (1972), Jonas turned the video camera as spectatorial device on herself and four other female performers. Wearing elaborate costumes and masks covered with feathers and jewels, the performers manipulated mirrors, cameras, and monitors to create a disjunctive collage of "real" and reflected images (fig. 6.9). Although these women might initially appear to be participating in the kind of unwitting self-objectification that Lippard warned against and that seemed epitomized in Wilke's work, the spatial and temporal fragmentation of the imagery and actions disrupted any possibility of their being recuperated into what Mulvey called "fetishistic scopophilia."[82] Fetishism is certainly alluded to by the costuming, but it is then circumvented by the mobile agency of the performers and by their constant disruption of the spectacle by holding mirrors and cameras up to one another. Moreover, by repeatedly putting on and removing their masks, they enacted that distance between the self and the image that is paradigmatic of the feminine masquerade.

Images from *Organic Honey's Visual Telepathy* were later incorporated into a video called *Vertical Roll* (1972), which disturbed the pleasures of viewing much more aggressively (fig. 6.10). Jonas played with the image by adjusting the frequency of the monitor so that a roll bar interrupts the image at regular intervals. She then rescanned the monitor, incorporating this "flaw" into the final tape to make it appear at different points as though the images are either being pulled down off the screen or jumping over the roll bar. This repetitious rupture of the image is intensified by the ear-shattering soundtrack of a spoon being banged on a mirror or by pieces of wood being clapped together to mark the moment when the roll bar strikes the bottom of the monitor. By confronting the viewer with these severe distortions, Jonas makes watching her roam the screen and negotiate its rolling barrier a disconcerting and

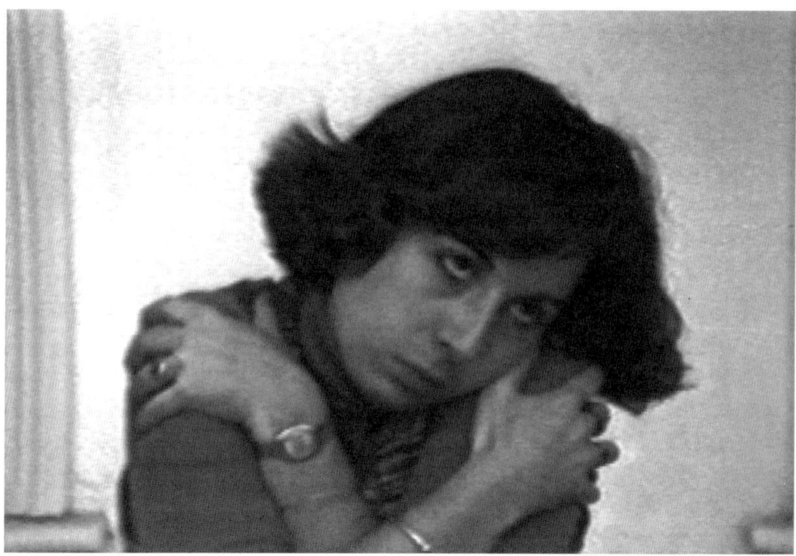

6.11 Dorit Cypis. *Exploring Comfort*, 1974. Black-and-white video, 10:30 min

confusing experience. The insistent artifice of the technical manipulations echoes and reinforces the artifice of the images, which forces us, through our extreme discomfort, into a conscious awareness of our role as viewer.

Extreme discomfort is also experienced watching Dorit Cypis's video *Exploring Comfort* (1974). Cypis was a student at the Nova Scotia College of Art and Design at the time and would have known of Martha Wilson's pioneering feminist example. *Exploring Comfort* was one of Cypis's first performance videos, and as Jan Peacock noted, like the fledgling explorations of many young women artists, it presented "a vulnerable female subject who sets the task of seeing herself under conditions of being seen" (fig. 6.11). Seated on a stool before the camera, Cypis announces "I need some comfort" and then, after a pause, "I *need* some comfort." She stares expectantly into the camera for what may be the longest forty seconds in video history. As Peacock says, to sit locked in Cypis's gaze (and for how long we do not know) "is to live without comfort – or rather live with discomfort: hers, our own, or both."[83] Suddenly Cypis breaks the tension and begins to caress her face and body. She then moves her face in close to the camera to practice facial expressions and laughter styles while checking her image against an off-screen monitor. Watching her on-screen affectations, we quail with embarrassment both for her and for ourselves because she seems to watch *us* as we look. Scrutiny becomes a form of torture, and we find ourselves most decidedly in the realm of visual un-pleasure. As Anne Wagner has proposed, this kind of video aimed "to summon you into the present moment, as an audience, and sometimes, under selected circumstances, to make you all-too-conscious of that fact."[84]

The presence of the camera/monitor was such a highly charged signifier of spectatorial structures that these devices were often incorporated into live performance. For example, in *Some Reflective Surfaces* (1976), Adrian Piper used film and video images to make the audience self-conscious of its position (fig. 6.12). She explained:

> I am a neutral object in black clothes, white face, moustache, dark glasses. I tell you, the audience, a story of myself as a disco dancer as I mimic and repeat the dancer's movements. Sometimes I stop to rest, practice, and refuel myself with whiskey. A film, of me, dancing with friends and watching you, is projected on and behind me as I dance to the song *Respect*. A man's voice criticizes my dancing in sharp commands. As I move into the spotlight my image appears on a video monitor. The film and music stop; I acknowledge you; the light goes out.[85]

6.12 Adrian Piper. *Some Reflective Surfaces*, 1976. Photodocumentation of performance at the Whitney Museum of American Art, New York.

As Piper obeyed these commands, the theme of Aretha Franklin's song (i.e., self-esteem and confidence, especially for young blacks) and the notion of popular dance as spontaneous and free self-expression were brutally undermined by this scrutinizing male presence watching her and exercising his authoritative ability to coerce her into compliance. This male voice seeks to assert its disembodied (transcendent) mastery, but in the end, it is Piper who acknowledges the audience and who asserts her own particularized subjectivity as a black woman.

For women, the devices of camera and monitor carry the burden of their own material and philosophical relation to the history of technology, wherein the "bachelor machine" has been imbued with a masculine auto-eroticism and the feminine has been instrumentalized. In tracing this history and attempting to address how women can enter the technological order, critic Nell Tenhaaf reiterates Luce Irigaray's question: "If machines, even machines of theory, can be aroused all by themselves, may women not do likewise?"[86] In response, Tenhaaf proposes that many early feminists did exactly this by merging their bodies with the video apparatus itself. In *Delicate Issue* (1979), for example, Kate Craig turns the machine on herself in the most intimate scrutiny of the elusive boundary between private and public, closeness and distance, flesh and machine (fig. 6.13). The camera, while operated by her partner, is fully under her control as it scans her body inch by visceral inch. The embodied sounds of amplified breath and heartbeat rise and fall. As the camera probes the scarcely identifiable landscape of Craig's body, her voice addresses us with equally probing questions: "At what distance does the subject read? How close can a camera be? How close do I want to be? How close do you want to be?" In the end, as the camera closes in on her glistening clitoris, Craig again asserts her control over our desire to look, to take in her body: "This is as close as you get," she says, "I can't get you any closer." We are, says Tenhaaf, on a threshold, literally and metaphorically, where the feminine merges with the technological without being subsumed by it.[87]

## BODIES OF DISCOURSE

As Craig's embodied encounter with the machine implies, bodies always exist within the complex signifying practices of social meaning. From the late 1970s through the 1980s, especially in the work of artists like Victor Burgin, Barbara Kruger, Cindy Sherman, Jeff Wall, and others, who explored photography's relation to commerce and popular culture,

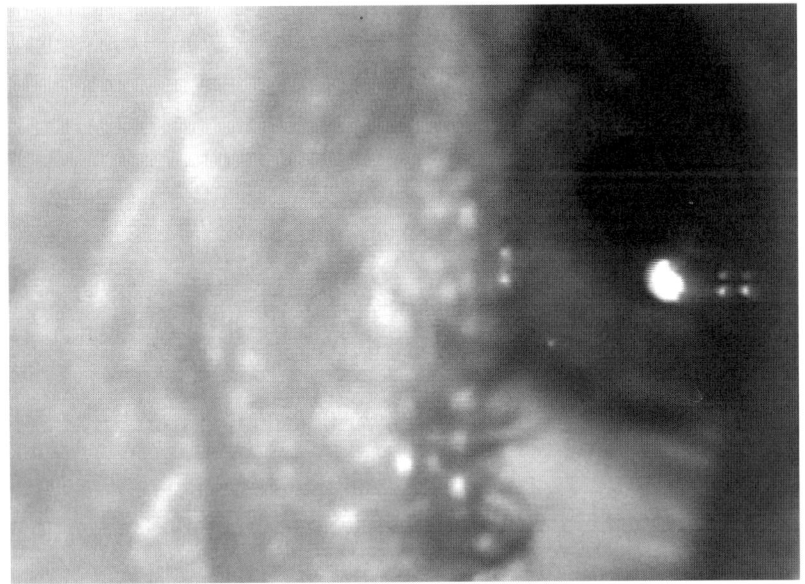

6.13 Kate Craig. *Delicate Issue*, 1979. Colour video, 12:36 min.

art's dominant discourse shifted to a focus on the role of representation as a potent form of mediation within ideological and cultural discourse. The goal of such work was not to escape or provide alternatives to the representational myths and ideologies produced within culture but to interrupt their flow, to diagnose and reveal their mechanisms, and thus to play a role in liberating people from the institutions that control their lives.[88]

Yet much of the critical groundwork for these investigations came from the ideas and issues first articulated within feminist art practice of the 1970s. Not only had early feminists been committed to a critique of representation, but they had also expanded our understanding of politics beyond the traditional class-oriented language of the Left by exposing its lingering humanism as a gendered construct blind to sexual difference. Moreover, because feminist artists saw themselves as part of a large social movement, they were especially concerned with the need for their work to be meaningful both within and beyond the art world; that is, they saw it as explicitly political. Unlike the dominant art practices of the period, such as Minimalism and Conceptualism, which, for all their claims to having "political implications," remained confined to

6.14 Martha Rosler. *Vital Statistics of a Citizen, Simply Obtained*, 1977. Black-and-white video, 38:00 min.

self-reflexive critiques of the art world and its systems, early feminist art aimed to reach new audiences by means of an aesthetic discourse that was clearly and broadly legible. This predilection for a culturally shared language through which women could refer to and critique the contingencies of experience in the contemporary world enabled feminists to articulate a new form of avant-garde engagement.

The feminist concern with questions of how identity, the body, and its representations are embedded within social relations and historical contingencies was always explicit in the work of Martha Rosler. Rosler's preoccupation has been to show the inadequacy of all systems of representation not just as art world constructs, but also as social discourse. In her view, these systems constitute the "mythologies of everyday life."[89] In her *Vital Statistics of a Citizen, Simply Obtained*, originally performed live (1973) and reenacted as a video (1977), Rosler presents a dark parody of positivist science in which a male researcher and assistant verbally interrogate a woman (Rosler) in a clinical setting (fig. 6.14).[90] As the examination proceeds to physical information, Rosler gradually undresses, and every inch of her body is scrupulously measured by the two men, while three female assistants register with bells, whistles, or kazoos how her measurements compare to the "standard." The video is accompanied by Rosler's voiceover reciting a litany of "crimes against women." *Vital Statistics* is a searing indictment of how society circumscribes and controls female behaviour and roles through both mythical ideals and the "objective" categories of science.

Her voiceover also reflects upon how one learns to "manufacture" oneself as a being in a state of culture by simulating an idealized version of the self as "natural," thus proposing, as Henry Sayre suggests, that the external appearance of the self does not *conceal* the true or natural self but is a *representation* of the self as natural.[91]

Although we have seen that a number of early feminist artists like Rosler, Piper, Mendieta, Michishita, and Idemitsu addressed gender in relation to economies of production and to the particularities of racial or cultural identity, the focus of most feminist performance art in the 1970s was primarily on gender alone. This tendency within early feminism in general has subsequently resulted in harsh critiques of it as exclusionary, especially of women of colour.[92] These critiques were also made in the art world. Although feminism always claimed to uphold inclusiveness and collectivism, feminist artists were seen by some to have betrayed this egalitarian vision as soon as they had themselves attained a degree of recognition within the art world's mainstream institutions. American artist Lorraine O'Grady made precisely this point when she staged a kind of guerrilla attack at the opening of the "Personae" show in 1981 at the New Museum of Contemporary Art in New York. In a defiant gesture reminiscent of the intrusion of Robin Morgan and her feminist cohort at the 1968 Miss America pageant, O'Grady appeared as *Mlle Bourgeoise Noire*, wearing a tiara and a gown made of 180 pairs of white gloves, and proceeded to disrupt the opening by shouting angry poems against the racial politics of the art world that had sponsored the "Nine-White-Personae" show (fig. 6.15).[93] O'Grady's Mlle Bourgeois Noire character had in fact already debuted in 1980 in a similar invasion of the Just Above Midtown Gallery, which was conceived by its founder/director, Linda Goode-Bryannt, to serve as the only black avant-garde art gallery in New York at the time. Although the boldness of Goode-Bryannt's vision was indicated by her choice to locate the gallery in the heart of the mainstream New York art scene, O'Grady felt that the work of too many of the gallery artists was simply not living up to the gallery's radical potential. While the punch line of her poem at the New Museum was "Now is the time for an invasion!" her poem at Just Above Midtown was an exhortation to its artists that "Black art must take more risks!" All in all, Mlle Bourgeois Noire was an equal-opportunity critic, shouting out in tough terms against the conventions and hypocrisies of both the black and white art world milieus.[94]

6.15 Lorraine O'Grady. *Mlle Bourgeoise Noire Goes to the New Museum*, 1981. photodocumentation of performance at the New Museum of Contemporary Art, New York. Photograph: Coreen Simpson.

During the 1980s and 1990s, American artists like O'Grady, Coco Fusco, and Lorna Simpson and Canadians like Jin-Me Moon, Lori Blondeau, and Shelley Niro addressed more directly the questions of how race, identity, power, and politics intersect with feminism. For Martha Rosler, however, it was just as problematic to focus on race at the expense of class as it was to focus exclusively on gender. In particular, she argued that demands for inclusion missed a crucial point because they do not sufficiently address the question of art audiences and their investments in the economics and prestige of class hierarchy and, moreover, that such demands are all too easily co-opted into the desires of the art world's controlling institutions to appear progressively liberal: "Looked at from the perspective of a fashion-driven industry, the advent of art world identity politics, or multiculturalism, represents the incorporation of marginal producers, who bring fresh new 'looks' to revivify public interest ... Powerful cultural institutions like the Rockefeller Foundation and many universities, which didn't care for the older [Marxist] version of political art, have been quick to sponsor multiculturalism, which is, after all, a demand for inclusion rather than for economic restructuring."[95]

No doubt Rosler's comments will be seen as highly contentious in some circles, but her point is that feminism should not merely expand its discourse to include the politics of race, ethnicity, and sexuality, but also maintain a focus on the historically specific context of capitalism and the bourgeois ideology that sustains it. As a result of Rosler's presence, as well as that of British feminists like Mary Kelly and Sandy Flitterman as visiting artists or teachers at the Nova Scotia College of Art and Design in the late 1970s and early 1980s, the question of gender *and* class became an important reference point for students there at this time. In 1982, for example, Wendy Geller produced the video *48-Hour Beauty Blitz*, the premise of which was taken directly from a *Glamour* magazine article designed to instruct the reader in carrying out a weekend-long regimen for self-renewal centred on a beauty makeover.[96] Feminists had long seen such representations of women as responsible for inculcating prescriptive ideals of femininity. Yet Geller's intention was not simply to expose such representations as oppressive, but also to understand her own fascination with them.

As Geller works through her weekend beauty regimen, we see that there is more going on here than an interrogation of the allure of women's popular culture. It has something to do with the discrepancy

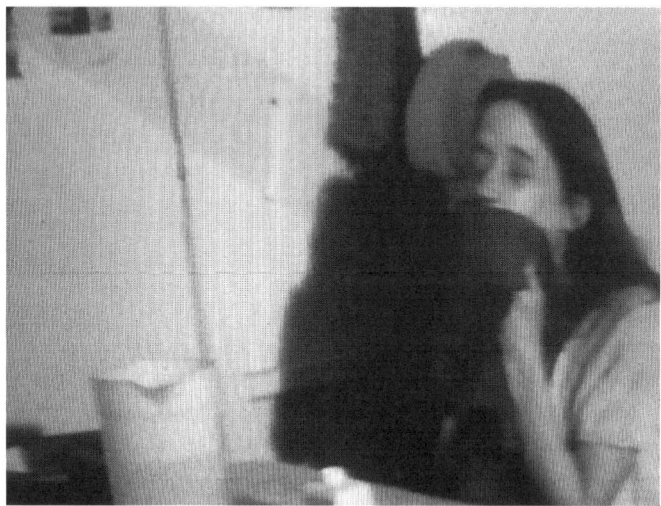

6.16 Wendy Geller. *48-Hour Beauty Blitz*, 1982. Colour video, 38:00 min.

6.17 Wendy Geller. *48-Hour Beauty Blitz*, 1982. Colour video, 38:00 min.

between the makeover's intended results and the results that Geller actually experienced, which came not only from the fact that beauty work turns out to be isolating, tedious, and exhausting, but also from the stark contrast between Geller's efforts to inhabit the feminine fantasy and the persistent hindrances of her impoverished reality. Geller tells us, for example, with a dour and deadpan expression, that she is supposed to use her best china and crystal so as to make the beauty blitz as pleasant as possible, but what she holds up for view are a few chipped dishes from a thrift store (fig. 6.16). Later we see her cooking the prescribed "low-cal" dinner – an egg-white omelette – in a pie pan on a hot plate. With devastating satire emulating Rosler's *Semiotics of the Kitchen*, Geller repeatedly uses the magazine as a cover for the broken blender in which she buzzes raw vegetable "soups." Later, realizing that her rooming-house bathroom is occupied at a critical moment, she is forced to improvise a facial at her kitchen table with a bowl of water and a ragged scrap of towel (fig. 6.17). This discrepancy between the fantasy and the reality is not just a matter of Geller's inability to live up to the impossible ideals of feminine beauty. Rather, the most debilitating obstructions to the presumed pleasures of the *Beauty Blitz* result from the hardships of her economic reality. In revealing how her beauty tasks are thwarted by her poverty, Geller's "disclosure of class relations" casts a glaring light on how her ideological purchase on femininity is determined by the limitations of her economic purchase on consumption.[97]

As much as Geller satirizes the fantasies of women's popular culture, she does not disavow their allure and significance. We have seen how other feminist artists have deftly appropriated the discourses of popular culture while intervening in their prescriptive ideologies. This often takes the form of a self-mocking defiance that reminds us of Freud's observation that "Humour is not resigned; it is rebellious." And because it is the sign of "the ego's victorious assertion of its own invulnerability," it is empowering.[98] Such rebelliousness is clearly evident in the work of Lori Blondeau, who uses parody to define a positive identity in the midst of a hostile social environment. One response to her experience of the clash between her Aboriginal identity and the dominant ideals of white femininity was her creation of the character CosmoSquaw, in whose guise she appeared in 1996 as the bosomy cover girl of her mock magazine, *CosmoSquaw* (fig. 6.18). Recuperating the term "squaw," which means "woman" in the Cree language, was an act of defiance both against the teenaged boys who had called her "a fucking

6.18 Lori Blondeau. *CosmoSquaw*, 1996. Cover of mock magazine. Collaboration and photograph: Bradlee LaRocque.

6.19 Lori Blondeau. *Lonely Surfer Squaw*, 1997. Digital image for the Internet exhibition "Virtual Postcards from the Feminist Utopia," sponsored by Mentoring Artists for Women Artists, Winnipeg, Manitoba. Photograph: Bradlee LaRocque.

ugly squaw" and against the way that *Cosmopolitan* magazine targets single white women looking for tips to find a man – tips that were of no help to a single and Aboriginal woman.[99] Blondeau's magazine satirizes the exclusionary presumptions and bombastic prose of *Cosmopolitan* with cover lines such as "Learn How to Spoon Feed *Your* Man!" and "10 Easy Tips for a Killer Bingo-Face!" In *Lonely Surfer Squaw* (1997), which was designed for the web-based exhibition "Virtual Postcards from the Feminist Utopia," Blondeau posed with a pink surfboard, like a displaced *Baywatch* babe, on the bank of a frozen Saskatchewan river wearing nothing but a fur bikini and mukluks (fig. 6.19).[100] Blondeau shows that humour can indeed repudiate reality and thus enable the humorist to resist her own subjection. It is, finally, as Judith Butler would say, a way to "make trouble" for the status quo of hegemonic power structures.

Winnipeg-based performance artists Shawna Dempsey and Lorri Millan have been making similar trouble for over a decade now. As emphatically "out" lesbians, their work addresses sexism, homophobia, and the social negotiations of identity. They use costume and dress as metaphor, symbol, or dramatic prop for narrative skits and vaudevillian gags that

6.20 Lorri Millan and Shawna Dempsey. *Arborite Housewife*, 1994. Studio photograph of performance costume. Photograph: Sheila Spence.

are wickedly parodic inversions of what is "normal," legitimate, and officially sanctioned. Nothing is sacrosanct in their comedic repertoire. As the *Arborite Housewife* (1994), Dempsey wears a pink dress made from one of the new "wonder" materials that furnished the postwar suburban boom (fig. 6.20).[101] Reciting a parable about marriage being like driving the family car, she warns of the dangers that ensue if family members deviate from their prescribed roles. Yet there is little danger of us taking her morality tale seriously, for it is as rigid and artificial as her dress. In *Growing Up* (1996), however, Dempsey confides that such rigid and artificial constructions could also be the object of queer desire (fig. 6.21). As an adolescent in the late sixties, she didn't know what erotica or porn were, but she did know what turned her on: the ladies in the lingerie pages of Eaton's catalogue wearing "industrial-strength underwear concealing unimaginable body parts so powerful they needed architecture to keep them in place."[102] Humour cuts like a knife here, as always for Dempsey and Millan, serving both as a means to expose the cultural contradictions and confinements that oppress them and as a force for liberatory release, theirs and ours.[103] From that "empty stage where feminist women can experiment with their own subjective becoming," their gift of laughter rises defiantly.[104]

6.21 Lorri Millan and Shawna Dempsey. *Growing Up Suite*, 1996. Photodocumentation of performance. Photograph: Don Lee, Banff Centre, Banff.

# Conclusion

In concluding this study of the history of feminist performance art, I am reminded of the old joke "How many feminists does it take to change a light bulb?" The answer, of course, is "That's not funny!" But, to the contrary, the work of many of these artists shows that feminist humour can indeed be devastatingly funny. The aim of such humour, however, is not to soften the political point in order to make it more palatable and less offensive but to soften up the audience in order to make it more receptive to the political critique itself, for this has always been the point of feminist art. In addition to humour, feminist performance art has used many different strategies to advance its political objective of using art as a means to change the praxis of everyday life. As this study has argued, with this objective as its operative principle, feminist art since the early 1970s has had a major influence in shifting art practice away from its exclusive preoccupation with aesthetic concerns and toward a critical engagement with the social and political contingencies of our own times.

The art world, however, is an institution driven by market demands for innovation and fashionableness. In the last few years, a trend has emerged on the international art scene toward a fascination with the "ordinary" and the "everyday," on the one hand, and with the "sensational," on the other, both of which position themselves in distinct contrast to the preoccupation with "socially concerned" art that had previously predominated, especially in the more theory-driven forms that were prevalent the 1980s.[1] As Canadian art critic Dena Shottenkirk characterized it, this rejection of social concerns in recent art is the result of a fatigue with the "didactic presumption" and with artists' "claims to the ... grandiose status of social critic/shaman" associated with the politicized art "which proliferated in the '80s and '90s."[2] Inevitably, something that has been around as long as feminist art has often come to be regarded in this new context as no longer fashionable, as though feminist art were merely a period style now become passé.

This view of feminism as unfashionable, which I alluded to in reference to the work of Charmaine Wheatley in the Introduction to this book, is also manifested and perpetuated by the phenomenon of so-called "postfeminism." Postfeminism is often confused with third-wave feminism largely because both are associated with young women in particular and because both are perceived as having a critical or even hostile relation to feminism. The two terms, however, signify very different things. Unlike third-wave feminists, who retain a commitment to feminism while also seeking to alter its parameters in order to make it more responsive to the concerns of women today – especially younger women and those who seek to foster a transnational feminism – postfeminists maintain that feminism is, at best, obsolete and, at worst, a repressive and even puritanical force that imposes a victim mentality on women.[3] As Heather Anderson has argued in her thesis on contemporary Canadian performance art by women, postfeminism is in fact part of the feminist backlash, aligning it with a conservative, laissez-faire agenda which claims that, since women have now achieved equality with men, they should abandon their radical politics, shut up, and just get over it. Anderson points out further that postfeminism's rejection of collective social politics is also fuelled by the entertainment and consumer-culture industries' celebration of hypersexualization and "go-girl" individualism, whereby one's "politics" consist of having the right to acquire and express one's identity as a consumable lifestyle.[4]

In the context of art practice, specifically that of performance art, postfeminism is especially evident in works that assert women's sexualized bodies as manifestations of women's rights to be sexual subjects but that do so in ways leaving unchallenged the conventional expectations of women as objects of erotic, spectatorial display. As Anderson argues in her thesis, this is the case not only with Wheatley's strip-club performances and erotic merchandising (e.g., chocolate moulds made from the crack in her butt cheeks, available for US$100.00 from her website, http://www.chachacharmaine.com), but also with Vanessa Beecroft's "living art," in which nude or scantily-clad fashion models with "perfect" bodies pose or totter about in art galleries on designer stilettos, and with Canadian artist Tagny Duff's "interventions" in shopping malls where she briefly lies naked on the floor before being apprehended by security guards.[5] In such work, feminism is present as a validating framework ostensibly to "problematize" such objectified display. But given that any potentially critical challenges are subsumed, on the one hand, by simplistic, libertarian assertions of women's right to have "fun" with their sexuality (even though such works are not particularly funny) and, on the other hand, by acquiescence to the dominant culture's standardized and commodified ideals of desirable femininity (i.e., young, white, and thin), feminism here is little more than a hollowed-out signifier. Its challenge as a collective, political movement is reduced to marketable stylizations of the kind of mythological individualism that feminism and feminist art have long endeavoured to expose and critique.

As my study has shown, however, feminist art is much more than a style, and in this I concur with Lucy Lippard, who asserted in 1980 that feminist art is "neither a style nor a movement" but rather "a value system, a revolutionary strategy, a way of life," whose major contribution to the art world has been "complex, subversive, and fundamentally *political*."[6] This revolutionary strategy goes back to the earliest days of feminist art as an explicit challenge to the notions that the everyday can be stripped of the political and that the experiences of everyday life, no matter how intimate or personal, can be severed from social practices, macroeconomics, or state policies. Far from being obsolete, feminist art, like the feminist movement as a whole, is remarkable for its longevity. Roberta Hamilton's observation that "of all the social movements of the 1960s, the women's movement, however diversified it became, however its strategies were adapted to new circumstances, continued to grow in countries around the world" could be applied as well to the practices of feminist art and feminist art history.[7]

Across this arcing trajectory through both time and space, feminist art and art history have indeed modified and diversified their strategies. As Griselda Pollock has noted, "feminism is a historical project and thus is itself constantly shaped and remodeled in relation to the living process of women's struggles."[8] In the 1970s feminist art was utopian, celebratory, righteously angry, and defiant of the rigid precepts and exclusionary values that dictated what could be counted as art and who could legitimately make it. In the 1980s feminism was forced to confront the extent to which its claims to inclusiveness and sisterhood papered over or denied the racism, classism, imperialism, and heterosexism experienced by so many women the world over. In the 1990s, as Pollock wrote further, "difference and with it, the painful realization of conflict and even antagonism, structure a much more careful, self-conscious and chastened feminist discourse." What survives, however, both into the 1990s and into the twenty-first century, is feminism as a form of dissidence – a dissidence that Pollock identifies as a way of keeping *thought* alive in artistic and historical practices.[9]

This critical ethos of thought that fostered feminism as a social movement and made it such a radical force of change in the art world has become as passé in today's art world as feminism itself is often perceived to be – and, indeed, may account for *why* feminism is so often regarded in this way. To quote Richard Rhodes, the editor of Canada's most prominent art magazine, *Canadian Art*: "Something is astir in the art world again. Artists are finding a different tone of voice. They are beginning to put 20th-century 'criticality' behind them. The mood has shifted to favour the immediacy of everyday experience."[10] This disavowal of criticality, which can be traced to that strain within postmodernism that critics and historians like Fredric Jameson, Richard Sheppard, Hal Foster, and David Hopkins have identified as "conservative" and "assimilated" into the dominant, market-driven values of laissez-faire late capitalism, produces an art world in which art is a cultural product like any other.[11] With no consensus of goals, no authoritative positions to resist, and no prescriptive rules, it has become extremely difficult for art to maintain any oppositional stance or adversarial distance from the social mechanisms and market forces into which it has been merged. Within this vacuum of criticality, art has become a pluralistic field where "anything goes" – except, apparently, criticality itself!

This situation has its ramifications for feminist art as well. Not only does it comprise the cultural and historical context in which third-wave feminism and postfeminism have emerged simultaneously, but it also accounts for much of the confusion that exists between the two categories, or approaches – a confusion not unlike the one that often exists between "assimilated" and "oppositional" forms of postmodern art as a whole, frequently making the two modes hard to distinguish.[12] These confusions can also make it difficult to discern a distinctive critical ethos in work by women artists today that can be defined as feminist and, therefore, to determine how and why women artists continue to make feminist art.

On the one hand, there are those like Wheatley, Duff, Beecroft, and others whose work alludes to the critical discourses of historical feminist art while cancelling out any actual criticality. The Spanish artist Ana Laura Aleaz, for example, recently created an installation at the Palais de Tokyo in Paris in 2002 entitled *Prototype Beauty Cabinet*, which was ostensibly meant to provoke critical reflection on the relationship between femininity and beauty, when in reality, since the whole project was staffed and underwritten by the Japanese cosmetic company Shiseido, feminism merely served here as a thin veneer for a marketing opportunity.[13]

On the other hand, there are other contemporary women artists whose critical engagement with feminism remains explicitly evident. One example would be the Québécois performance ensemble Les Fermières obsédées, whose name, which roughly translates as the Obsessed Farm Wives, refers to the Cercles des fermières, an association mentioned in chapter 1, and thus to the long tradition of women's organizing and activism in Quebec. As part of their 2003 tour, the members of Les Fermières obsédées, Annie Baillargeon, Mélissa Charest, Eugénie Cliche, and Catharine Plaisance, performed in Halifax under the auspices of Eye Level Gallery. While Les Fermières obsédées tip their hats to the artisanal and communal traditions of the Cercles des fermières – for instance, by "knitting" with their heads and "preserving" fabric in jars – they also disrupt these traditions in absurd and playful ways. Wearing unruly wigs, ill-applied makeup, and feminine "uniforms" consisting of blouses and skirts, unwashed for the duration of the tour, Les Fermières obsédées interacted between the gallery's storefront window and the sidewalk, stripping down to their underwear and exchanging clothing with one another, throwing paint around, and binding themselves together with duct tape before trying to walk down the street in unison. As Heather Anderson has observed, their performances evoked the notion of femininity as masquerade and explored the tension between individual identity and the collective category "woman."[14] By alluding to these well-established feminist tropes, Les Fermières obsédées underscore the extent to which gender continues to be defined by a set of demarcated norms.

Like Les Fermières obsédées, Toronto artist Allyson Mitchell uses wit and irreverence to defy such norms, especially as they have been codified in the hypersexualized forms promulgated in contemporary popular culture. Her 2004 exhibition in Toronto, "The Fluff Stands Alone," for example, featured wall hangings of Rubinesque nudes made out of vividly coloured fun fur and crushed velvet fabric.[15] While aping the seductive allure of *Playboy* centrefolds, Mitchell's work snaps our attention to the gap between their slick eroticism and the crafty, low-art sensuality of these buxom babes. Like many young women today, Mitchell refuses the prescriptive ideals perpetuated by the powerful economies of popular culture not by turning away from this culture but rather by participating in a populist alternative network of feminist websites, zines, and filmmaking. Among Mitchell's enterprises was the founding, with her partner, Lex Vaughan, of the fat-activist performance troupe called Pretty Porky and Pissed Off, whose website declares: "Our brand of fat activism is about everyBODY. People come in all different sizes. One person's chubby is another person's chunky is another person's skinny is another person's svelt [*sic*] is another person's huge. From XXL to Super Size, we want to spread the word that everyBODY is a good body."[16]

The do-it-yourself ethic of Mitchell and her cohorts and their refusal to be subjugated to the regulatory norms of commodified and heterosexist female sexuality attest not only to the ongoing relevance of feminism as a way to address inequalities, but also to how women of their generation have creatively adapted strategies of feminist organizing to their particular concerns, time, and place. As Candis Steenbergen has pointed out, these are the women that the popular press has failed to take account of when it declares feminism dead, women whose "voices appear in independently-produced zines, in book reviews hidden in the backs of journals, on walls and across public advertisements [and] in non-mainstream publications."[17]

The art world, with its free-market imperatives and entrenched system of critical and curatorial mediation, certainly presents feminist artists with a different set of challenges than those faced by feminist writers. But while the art world today seems to have squandered its purchase on avant-garde criticality in order to exploit the market's predilection for capitalizing on what is *au courant,* it is clear that feminist artists continue to engage critically with the complexities of women's everyday experiences and with the social and structural relations affecting them. Like their predecessors in the 1970s and 1980s, artists like Collyer, Dragu, and Di Risio continue to work with the strategies of autobiography and narrative not so much to find and express their voices as to go on interrogating the subtle ways that oppression continues to operate at the juncture of the private and the public domains. Artists like Mars, Urban, Tourangeau, Lake, and Les Fermières obsédées continue to use the possibilities of roles and transformations not only to explode the persistent and mutating stereotypes of femininity, but also to assert transformation itself as a model for historical change. For their part, artists like Blondeau, Antoni, Mitchell, Dempsey, and Millan have taken up the enduring feminist preoccupation with how bodies are marked as sites of hierarchical social difference while pushing it into new areas of inquiry. Regardless of their age or generation, these current feminist artists demonstrate that feminism's commitment to aligning the political and the everyday can indeed continue to arrest us, challenge our comfortable ideas, and make us laugh at the same time. In this way, feminist art counters alienation and grounds us in the here and now. Its history lives on in the present.

# Notes

## INTRODUCTION

1 See Morgan, *Going Too Far*, 62–7.
2 See Darling-Wolf, "From Airbrushing to Liposuction," 280.
3 Wolff, "Prospects and Problems for a Postmodern Feminism," in F*eminine Sentences*, 1.
4 Charmaine Wheatley, quoted in Eyland, "Introduction," in Cliff Eyland, ed., *Charmaine*, 2.
5 Braidotti, *Nomadic Subjects*, 163, italics in the original.
6 Reinelt, Introduction to the section "Feminism(s)," in Reinelt and Roach, eds, *Critical Theory and Performance*, 225.
7 de Beauvoir, *The Second Sex*, 143.
8 Lippard, "The Pains and Pleasure of Rebirth: European and American Women's Body Art," in *From the Center*, 124, italics in the original.
9 Use of the term "waves" to describe various phases of feminism has become common practice, although like most aspects of feminism, it does not go uncontested. The first wave refers to the period between 1850 when women began to mobilize for legal status and the granting of female suffrage after the First World War. The second wave refers to the period since 1960, although there is much debate as to whether it has been superseded by a third wave in the form of a "postfeminist" backlash or a more diverse "transnational" feminism. For a summary of the waves and related debates, see Hamilton, *Gendering the Vertical Mosaic*, 5.
10 Goldberg, *Performance Art from Futurism to the Present*, 9.
11 There are also some general surveys of performance art, such as that cited above by Goldberg as well as her more recent *Performance: Live Art since 1960*. There are also regional or national studies, such as Loeffler and Tong, eds, *Performance Anthology*; and Richard and Robertson, eds, *Performance au/in Canada, 1970–1990*.

12 Sayre, *The Object of Performance*; Brentano and Georgia, *Outside the Frame*; and Schimmel, ed., *Out of Actions*.
13 Licht, *Bodyworks*; Mayer, "Performance and Experience," 33–6; and Nemser, "Subject-Object: Body Art," 38–42.
14 Phelan, *Unmarked*, 146, 149–52.
15 O'Dell, "Toward a Theory of Performance Art," 43–4; Jones, "'Presence' in Absentia," 11–18; Wagner, "Performance, Video and the Rhetoric of Presence," 59–80; and Auslander, "Liveness: Performance and the Anxiety of Simulation," in *From Acting to Performance*, 196–213, and *Liveness: Performance in a Mediatized Culture*, especially the chapter "Against Ontology," 38–54.
16 Elwes, "On Performance and Performativity," 193–7.
17 Vergine, *Il corpo come linguaggio*; O'Dell, *Contract with the Skin*; and Jones, *Body Art*.
18 Roth, ed., *The Amazing Decade*. In addition to Lippard's groundbreaking article cited above, some of the major essays on feminist performance include Straayer, "I Say I Am," 8–12; Elwes, "Floating Femininity," 164–93; Barry, "Women, Representation, and Performance Art," 439–68; Fuchs, "Staging the Obscene Body," 33–58; Wolff, "Reinstating Corporeality: Feminism and Body Politics," in *Feminine Sentences*, 120–41; Withers, "Feminist Performance Art," 158–73; Jones, "Interpreting Feminist Bodies," 223–314; and Potkin, "Performance Art," 75–88.
19 This term was devised in the mid-1960s as a way to expand the discipline of theatre and drama into what Richard Schechner has described as an inclusive and "in-between" category comprising all kinds of performative practices that do not fall within the area of performing arts; see Schechner, "What is Performance Studies Anyway?" 357–66.
20 A broad perspective of this body of theory can be gleaned from these key texts and anthologies: Case, ed., *Performing Feminisms*; Dolan, *Presence and Desire*; Hart and Phelan, eds, *Acting Out*; Martin, ed., *A Sourcebook of Feminist Theatre and Performance*; Diamond, *Unmaking Mimesis*; and Reinelt and Roach, eds, *Critical Theory and Performance*.
21 See Rosenberg, "The American Action Painters," 22–3, 48–50; Kaprow, "The Legacy of Jackson Pollock," 24–6, 55–7; and Fried, "Art and Objecthood," 12–23.
22 Tanya Mars, for example, who is described by art critic Sarah Milroy as "Canada's senior stateswoman of performance art," clearly identifies herself as an artist; see Milroy, "Mars Attack," *Globe and Mail*, 10 June 2004, national edition, sec. R, 1, 9.

## CHAPTER ONE

1 These events demonstrate the extent to which the student movement in the 1960s was too widespread to be explained by local politics or ad hoc phenomena, beyond the generalization that in Communist countries student

radicalism led to demands for democracy, while in capitalist countries it leaned distinctly to the Left; see Hobsbawm, *The Age of Extremes*, 298–301. The instability of these political affiliations was made poignantly evident when the uprising of the New Left students in Paris was condemned by their erstwhile allies of the Old Left, the French Communist Party. For the French intellectual Jean-François Lyotard, this betrayal was the razor's edge that severed the modernist, Marxist metanarrative from what he saw as the inevitability of postmodernity's micronarratives, which he then theorized in 1979 in *The Postmodern Condition*.

2 The Vietnamization policy essentially involved turning the ground war over to the Saigon Army, while American troops, in fewer numbers, focused on air bombings of North Vietnam and – in secret – Cambodia. See Gitlin, *The Sixties*, 377–8.

3 See [Weatherman], "Look At It: America 1969," 167–8, 172. Ted Gold, Diana Oughton, and Terry Robbins died that night, while several others escaped, including Cathy Wilkerson, whose father owned the townhouse.

4 Gitlin, *The Sixties*, 381, 389.

5 Rae, "Canada: As Good as It Gets," *Globe and Mail*, 19 May 2001, national edition, sec. D, 2.

6 Gitlin, *The Sixties*, 6.

7 Said, *Culture and Imperialism*, 291.

8 Harris, "Modernism and Culture in the USA, 1930–1960," 71.

9 Part of this statement is reprinted in Schwartz, "The Politicalization of the Avant-Garde," prt. 1, 97.

10 Ibid., prt. 2, 71.

11 Ibid., prt. 3, 69–71.

12 Quoted in Sandler, *American Art of the 1960s*, 293, citing LeWitt in "La Sfida del Sistema," 44–5.

13 Quoted in Sandler, *American Art of the 1960s*, 301 n. 10, n. 18, citing Judd and Kaprow in "La Sfida del Sistema," 38–40, 43. By contrast, that same year Guy Debord and other members of the French group called the Situationist International, which was dedicated to the integration of art and politics, played a central role in mobilizing students during the *événements* in France, especially at Nanterres University. See Wollen, "Bitter Victory," 20–61.

14 This episode between the AWC and the MOMA over the My Lai poster is discussed in Frascina, "The Politics of Representation," 106–8.

15 "The Artist and Politics," 35. The artists whose responses to this question were printed include Carl Andre, Jo Baer, Walter Darby Bannard, Billy Al Bengston, Rosemarie Castoro, Rafael Ferrer, Don Judd, Irving Petlin, Ed Ruscha, Richard Serra, Robert Smithson, and Lawrence Weiner. This topic was also addressed in numerous other articles from this period. See, for example, Ashton, "Response to Crisis in American Art," 24–35; Lippard, "The Dilemma," 27–9; Leider, "How I Spent My Summer Vacation," 40–9; Andre, "Carl Andre: Artworker," 175–9; and the proceedings of a symposium on "The Role of the Artist in Today's Society," 327–31.

16 Bannard in "The Artist and Politics," 36.
17 Weiner in "The Artist and Politics," 39.
18 Ruscha in "The Artist and Politics," 38.
19 Smithson in "The Artist and Politics," 39.
20 For a thorough account of Minimalism's attack against Modernism, see Foster, "The Crux of Minimalism," in *The Return of the Real*, 35–68.
21 Fried, "Art and Objecthood," 12–23.
22 Morris, "Notes on Sculpture, Part 3," 29. As Charles Harrison and Paul Wood remarked, the appearance of both these essays in the same issue indicated that "If they had not been aware of it before, readers of *Artforum* were presented with powerful evidence of a deep schism within the professional world of modern American art"; see their "Modernity and Modernism Reconsidered," 190.
23 Andre in "The Artist and Politics," 35.
24 Baer in "The Artist and Politics," 35
25 Judd in "The Artist and Politics," 36–7.
26 Greenberg, "Avant-Garde and Kitsch," in *The Collected Essays and Criticism*, vol. 1, 5–22.
27 For an account of this depoliticization of the American intelligentsia, see Guilbaut, *How New York Stole the Idea of Modern Art.*
28 Kant, *Critique of Judgment*, 2.
29 Greenberg, "Avant-Garde and Kitsch," in *Art and Culture*, 3–21.
30 Greenberg, "Modernist Painting," in *The Collected Essays and Criticism*, vol. 3, 85–6.
31 Poggioli, *The Theory of the Avant-Garde.*
32 Bürger, *Theory of the Avant-Garde*, 27, 50, 59, 58, italics in the original.
33 Buchloh, "Theorizing the Avant-Garde," 21.
34 Foster, "Who's Afraid of the Neo-Avant-Garde?" in *The Return of the Real*, 14, 16, 24.
35 Judd in "The Artist and Politics," 36.
36 Harrison and Wood, "Modernity and Modernism Reconsidered," 214.
37 Judd in "The Artist and Politics," 37.
38 Kosuth, "1975," in Alberro and Stimson, eds, *Conceptual Art*, 345. In his introductory essay to this anthology, Stimson outlines his view of why Conceptual art remained a primarily aesthetic and institutionalized practice; see Stimson, "The Promise of Conceptual Art," xxxviii–lii.
39 Stimson, "The Promise of Conceptual Art," xli.
40 Smithson, "Production for Production's Sake," in Alberro and Stimson, eds, *Conceptual Art,* 284.
41 Alberro, "Mel Bochner: Thought Made Visible, 1966–1973," 81.
42 For a description of these works, see Wallis, ed., *Hans Haacke*, 86–7, 92–7.
43 Crow, *The Rise of the Sixties*, 179–80.
44 Buchloh, "Conceptual Art, 1962–1969," 141.
45 Phelan, "Survey," 21. As Phelan notes, for an in-depth discussion of the unique character and contributions of feminist art as a movement, see Parker and Pollock, eds, *Framing Feminism.*

46 See MacPherson and Sears, "The Voice of Women," 71–92.
47 See Dumont, "The Origins of the Women's Movement in Quebec," 462–78.
48 See Morris, "Determination and Thoroughness," 1–21.
49 See Information Canada, *Report of the Royal Commission on the Status of Women.*
50 Since then the NAC has broadened its original mandate and now lobbies on a vast array of issues relevant to women, from daycare and violence to self-determination for Aboriginal people and constitutional policy.
51 Dumont, *The Women's Movement*, 10. The first feminist text to express resistance to the entrenched roles and expectations of feminine bourgeois domesticity was Friedan's *The Feminine Mystique.* For a discussion of attitudes toward women, work, and domestic life during this period, see Strong-Boag, "Home Dreams," 375–401.
52 Anonymous quotation in Anderson and Zinsser, *A History of Their Own*, vol. 2, 406; original cited in Collins and Sayre, eds, *Les femmes en France*, 302.
53 Gitlin, *The Sixties*, 363, 367–71.
54 Evans, *Personal Politics*, 213.
55 Ibid., 218–19.
56 Ibid., 214.
57 Braidotti, *Nomadic Subjects*, 264.
58 Meehan, "Introduction," in Meehan, ed., *Feminists Read Habermas*, 8.
59 See Marcuse, *One Dimensional Man*; Lefebvre, *Everyday Life in the Modern World*; and Althusser, "Ideology and Ideological State Apparatuses," 121–73.

## CHAPTER TWO

1 The literature on this topic is extensive, but see especially Nochlin, "Why Have There Been No Great Women Artists?" 1–39; Parker and Pollock, *Old Mistresses*; and Chadwick, *Women, Art, and Society.*
2 Reg Butler, quoted in Parker and Pollock, *Old Mistresses*, 6–7, from a lecture at the Slade School of Art, London, 1962, published in *New Society*, 31 August 1978, 443. For a critique of sexism in the art world at this time, see Lippard, "Sexual Politics: Art Style," in *From the Center*, 28–37.
3 Pollock, "The Politics of Theory," 15.
4 Cottingham, "The Masculine Imperative: High Modern, Postmodern," in *Seeing through the Seventies*, 47–71.
5 Firestone, *The Dialectic of Sex*, 157.
6 Schneemann, *More Than Meat Joy*, 52, italics in the original.
7 Gagnon, "Work in Progress," 105.
8 Gaulke, "Performance Art of the Woman's Building," 156; see also Jacobs, "Introduction," in Roth, ed., *The Amazing Decade*, 11.
9 Roy, "Corporeal Returns," 61–2.
10 For a general history of performance art, see Goldberg, *Performance Art from Futurism to the Present.* For the origins of performance art in the cabaret, see Siegel, *Bohemian Paris.*
11 Goodnough, "Pollock Paints a Picture," 38–41.

12 Rosenberg, "The American Action Painters," 22.
13 Kaprow, "The Legacy of Jackson Pollock," 56.
14 A thoroughly documented account of these practices is found in Schimmel, ed., *Out of Actions*. The essay by Osaki, "Body and Place," 121–57, traces the impact of Pollock's example on the Gutai and other postwar Japanese artists.
15 Kaprow, *Assemblages, Environments and Happenings*.
16 Schechner, *Environmental Theater*, ix–xvii; see also his "What Is Performance Studies Anyway?" 357–62.
17 Jones, *Body Art*, 55, 62.
18 See Lippard, *Six Years*; and Goldstein and Rorimer, eds, *Reconsidering the Object of Art*.
19 Stiles, "Uncorrupted Joy," 228–9.
20 Brentano, "Outside the Frame," 42.
21 Schneider, *The Explicit Body in Performance*, 23.
22 Grimm, "Alienation in Context," 42–3.
23 Mulvey, "Visual Pleasure and Narrative Cinema," *Screen* 13, no. 3 (Autumn 1975): 6–18, reprinted in *Visual and Other Pleasures*, 14–26; subsequent citations refer to this reprint.
24 Pollock, "Screening the Seventies: Sexuality and Representation in Feminist Practice – A Brechtian Perspective," in *Vision and Difference*, 155–99.
25 Reinelt, Introduction to the section "Feminism(s)," in Reinelt and Roach, eds, *Critical Theory and Performance*, 225.
26 Diamond, "Brechtian Theory/Feminist Theory," 129.
27 Ibid, italics in the original.
28 Dolan, *The Feminist Spectator as Critic*, 2.
29 Ibid., 101.
30 Ibid., 106.
31 Dolan, "Gender Impersonation Onstage," 3–13. The original version of this article was published in *Women and Performance Journal* 2, no. 2 (1985): 5–11. For the reference to Pollock and Parker, see *Old Mistresses*, 119.
32 Case, "Introduction," in Case, ed., *Performing Feminisms*, 2.
33 Dolan, "Gender Impersonation Onstage," 8; and Case, "Introduction," in Case, ed., *Performing Feminisms*, 2.
34 Forte, "Women's Performance Art," 254.
35 Ibid., 259–61.
36 Hart, "Introduction," in Hart and Phelan, eds, *Acting Out*, 5–6.
37 Parker and Pollock, *Old Mistresses*, 157.
38 Banes, *Greenwich Village, 1963*, 13. Banes acknowledges that her model of a heterotopia comes from Michel Foucault, who described it as a countersite, "a kind of effectively enacted utopia in which ... all the other real sites that can be found within the culture, are simultaneously represented, contested and inverted" ("Of Other Spaces," 24).
39 For a history of Judson, see Banes, *Democracy's Body*.
40 Rainer, quoted in Lippard, "Yvonne Rainer on Feminism and Her Film," in *From the Center*, 273.

41 Banes, *Greenwich Village, 1963*, 72.
42 This work is described in more detail in Schneemann, *More than Meat Joy*, 234.
43 Schneemann's historical significance for feminist performance has been frequently noted. See Lippard, "The Pains and Pleasures of Rebirth: European and American Women's Body Art," in *From the Center*, 126; Banes, *Greenwich Village, 1963*, 225–8; Jones, *Body Art*, 1–5; and Schneider, *The Explicit Body in Performance*, 29–38.
44 In an essay first published in *Zero* 3 (July 1961), Yves Klein wrote that by painting "in this way I stayed clean. I no longer dirtied myself with color, not even the tips of my fingers ... I could salute [the paintings'] birth into the tangible world in a dignified manner, dressed in a tuxedo" ("Truth Becomes Reality," 230). For the instructions to, or "score" of, the Ben Patterson event, see Hendricks, ed., *Fluxus Etc.*, 229. Fluxus founder George Maciunus was famous for his lists of sanctioned and excommunicated members. According to Schneemann, Maciunus printed a note expelling her for her "expressionist tendencies" and banishing her to the realm of Happenings, even though he was willing to admit the equally "messy" work of Wolf Vostell and Claes Oldenburg (*More than Meat Joy*, 52). See also Schneider, *The Explicit Body in Performance*, 189 n. 24.
45 Schneider, *The Explicit Body in Performance*, 33.
46 Friedan, *The Feminine Mystique*.
47 Schneemann, from an unpublished interview with Schneider, quoted in Schneider, *The Explicit Body in Performance*, 38.
48 For discussion of such films, see Banes, *Greenwich Village, 1963*, 212–19.
49 The Paris, London, and New York performances of *Meat Joy* are described and documented in Schneemann, *More Than Meat Joy*, 63–87.
50 Johnston, "Meat Joy," 13, quoted in Banes, *Greenwich Village, 1963*, 217.
51 Banes, *Greenwich Village, 1963*, 216.
52 See especially Foucault, *The History of Sexuality* and *Discipline and Punish*.
53 For a study of the relationship between the body, transgression, and the politics of power since the seventeenth century, see Stallybrass and White, *The Politics and Poetics of Transgression*.
54 Banes, *Greenwich Village, 1963*, 217.
55 For the relationship between Minimalist sculpture and the postmodern dance developed by the Judson Dance Theatre, see Haskell, *Blam! The Explosion of Pop, Minimalism and Performance, 1958–1964*, 61–7.
56 Schneider, *The Explicit Body in Performance*, 31.
57 Berger, *Labyrinths*, 82.
58 See Banes, *Greenwich Village, 1963*, 225–6; Sayre, *The Object of Performance*, 66–76; and Crow, *The Rise of the Sixties*, 138–9.
59 Schneemann, *More than Meat Joy*, 196, capitals in the original.
60 Sayre, *The Object of Performance*, 75–6. Schneemann's role in *Site* is also briefly discussed in Strauss, "Love Rides Aristotle through the Audience," 320–1, but no new interpretation is offered to explain her participation.

61 For the full text and description of *Interior Scroll*, see Schneemann, *More than Meat Joy*, 234–9.
62 Patraka, "Binary Terror and Feminist Performance," 163–85.
63 Schneider, *The Explicit Body in Performance*, 36.
64 Stiles, "Between Water and Stone," 77.
65 See Munroe and Hendricks, eds, *Yes Yoko Ono*, 158.
66 For discussion of the body in such Fluxus works, see Stiles, "Between Water and Stone," 84–5.
67 Crow, *The Rise of the Sixties*, 133.
68 Jones, *Body Art*, 62.
69 Stiles, "Between Water and Stone," 77.
70 Schneemann, *More Than Meat Joy*, 52.
71 Schneider, *The Explicit Body in Performance*, 38.
72 These and other early feminist art organizations in the US are discussed in Lippard, "Sexual Politics," in *From the Center*, 28–9.
73 For the history of Galerie Powerhouse, now operating as La Centrale, see Nash, "Montréal's Powerhouse Gallery," 85–91.
74 Tenhaaf, "A History, or A Way of Knowing," 81.
75 Arbour, "Art et féminisme," 3–14.
76 See Côté, ed., *Réseau art-femme*.
77 For a history of feminist film and video collectives in Vancouver, see Diamond, "Daring Documents," 180–4.
78 For a review of the Women and Film (1896–1973) International Festival, see Zemel, "Women and Video," 30–40.
79 The Guerrilla Girls are an anonymous group of women who formed in 1985 in New York City to expose sexism and racism in politics, the art world, and the culture at large. The history of their activities is documented on their website, http://www.guerrillagirls.com.
80 Chicago, *Through the Flower*, 56–7, 63.
81 Chicago, quoted in Lippard, "Judy Chicago Talking to Lucy Lippard," in *From the Center*, 217–18.
82 Chicago, *Through the Flower*, 66.
83 See Roth, "Toward a History of California Performance: Part Two," 117.
84 "The Artist and Politics," 35–9.
85 Chicago, *Through the Flower*, 75. It must be noted that Chicago was also very concerned that her students develop the basic skills necessary to succeed as professionals. She had them find an off-campus studio to rent and fix up, thus forcing them to assert themselves with real estate agents, to work independently and collaboratively, and to become competent using the tools and materials that men took for granted but that were completely unfamiliar to most women of their generation.
86 In addition to Chicago's accounts of the activities of her class at Fresno State College in *Through the Flower*, 70–92, see Roth, "Toward a History of California Performance: Part Two," 117–19; and Wilding, *By Our Own Hands* and "The Feminist Art Programs at Fresno and CalArts."

87 Chicago, *Through the Flower*, 87.
88 These quotations from Chicago, Wilding, and Hall are cited in Roth, "Towards a History of California Performance: Part Two," 117.
89 For first-hand accounts of the Womanhouse project, see Chicago, *Through the Flower*, 112–32; Schapiro, "The Education of Women as Artists," 268–70; and the Feminist Art Program's exhibition catalogue, *Womanhouse.* For a more recent historical reappraisal, see Raven, "Womanhouse," 48–65.
90 Statement by artists Karen LeCoq and Nancy Youdelman, quoted in Raven, "Womanhouse," 60.
91 For a full description of the Womanhouse performances, see Chicago, *Through the Flower*, 207–19.
92 Withers, "Feminist Performance Art," 168.
93 For the most complete account of West Coast performance, see Loeffler and Tong, *Performance Anthology*, which includes detailed chronological accounts of individual performances as well as several critical essays. For an overview of how California performance related to activities in other areas, see Brentano, "Outside the Frame," 46–54.
94 Brentano, "Outside the Frame," 49.
95 Roth, "Towards a History of California Performance: Part Two," 117.
96 Lacy and Lippard, "Political Performance," 23, italics in the original.

## CHAPTER THREE

1 For early examples of such coalition building, see Evans, *Personal Politics*, 237.
2 The issues of essentialism and difference have been widely discussed across every field of feminist study. For key theoretical debates, see especially Schor and Weed, eds, *The Essential Difference*; Fraser and Nicholson, "Social Criticism without Philosophy," in Nicholson, ed., *Feminism/Postmodernism*, 19–38; Fuss, *Essentially Speaking*; Spelman, *Inessential Woman*; and Eisenstein and Jardine, eds, *The Future of Difference.*
3 Thornham, "Postmodernism and Feminism," 42–3.
4 De Beauvoir, *The Second Sex*, 267.
5 Firestone, *The Dialectic of Sex;* and Millett, *Sexual Politics.* Unlike liberal feminism, which seeks equal rights, radical feminism makes the distinction of seeking equal power in society. For a more detailed discussion of radical feminism, see Tong, *Feminist Thought*, 71–138.
6 See Tong, *Feminist Thought*, 212–13.
7 Irigaray's body of work is extensive, but the two main sources that English readers have drawn upon are *Speculum of the Other Woman*, originally published in French in 1974, and *This Sex Which Is Not One*, originally published in French in 1977.
8 Schor, "The Essentialism Which Is Not One," 47.
9 Ibid., 48.
10 Rose, "Vaginal Iconology," 59.

11 For an overview of these various approaches, see Gouma-Peterson and Matthews, "The Feminist Critique of Art History," 332–43.
12 McTavish, "Body Narratives in Canada, 1968–99," 5–11.
13 The main texts that addressed the history of women artists include the massive dictionary by the Women's History Research Center, *Female Artists Past and Present*; Tufts, *Our Hidden Heritage*; Petersen and Wilson, *Women Artists*; and Harris and Nochlin, *Women Artists 1550–1950*. While these texts aimed mainly to add forgotten women to the history of art, Parker and Pollock, *Old Mistresses,* signaled a new departure in that it examined women artists in relation both to the ideology of cultural production and to the discipline of art history itself. Nevertheless, the survey approach persists, as in Tippett, *By a Lady*.
14 For a recent study of this important work and its controversial reception, see Jones, ed., *Sexual Politics*.
15 Many texts were produced at this time that linked archeological evidence of ancient goddess worship to the contemporary women's spirituality movement. See Davis, *The First Sex*; Daly, *Beyond God the Father* and *Gyn/Ecology*; Stone, *When God Was a Woman*; Griffin, *Women and Nature*; and Spretnak, *The Politics of Women's Spirituality*.
16 Lippard, "Sweeping Exchanges," 364.
17 See Roth, ed., *The Amazing Decade*, 22–7; and Orenstein, "Recovering Her Story," in Broude and Garrard, eds, *The Power of Feminist Art*, 174–89.
18 Schneemann, *More Than Meat Joy*, 234.
19 Damon, "The 7,000 Year Old Woman," 12.
20 For a detailed description of this work, see Edelson, *Seven Cycles,* 17.
21 Edelson, quoted in Lippard, "Freelancing the Dragon," in *From the Center*, 21.
22 Edelson, "Pilgrimage/See for Yourself," 96–9.
23 For further description, see Roth, ed., *The Amazing Decade*, 92–3.
24 Gimbutus, *The Goddesses and Gods of Old Europe*.
25 Rosler, "The Private and the Public," 67. Like the Feminist Art Program, the origins of the Los Angeles Woman's Building go back to Judy Chicago. In 1972 Chicago wanted to opt out of the CalArts program, and along with art historian Arlene Raven and designer Sheila Levrant de Bretteville, she set up an entirely independent program called the Feminist Studio Workshop. Joining forces with several other groups from the women's community, they opened the Woman's Building in 1973. In addition to the Feminist Studio Workshop (which had thirty students), the Woman's Building housed several galleries, a theatre workshop, a printmaking studio, a performance coordination centre, a bookstore and several small publishers, the Los Angeles chapter of the National Organization of Women, the offices of the Women's Liberation Union, and the Center for Art-Historical studies, run by Raven and Ruth Iskin, which contained the Los Angeles West-East Bag slide registry of women artists' work. See Chicago, *Through the Flower*, 178–206; and Lippard, "The L.A. Woman's Building," in *From the Center*, 96–100.
26 See Lippard, *Overlay*.

27 For example, although many of Robert Smithson's earthworks were anti-heroic monuments that critiqued Minimalism's industrial fetishism and although he was more aware than most of the impossibility of escaping what he called the "cultural confinement" of the art world (see Smithson, "Cultural Confinement," 32), the irony of his claims for the "ecological" basis of his work as an opposition to the market-driven corruption of contemporary art and society has been noted by Frascina, "The Politics of Representation," in Wood, Frascina, Harris, and Harrison, *Modernism and Dispute*, 105. Frascina writes: "To make *Spiral Jetty*, 6,650 tons of material were moved, involving 292 truck-hours and 625 hours' work in total. Approximately $9,000 (not including the many administrative expenses) was spent on constructing the earthwork alone, by Virginia Dwan of Dwan Gallery, New York; and another $9,000 was provided by Douglas Christmas of Ace Gallery, Vancouver, and Venice, California, for a film of the work."
28 Lippard, *Overlay*, 52–5, notes that although artists like Oppenheim and Long appear to take a more sensitive approach in their interactions with nature than did most earthwork artists, their work often manifests an ambivalence toward nature that can been seen in their predilection for scarring the landscape with huge lines or marks, especially when their creations have, as in Oppenheim's case, entailed plowing down crops or decapitating fields of daisies.
29 The notion of earthworks as "rearrangements" of nature was articulated by Philip Leider, editor of *Artforum*, in a 1970 article chronicling his visits to a number of recent projects in the American West; see Leider, "How I Spent My Summer Vacation," 48–9.
30 See Lippard, "Quite Contrary," 31–47.
31 Roth, ed., *The Amazing Decade*, 24.
32 Henes, "Spider Woman Series," 61, and "Spider Woman: Donna Henes Interviewed by Linda Burnham," 27–8.
33 Henes, "Cocoon Ceremony," 38–9.
34 It should be noted, however, that any putative exploitation in Henes's work might be militated by the fact that she had previously collaborated with the New York experimental theatre group Spiderwoman, which had originated with a 1975 workshop that aimed to bring Aboriginal and non-Aboriginal women together.
35 Ana Mendieta died in 1985 as a result of a fall from the window of the New York loft she shared with Carl Andre. The cause of death, whether by suicide, accident, or murder, has never been conclusively determined. See Katz, *Naked by the Window*.
36 This 1981 exhibition statement is now among the documents in the Mendieta Estate and was quoted in del Rio, "Ana Mendieta," 28.
37 Mendieta, quoted in Perreault, "Earth and Fire," 14.
38 This previously unpublished statement is quoted in ibid., 10.
39 Mendieta's library contained a full collection of texts by Lydia Cabrera, the foremost scholar on Santería traditions in Cuba; see del Rio, "Ana Mendieta," 29.

40 Raquelin Mendieta, "Ana Mendieta," 39.
41 Kwon, "Bloody Valentines," 168.
42 Lippard, *Overlay*, 47.
43 Ana Mendieta, Introduction to *Dialectics of Isolation,* quoted in Perreault, "Earth and Fire," 17 n. 2.
44 Phelan, "Survey," 23. As Phelan notes, the best discussion of these complicated "feminist sex wars" is to be found in Hart, *Between the Body and the Flesh*, 36–82. See Moraga and Anzaldúa, eds, *This Bridge Called My Back*.
45 For a thorough overview of the history and debates of feminism in Canada, see Hamilton, *Gendering the Vertical Mosaic,* especially 39–70.
46 Million, "Telling Secrets," 99.
47 Anderson, "Contemporary Canadian Women's Performance Art," 83–4.
48 See Ortner, "Is Female to Male as Nature Is to Culture?" 67–87.
49 Gornick, "Toward a Definition of Female Sensibility," 112.
50 The critique of metanarratives as the basis for modern Enlightenment philosophy was first articulated in Lyotard, *The Postmodern Condition.*
51 See Fraser and Nicholson, "Social Criticism without Philosophy," 21–3.
52 Harding, "Feminism, Science, and the Anti-Enlightenment Critiques," 90.
53 For a succinct feminist summary of Lacan's major precepts, see Mitchell, "Introduction I," 1–26, and Rose, "Introduction II," 27–57, in Mitchell and Rose, eds, *Feminine Sexuality*. See also Grosz, *Jacques Lacan*, 31–49.
54 See Derrida, *Of Grammatology*.
55 See especially Irigaray, *Speculum of the Other Woman* and *This Sex Which Is Not One*; Kristeva, *Desire in Language*; and Cixous, *The Newly Born Woman.*
56 Kristeva, "Le sujet en procès," "L'expérience et la pratique," and "Matière, sense, dialectique," in *Polylogue*, 55–136, 263–86.
57 Crenshaw, "Beyond Racism and Misogyny," 111–32.
58 Rich, "Compulsory Heterosexuality and Lesbian Existence," 631–60.
59 Cottingham has also discussed the history and role of lesbianism and lesbian politics in the work of a number of visual artists from the 1970s, although she does not address the practice of performance art per se; see her "Eating from the *Dinner Party* Plates," 133–59, and "Notes on Lesbian," in *Seeing Through the Seventies*, 175–87.
60 De Lauretis, "Sexual Indifference and Lesbian Representation," 17.
61 Ibid., 18. For the use of the term "hommo-sexuality," see Irigaray, *This Sex Which Is Not One*, 86.
62 De Lauretis, "Sexual Indifference and Lesbian Representation," 39.
63 See especially Davy, "From Lady Dick to Ladylike," 55–84; Solomon, "The WOW Café," 42–51; and Case, ed., *Split Britches*.
64 In this instance, I have adopted the nomenclature "Native," "non-Native," and "Native American" from the Spiderwoman Theatre webpage on the Native American Women Playwrights Archive website, http://staff.lib.muohio.edu/nawpa/origins.html. The preferred usage in the Canadian context is Aboriginal or Indigenous or, for those living on reserves,

First Nations people.

65 For a study of Spiderwoman and an account of this breakup, see Schneider, "See the Big Show," 227–55.

66 Case, "Introduction," in Case, ed., *Split Britches*, 5.

67 Patraka, "Split Britches in *Split Britches*," 216.

68 Case, "Toward a Butch-Femme Aesthetic," 282–6.

69 Ibid., 296–7.

70 Ibid., 298.

71 Case, "Introduction," in Case, ed., *Split Britches*, 11.

72 See Solomon, "The WOW Café," 42–51; Davy, "Fe/male Impersonation," 231–47; and Dolan, "The Dynamics of Desire," 156–74.

73 Case, Introduction to *Split Britches*, 13.

74 Hart, "Identity and Seduction," 120. For examples of writers who have raised questions about lesbian performance within and outside the WOW Café, see Davy, "Reading Past the Heterosexual Imperative," 136–56; and Dolan, *The Feminist Spectator as Critic*, 119–21.

75 Hart, "Identity and Seduction," 126, italics in the original.

76 Ibid., 130.

77 Butler, *Bodies that Matter*, 21, 232.

78 Case, "Introduction," in Case, ed., *Split Britches*, 13–14.

79 Thornham, "Postmodernism and Feminism," 46.

80 Di Stefano, "Dilemmas of Difference," 65, 76.

81 For a useful summary of these debates, which, at least originally, boiled down to a difference between the pursuit of equality for women (associated with Anglo-American feminism) and the articulation of women's difference from men (associated with French feminism), see Buhle, *Feminism and Its Discontents*, 318–58.

82 Flax, "Re-membering the Selves," 106. See also Brown, "Where Is the Sex in Political Theory?" 3–23; Hartsock, "Rethinking Modernism," 187–206; and Miller, "Changing the Subject," 102–20.

83 Butler, "Gender Trouble, Feminist Theory, and Psychoanalytic Discourse," 327.

84 See Haraway, "A Manifesto for Cyborgs," 65–107; and Braidotti, *Nomadic Subjects*.

85 Nicholson, "Introduction," in Nicholson, ed., *Feminism/Postmodernism*, 6–9.

86 Thornham, "Postmodernism and Feminism," 52.

87 See Modleski, *Feminism without Women*.

88 Fuss, *Essentially Speaking*, 20–1.

89 Spivak, "Subaltern Studies," 205.

90 Hart, "Identity and Seduction," 128.

91 Butler, *Gender Trouble*, 4.

92 Case, "Introduction," in Case, ed., *Performing Feminisms*, 12.

93 Ibid., 13.

94 Kwon, "Bloody Valentines," 166. Although Kwon herself does not berate one camp or another, she uses such terms to frame the tone of the debate itself.

95 Rosler, "The Private and the Public," 68.
96 For a discussion of the enormous popularity of *The Dinner Party*, see Jones, "The 'Sexual Politics' of *The Dinner Party*," 89–92.
97 Kwon, "Bloody Valentines," 166.
98 Dolan, *The Feminist Spectator as Critic*, 3.
99 Gornick, "Woman as Outsider," 144.
100 Kristeva, "Women's Time," 41–2.

## CHAPTER FOUR

1 Austin, *How to Do Things with Words*.
2 Stiles, "Uncorrupted Joy," 246. For an account of terminology used to classify performance-based practices, see Barber, "Indexing," 184–204.
3 Derrida, "Signature Event Context," 321–7.
4 Phelan, "Reciting the Citation of Others," 21.
5 Phelan, "Survey," 20.
6 See Marks and de Courtivron, "Introduction I," in Marks and de Courtivron, eds, *New French Feminisms*, 6.
7 Barthes, "The Death of the Author," 143.
8 Marchessault, "Is the Dead Author a Woman?" 12.
9 Lesage, "The Political Aesthetics of Feminist Documentary Film," *Quarterly Review of Film Studies* (Fall 1978), 518, quoted in Marchessault, "Is the Dead Author a Woman?" 12. For Rich's poem, see her *Diving into the Wreck*, 22–4.
10 Felski, *Beyond Feminist Aesthetics*, 48.
11 Bürger, *Theory of the Avant-Garde*, 49.
12 Stiles, "Uncorrupted Joy," 238.
13 Ward, "Some Relations between Conceptual and Performance Art," 36–40.
14 Lippard, "The Pains and Pleasures of Rebirth: European and American Women's Body Art," in *From the Center*, 122.
15 Kelly, "Re-Viewing Modernist Criticism," 97.
16 Lippard, "Making Up: Role-Playing and Transformation in Women's Art," in *From the Center*, 102.
17 Kozloff, "The Women's Movement," 49.
18 Lacy, "Visions and Re-Visions," 43, italics in the original.
19 Frascina, "The Politics of Representation," 82, 165.
20 Owens, "The Discourse of Others," 59.
21 Tickner, "The Body Politic," 237.
22 Sayre, *The Object of Performance*, 96.
23 Ibid.
24 Roth, "Toward a History of California Performance: Part Two," 122.
25 Hutcheon, "Splitting Images," 257.
26 Ostriker, *Stealing the Language*, 11.
27 Hutcheon, "Splitting Images," 261–2.
28 Howells, *Private and Fictional Words*, 184.

29 Hutcheon, "Splitting Images," 256.
30 The differences in male and female artists' approaches to body and performance art were first noted by Lippard in "The Pains and Pleasures of Rebirth," in *From the Center*, 125. More recently, several art historians have attempted to explain what accounts for the self-inflicted violence of artists like Vito Acconci, Chris Burden, Paul McCarthy, Barry Le Va, and the Viennese Aktionists. Stiles, "Uncorrupted Joy," 244, argues that such actions work to negate the things that the actions themselves exhibit and deplore. Jones, *Body Art*, 103–50, views Acconci's masochism as a conscious repudiation of the assumptions of power and privilege normally accorded to masculine subjectivity. O'Dell, *Contract with the Skin*, has read the preoccupations with masochism in this period as cathartic responses to social alienation caused by repressive institutional domination.
31 Krauss used this term in "Notes on the Index," 196–219, to identify a principle that could encompass the diversity and pluralism of art during the 1970s, which she felt resulted from a crisis of representation brought about by Pop, Minimalism, and Conceptualism. Recognizing that no stylistic term could serve this purpose, she proposed that the unifying principle of the body art, installation work, and much of the video of that decade was to be found in its desire to reground art in the physical, or indexical, marks of the presence of the artist.
32 Hanley, "The First Generation," 21.
33 Peacock, *Corpus Loquendi*, 14.
34 Wagner, "Performance, Video and the Rhetoric of Presence," 74, 80.
35 For her personal history, see Montano, "Art in Everyday Life," in *Art in Everyday Life*, n.p.
36 See Montano, "*Home Endurance* March 26, 1973–April 2, 1973," in *Art in Everyday Life*, n.p.
37 See Montano, "*Three Day Blindfold/How to Become a Guru*," in *Art in Everyday Life*, n.p.
38 See Roth, *Linda Montano;* and Fisher, "*Seven Years of Living Art*," 23–8.
39 Montano, "Matters of Life and Death," 6.
40 Fisher, "*Seven Years of Living Art*," 28, provides a résumé of Montano's healthcare and counseling work.
41 Montano, "Linda Montano," interview by Andrea Juno, in Juno and Vale, eds, *Angry Women*, 63. In recent years, Montano's attitude toward the media and the larger social world has changed dramatically. During the period between 1998 and 2004, when she cared for her ill father in a performance that she titled *Dad Art*, Montano used the TV as a helper, turning on the Catholic channel as inspiration to herself and her father, who liked to hear the Rosary. Montano found not only that the television gave her spiritual company, even though it was technological, but also that she began to read the paper that arrived at the house and even took daily respite breaks from care giving to read the *New York Times* at the library. This once rigourously detached and self-declared "art-mystic" reports that she has now developed such a habitual

attachment to TV and newspapers that she has become a "media-alholic." Linda Montano, e-mail message to author, 27 July 2005. For more information on Montano's *Dad Art* and the related video performance called *Dad Art: Old Age, Sickness and Death*, see her book, *Letters from Linda M. Montano*.

42 Rosler, "Well, *Is* the Personal Political?" 96.

43 Wordsworth, "The World Is Too Much with Us; Late and Soon," 353.

44 Kaprow's relation to Schapiro and Cage is discussed in Haywood, "Critique of Instrumental Labor," 27–46, and in Buchloh, "Robert Watts," 9–10. Buchloh (8) also makes a connection between Cage's aesthetic model and the alienation strategies of Bertolt Brecht, which are in part derived from Hegel's philosophical principle that the well-known or familiar, precisely because it is well-known or familiar, is not really understood at all. For a summary of Brecht's theory and practice, see Grimm, "Alienation in Context," 35–46. For Kaprow's own version of this principle, see "Performing Life," 195–8.

45 Marioni's Museum of Conceptual Art is discussed in Loeffler, "From the Body into Space," 376–8. For Montano on *Handcuff*, see "Matters of Life and Death," 3, 5.

46 See Grey and Grey, "Linda Montano and Tehching Hsieh's *One-Year Art/Life Performance*," 24–9; and Carr, "Roped," 3–9. Information about this and other one-year performances by Teching Hsieh can be found on his website, http://www.one-year-performance.com.

47 Barry, "Women, Representation, and Performance Art," 442.

48 Wooster, "The Way We Were," 21.

49 For feminist analyses of the divisions between the public and private spheres in the history of art, see Pollock, "Modernity and the Spaces of Femininity," in *Vision and Difference*, 50–90; and Wolff, "The Culture of Separate Spheres: The Role of Culture in Nineteenth-Century Public and Private Life," in *Feminine Sentences*, 12–33.

50 Sally Potter, quoted in Elwes, "Floating Femininity," 177.

51 Lynda Benglis, e-mail message to author, 18 June 2004, has identified this man as Klaus Kertess, a well-known art historian, critic, curator, and fiction writer who now teaches at the School of the Visual Arts in New York, at Yale University, and at the University of Iowa. Although the viewer of *Home Tape Revised* would not know who he is, he clearly represents the writer as the creator of stories and was someone Benglis identified as a friend and perhaps as a voice of authority in the art world.

52 This quotation is from an anonymous statement describing Lynda Benglis's work in the Video Data Bank catalogue, *Early Video Art in the United States*, 9.

53 Kurtz, "Video is Being Invented," 40.

54 See, for example, Cameron, "Structural Videotape in Canada," 188–95.

55 Holt, quoted in Wooster, "The Way We Were," 32.

56 The key text that traces the double stance of photography as both presence and absence is Sontag, *On Photography* (1978); see also Barthes, *Camera*

*Lucida* (French original, 1980).

57 See Rosler, "In, Around, and Afterthoughts," 59–86, and "Shedding the Utopian Moment," 27–33.

58 Diamond, "Daring Documents," 183.

59 Bellour uses this term in "Video Writing," 421.

60 Lisa Steele, interview by author, Toronto, 5 May 1994.

61 Wooster, "The Way We Were," 36.

62 Nam June Paik is said to be the first artist to use the new medium of video when he brought the first Sony Portapak into North America in 1965. He allegedly recorded his trip from the airport to downtown New York and then played the tape at the Café a Go Go in Greenwich Village. See Peacock, *Corpus Loquendi*, 10.

63 This quotation is from an anonymous statement describing Kubota's work in the Video Data Bank catalogue, *Early Video Art in the United States*, 20.

64 hooks, "bell hooks," interview by Andrea Juno, in Juno and Vale, eds, *Angry Women*, 78–9, italics in the original.

65 Ibid., 86, italics in the original.

66 Wooster, "The Way We Were," 36.

67 Segalove, quoted in Linda Podheiser, "Ilene Segalove, Girl Video Artist," *Boston Review* 9, no. 3 (1984): 14, and cited in Hanley, "The First Generation," 15.

68 Wooster, "The Way We Were," 40.

69 Rosler, "Place, Position, Power, Politics," 58.

70 These series are illustrated in de Zegher, ed., *Martha Rosler*, 14–22, 146–52. See also my article, "Conceptual Art and Feminism," 44–5.

71 Fried, "Art and Objecthood," 12–23. For an analysis of Fried's criticism of the "theatricality" of Minimalism, see Kaye, "Theatricality and the Corruption of the Modernist Work," 24–45.

72 Rosler, "Place, Position, Power, Politics," 58.

73 Rosler, quoted in Frascina, "The Politics of Representation," 161.

74 Rosler, "An Interview with Martha Rosler," interview by Martha Gever, 11.

75 See Amy Taubin, "'And what is a fact anyway?' (On a Tape by Martha Rosler)," *Millennium Film Journal* 4–5 (Summer–Fall 1979), cited in Cottingham, "The Inadequacy of Seeing and Believing," 159.

76 Rosler, "Interview with Martha Rosler," interview by Jane Weinstock, 85.

77 Peacock, *Corpus Loquendi*, loose insert on Martha Rosler, n.p.

78 Rosler, "Interview with Martha Rosler," interview by Jane Weinstock, 86.

79 Rosler, quoted from an undocumented source in the Video Data Bank catalogue, *Early Video Art in the United States*, 28.

80 For brief essays on Di Risio's work, see Murchie, "A Third Language," 6–14; Edelstein, "Tonia Di Risio," n.p.; and Garnett, "Homemade," n.p.

81 For an overview of Collyer's work from this period, see Metcalfe, *Cozy*.

82 See Dykhuis, *Gillian Collyer;* and my essay for a second version of this exhibition, "Gillian Collyer."

83 Gillian Collyer, interview by author, Halifax, 12 June 2001. See also Winnicott,

"Transitional Objects and Transitional Phenomena," in *Playing and Reality*.
84 Dragu, "Confessions," 96–7.
85 On 15 June 2000, the Ontario Coalition Against Poverty (OCAP) organized a protest against the deep cuts to social services implemented by Mike Harris's Conservative provincial government. The demonstration soon turned violent, with protesters and police attacking one another. For information on this protest, and on the ensuing legal trials, see the OCAP website, http://www.ocap.ca/.
86 Hamilton, *Gendering the Vertical Mosaic*, 116.
87 Philip, "Breadwinner Now Likely to Be a Woman."
88 Arat-Koc, "In the Privacy of Our Own Home," 52. For a summary of the immigration and working conditions for female domestics in Canada, see Hamilton, *Gendering the Vertical Mosaic*, 121, 131–2, 137.
89 For a recent assessment of such inequalities, see Hadley, "'And We Still Ain't Satisfied,'" 3–18. See also Bezanson, Luxton, and Side, eds, "Never Done," a special issue of *Atlantis* on unpaid work.
90 Raven, "The New Culture," 8.
91 Bürger, *Theory of the Avant-Garde*, 49.

## CHAPTER FIVE

1 De Beauvoir, *The Second Sex*, 679–715.
2 Butler, *Gender Trouble* and *Bodies that Matter*. See also Derrida, "Signature Event Context," 321–7.
3 See Sartre, *Being and Nothingness*; Lacan, *The Four Fundamental Concepts of Psycho-Analysis*, especially "Of the Subject Who Is Supposed to Know, of the First Dyad, and of the Good," 230–43, and "From Interpretation to Transference," 244–60; and Merleau-Ponty, *Phenomenology of Perception* and "The Intertwining – the Chiasm," 130–55.
4 See Descartes, *Discourse on Method, Optics, Geometry, and Meteorology*.
5 For discussion of the phenomenological critique of the Cartesian subject, see Jay, *Downcast Eyes*. These theories are examined in relation to body art and performance in Jones, *Body Art*, 37–42.
6 De Beauvoir, *The Second Sex*, xxix.
7 Butler, "Sex and Gender in Simone de Beauvoir's *Second Sex*," 43.
8 De Beauvoir, *The Second Sex*, 267.
9 Butler, "Performative Acts and Gender Constitution," 412.
10 De Beauvoir, *The Second Sex*, xxix.
11 Diamond, *Unmaking Mimesis*, 46.
12 Butler, *Gender Trouble*, 25.
13 Butler, *Bodies that Matter*, 234.
14 Harris, *Staging Femininities*, 174–5, italics in the original. I am indebted to Heather Anderson for introducing me to Harris's argument; see her "Contemporary Canadian Women's Performance Art," 27–8.
15 Diamond, *Unmaking Mimesis*, 47. For further discussion of the relationship between performativity and performance, see Solomon, *Re-Dressing the*

*Canon*, 3.

16 Schneider, *The Explicit Body in Performance*, 106.

17 Roth, ed., *The Amazing Decade*, 19.

18 Although much of the writing about performance from the 1970s and early 1980s maintains that it provided the audience an unmediated experience of the "presence" of the artist's body/self, this view has been emphatically countered by Jones, *Body Art*, 32–7, and by O'Dell, *Contract with the Skin*, 8–9.

19 For a comparison between the acting methods of Bertolt Brecht and Constantine Stanislavsky, see Eddershaw, "Acting Methods," 128–44.

20 Diamond, "Brechtian Theory/Feminist Theory," 129, italics in the original. Diamond has also published a revised version of this essay in *Unmaking Mimesis*, 43–55.

21 Schneider, *The Explicit Body in Performance*, 23, italics in the original; and Solomon, *Re-Dressing the Canon*, 11.

22 These works are discussed in Fox, "Waiting in the Wings," 20–32, and in my "Conceptual Art and Feminism," 47–8.

23 Antin, artist's statement, quoted in Raven, "At Home," 136.

24 Antin, "Dialogue with a Medium," 23.

25 Antin, "Interview with Eleanor Antin," 35.

26 Antin, "Dialogue with a Medium," 24.

27 See Burnham, "Performance Art in Southern California," 408–10.

28 Antin, *The Angel of Mercy*, 2.

29 Antin, "Dialogue with a Medium," 23.

30 Antin's arrival in New York was announced as the world premiere of *Before the Revolution: A Ballet Designed, Costumed, Painted, Choreographed, Written, and Performed by the Celebrated Black Ballerina of Diaghilev's Ballet Russes, Eleanora Antinova*, which was held at the Kitchen Center for Video, Music and Dance on 22 February 1979. For her memoir of her preparations for this performance, see Antin, *Being Antinova*.

31 Antin, quoted in Raven, "At Home," 138.

32 Fox, "Waiting in the Wings", 155.

33 Bloom, "Rewriting the Script," 184.

34 Antin, quoted in Lippard, "Making Up: Role-Playing and Transformation in Women's Art," in *From the Center*, 105.

35 Brentano, "Outside the Frame," 49–50.

36 For excerpts of Roberta Breitmore's diary, see Hershman, "Roberta Breitmore," 24–7.

37 Withers, "Feminist Performance Art," 167.

38 Rosler, "The Private and the Public," 73–4.

39 Hershman, "Roberta Breitmore," 26.

40 Linda Montano was another California artist who created characters and personae, the best known of which was Chicken Woman, who appeared in public in a ball gown with feathered headpiece and wings, sometimes dancing absurdly, sometimes quietly meditating. Unlike Antin and Hershman, however, Montano's character performances were focused on self-expression and personal fulfilment rather than on a specifically feminist inquiry into identity

formation.

41 For a discussion of this group, see Watson, "Hand of the Spirit," 5–28. It included Michael Morris, Vincent Trasov, Glenn Lewis, Robert Fones, Gary Lee-Nova, Eric Metcalfe, and Kate Craig.
42 See Watson, "Return to Brutopia," 19–20.
43 For a study of the history of fetish gear and its assimilation into fashionable dress, see Steele, *Fetish: Fashion, Sex and Power.*
44 Craig, "Personal Perspectives," 262, italics in the original.
45 Arnold, "Kate Craig: Skin," 5.
46 For a history of Western Front, see Wallace, ed., *Whispered Art History.*
47 See Lum, "Canadian Cultural Policy," 76–83.
48 Kate Craig, letter to author, 9 February 2001.
49 Frenkel, in Frenkel, Tuer, and Robertson, "The Story Is Always Partial," 8.
50 Stimson, "The Promise of Conceptual Art," xlvi.
51 The rejection of subject-centred inquiry in Conceptual art has been frequently noted. See Buchloh, "Conceptual Art, 1962–1969," 139–40; and the round-table discussion with Buchloh et al., "Conceptual Art and the Reception of Duchamp," 140–4.
52 Lippard, "Escape Attempts," 23.
53 In 1969, for example, two of Piper's *Untitled* works were published in Vito Acconci's magazine, *0 to 9*. She had also exhibited in New York at the Dwan Gallery and the Paula Cooper Gallery as well as in Europe at the Städtisches Museum Leverkusen and the Kunsthalle Bern.
54 Adrian Piper, letter to author, 28 April 1996.
55 Piper, *Talking to Myself*, 38–9.
56 Piper's statement was not included in the catalogue for "Conceptual Art and Conceptual Aspects" but is quoted in Lippard, *Six Years*, 168.
57 Piper, *Talking to Myself*, 39–40, italics in the original. Although Piper's personal background would become more pertinent to the content of her later work, her awareness of the significance of such social factors was already evident at this time. Raised in Harlem by well-educated parents, Piper was a precocious child who earned scholarships to attend private school. Fitting in neither with the children from her own neighbourhood, who called her "Paleface" on account of her fair skin, nor with her affluent, white schoolmates, who regarded her as a curiosity, she grew up feeling alienated from both communities. From the mid-1970s to the present, Piper's work has focused on marginality, alienation, and racism. See Wilson, "In Memory of the News and of Our Selves," 39–64.
58 Piper, *Talking to Myself*, 53.
59 Piper, quoted in Lippard, "Two Proposals," 45.
60 Ibid.
61 Piper, *Talking to Myself*, 54, italics in the original.
62 Ibid., 47.
63 Piper "Catalysis: An Interview with Adrian Piper," in Lippard, *From the Center*, 170.

64 Piper, *Talking to Myself*, 62.
65 See Piper, "Food for the Spirit, July 1971," 34–5. Lorraine O'Grady has argued that Piper's naked self-portraits signalled "the catalytic moment for the subjective black nude"; see O'Grady, "Olympia's Maid," 155.
66 Berger, "Styles of Radical Will," 18.
67 Piper, "Xenophobia and the Indexical Present," 289.
68 Lippard, quoted in Wilson, "In Memory of the News and of Our Selves," 47.
69 Piper, "Supplementary Material, No. 17," unpublished manuscript, quoted in Wilson, "In Memory of the News and of Our Selves," 48.
70 Wilson, "In Memory of the News and of Our Selves," 48.
71 Piper, "Xenophobia and the Indexical Present," 290.
72 Piper, "The Critique of Pure Racism," 91.
73 For example, Jones, *Body Art*, 162, 303 n. 43, offers this kind of poststructuralist reading of Piper's work, but Jones also acknowledges that Piper has expressed strong disagreement with it.
74 As with many Americans at the time, this relocation to Canada was partly in protest against Vietnam; see Wilson, "Artist's Book Beat," 62.
75 Martha Wilson, interview by author, New York, 12 April 1995.
76 Four of the *Chauvinistic Pieces* were published in Lippard, *Six Years*, 227. The whole series, which consists of two pages of typescript, was exhibited for the first time at NSCAD's Anna Leonowens Gallery in 1994 but was not illustrated in the exhibition catalogue by Barber, ed., *Conceptual Art: The* NSCAD *Connection, 1967–1973*.
77 For the metaphor of women in the blind spot of patriarchy, see Irigaray, "The Blind Spot of an Old Dream of Symmetry," in *Speculum of the Other Woman*, 11–129. I am indebted to Lee Rodney, who adopted this metaphor to assess the role of representation in the work of Wilson and Suzy Lake in her unpublished curatorial essay, "Deflecting the Blind Spot: Suzy Lake and Martha Wilson."
78 Jones, *Body Art*, 50.
79 Schneider, "After Us the Savage Goddess," 157.
80 Buchloh, "Conceptual Art, 1962–1969," 107.
81 Owens uses this phrase in "The Medusa Effect," 97–105.
82 Butler, "Performative Acts and Gender Constitution," 412.
83 Jones, *Postmodernism and the En-Gendering of Marcel Duchamp*, 180.
84 For a more in-depth discussion of the historical reception of Wilson's work, see my article, "Martha Wilson," 24–6.
85 Jones, "Sexual Politics: Feminist Strategies, Feminist Conflicts, Feminist Histories," in Jones, ed., *Sexual Politics*, 28.
86 Wilson, quoted in Lippard, "Making Up: Role-Playing and Transformation in Women's Art," in *From the Center*, 106.
87 Martha Wilson, interview by author, New York, 12 April 1995.
88 Peacock describes the development of feminist politics at NSCAD at this time in *Corpus Loquendi*, 5–6. Among other things, she cites the importance of an unpublished paper written in 1976 by MFA student Barbara England titled

"An Examination of Masculinism at NSCAD."

89 Brentano, "Outside the Frame," 50.

90 Peacock, *Corpus Loquendi*, loose insert on Susan Britton, n.p.

91 Hutcheon, *A Theory of Parody*, 5.

92 Braidotti, *Nomadic Subjects*, 7.

93 Householder, quoted in Robertson, "The Complete Clichettes," 12.

94 The Clichettes often enacted performances like *Having My Baby* and *Go to Hell* as stand-alone pieces in various venues during the mid-1980s, but both were also incorporated into their important 1986 epic production, *She-Devils of Niagara*, co-written with Marni Jackson and performed at the Factory Theatre in Toronto.

95 Robertson, "The Complete Clichettes," 14.

96 Isaak, *Feminism and Contemporary Art*, 5.

97 Ibid., 31–2.

98 Tenhaaf, "A History, or A Way of Knowing," 84 n. 2.

99 Kibbins, "Elizabethan," 17.

100 Tuer, "The Women Men Love to Hate," 15. Tuer quotes here from Derrida, *Spurs: Nietzsche's Style*, 55.

101 Rodney, "Deflecting the Blind Spot," 5.

102 Irigaray, *This Sex Which Is Not One*, 76.

103 See Reid, *15 Minutes*, 13. For an overview of Lake's output, from her work of the early 1970s to those works created between 2000 and 2002 that focus on aging, see Fortin, *Attitudes et comportements, Suzy Lake*.

104 This characteristic of camp is discussed in Babuscio, "Camp and Gay Sensibility," 40–57, and in Kleinhans, "Taking Out the Trash," 187. Meyer, in his "Introduction" to Meyer, ed., *The Politics and Poetics of Camp*, 1–22, makes a distinction between "Camp" and "camp." Meyer uses the upper-case form to refer to Camp as an explicitly queer form of parody that is political and critical and uses the lower-case form to refer to the version of camp that constitutes a depoliticized set of aesthetic stylizations based on the ironic appropriation of "bad taste" in popular culture, which was made available through Susan Sontag's 1964 essay "Notes on Camp." Although the parodic forms of camp that I discuss here have more in common with the political and critical practices that Meyer designates as Camp than with camp as an aesthetic of "bad taste," I have maintained the lower-case form.

105 Fischer, "Of Children's Rhymes," 29.

106 Sylvie Tourangeau, interview by author, Joliette, QC, 9 July 2000. For brief descriptions of these performances, which included the participation of Danielle Lapointe, Claude Arteau, and Franceline Carbonneau, see Richard and Robertson, eds, *Performance au/in Canada*, 149, 165, 181, 187.

107 Tourangeau, "An Art of Manner," 152.

108 In 1989 Tourangeau pursued her interest in the relationship between performance and its artifacts in the exhibition "Performances + artefacts," of which she was co-curator with Denis Lessard. Tourangeau has also discussed the importance of movement and artifacts in her performances in Bergeron et al.,

*Parcours désordonné*, 18–20, 98–100.

109 See Tourangeau, *Objet(s) de présence*, 7–12, 28–9, 34.

110 Lippard, "Making Up: Role-Playing and Transformation in Women's Art," in *From the Center*, 107.

## CHAPTER SIX

1 Schneider, *The Explicit Body in Performance*, 2.

2 Jones, *Body Art*, 5.

3 Douglas, *Purity and Danger*, 125.

4 Wolff, "Reinstating Corporeality: Feminism and Body Politics," in *Feminine Sentences*, 125. The studies that Wolff cites are: Foucault, *Discipline and Punish* and *The History of Sexuality*; Elias, *The History of Manners*; Stallybrass and White, *The Politics and Poetics of Transgression*; and Barker, *The Tremulous Private Body*.

5 De Beauvoir, *The Second Sex*, xv–xvi, 37.

6 See Braidotti, *Nomadic Subjects*, 160.

7 Irigaray, *This Sex Which Is Not One*, 33.

8 Braidotti, *Nomadic Subjects*, 161.

9 See de Lauretis, "The Technology of Gender," 1–30; Wittig, *The Straight Mind and Other Essays*; Butler, *Gender Trouble*; and Haraway, "A Manifesto for Cyborgs," 190–233.

10 Riley, *"Am I That Name?"* 105.

11 Braidotti, *Nomadic Subjects*, 173–90.

12 For a brief summary of these debates, see Wolff, "Reinstating Corporeality: Feminism and Body Politics," in *Feminine Sentences*, 121–8.

13 This third position is vigorously advocated in Jones, "The 'Sexual Politics' of *The Dinner Party*," 90, 97–8, and *Body Art*, 22–5.

14 Kandel, "Beneath the Green Veil: The Body in/of New Feminist Art," in Jones, ed., *Sexual Politics*, 190.

15 Pollock, "The Politics of Theory," 19.

16 Tickner, "The Body Politic," 237.

17 De Lauretis, "The Technology of Gender," 20.

18 Key historical sources for body art include Sharp, "Body Works," 14–17; Nemser, "Subject-Object: Body Art," 38–42; Vergine, *Il corpo come linguaggio*; Kozloff, "Pygmalion Reversed," 30–7; and Frank, "Auto-art: Self-indulgent? And How!" 43–8.

19 Lippard, "The Pains and Pleasures of Rebirth: European and American Women's Body Art," in *From the Center*, 125. The kind of work by male artists that Lippard was referring to would include Bruce Nauman's early video recordings of sustained, repetitious activities in his studio, such as *Stamping in the Studio*, *Revolving Upside Down*, *Bouncing in the Corner*, and *Wall/Floor Positions* (1968); Vito Acconci's *Seed Bed* (1971), in which the artist masturbated beneath a false floor in a gallery for the duration of a two-week exhibition; Barry Le Va's *Velocity Piece* (1969), in which Le Va ran

back and forth crashing into two walls fifty feet apart until he collapsed; and Dennis Oppenheim's *Reading Position for 2nd Degree Burn* (1970), in which the artist exposed his torso to the sun long enough to sustain a second-degree burn. Although Lippard does not mention him, Chris Burden would also fit into this category. For an assessment of the predominance of violence and masochism in body art of this period, see O'Dell, *Contract with the Skin.*

20 Kristeva, *Powers of Horror*. For discussions of abjection in art since the 1970s, see Craig Houser, Leslie C. Jones, and Simon Taylor, eds, *Abject Art*; Foster, *The Return of the Real*, 153–68; and Betterton, "Body Horror?" 130–60.

21 Tickner, "The Body Politic," 246.

22 Other examples of work dealing with menstruation include Judy Chicago's *Menstruation Bathroom,* installed at Womanhouse in 1972; Leslie Labowitz-Starus's *Menstruation Wait* (1971), in which she invited visitors to her Los Angeles studio to wait with her until her bleeding started; a similar performance by Catherine Elwes, who enclosed herself for several days in 1979 in a glass compartment at the Slade School of Art while bleeding visibly; and *Trop(e)ism* (1980), a video by Montreal artist Marshlore in which, after a sequence of silent screams, she inserts her fingers into her vagina, smears her face with menstrual blood, and then takes a long drag on a cigarette, exhaling slowly.

23 Irigaray, *This Sex Which Is Not One*, 76–7. Interestingly, in her discussion of mimicry as a riposte to imposed mimesis, Irigaray alludes directly to menstruation: "It is here, of course, that the hypothesis of a reversal – within the phallic order – is always possible. Re-semblance cannot do without red blood. Mother-matter-nature must go on forever nourishing speculation. But this re-source is also rejected as the waste product of reflection, cast outside as what resists it: as madness" (77).

24 Mogul's tape is briefly but perceptively discussed in Straayer, "I Say I Am," 8.

25 Jones, *Body Art*, 104.

26 One exception is Mira Schor's feminist reading of Acconci's work as exploring masculinity only to reaffirm its privileges; see Schor, "Representations of the Penis," 7. Jones, *Body Art*, 137–8, mentions this article but does not examine further the question of how women perceived Acconci's work in the 1970s.

27 Acconci, quoted in Greenberg, "Vito Acconci," 122.

28 Lippard, "Making Up: Role-Playing and Transformation in Women's Art," in *From the Center*, 104.

29 Alloway, Kozloff, Krauss, Macheck, and Michelson, letter from editors, *Artforum* 13, no. 4 (December 1974): 9. Lippard gives an account of the uproar in "Making Up," in *From the Center*, 104–5.

30 Pincus-Witten, "Lynda Benglis," 59.

31 Lynda Benglis, quoted in Lippard, "Making Up," in *From the Center*, 105.

32 Susan Krane, *Lynda Benglis*, 40–1, discusses both the Benglis and Morris images, describes their personal relationship at the time as a partnership, and,

like Lippard, implies that Benglis's image was dependent on Morris's. In telephone interviews with the author (26 August 2003; 15 July 2005), however, Lynda Benglis categorically denied this assertion. According to Benglis, she had been working on the theme of the girlie pinup and pornographic representations of women since 1971–72 in relation to the idea that, although one could not control one's own image or the images of women circulated within media culture, the creation of art was one place where the control of such images could be reappropriated for both an individual and feminist agenda. While denying any personal relationship, Benglis maintains that she and Morris were in close professional communication during this period and that prior to publicizing his own advertisement in the April 1974 issue of *Artforum,* he was aware of her own investigations into the themes and motifs of the pornographic pinup and of her intention to produce such an image in an art magazine. Because Benglis's own pinup image, which she regards more as an "artist pages" piece than as an advertisement, came out later in the November 1974 issue of *Artforum* (13, no. 3: 4–5), the erroneous and unfortunate result, according to Benglis, is that her work has become widely assumed to be derivative of Morris's. Benglis also points out that her *Artforum* image was intended to be a cryptic but metaphoric indictment of the media's exploitation and dishonesty, especially as it had propped up Richard Nixon during the 1973–74 Watergate scandal and had suppressed his lies and deceptions. Disturbed by the exclusively sexual reading of the *Artforum* image, Benglis subsequently produced two related videos that attempted to shift its metaphoric associations toward more explicit references to media duplicity and ruthless greed by invoking the sleight of hand of magic (*How's Tricks*, 1976) and the exploitation of those vulnerable cultural oddities who, like artists, seek to uphold a moral position within a corrupt society (*The Amazing Bow-Wow,* 1976–77).

33 Jones, *Body Art*, 114, erroneously says that Benglis's image was only recently given a feminist recuperation. This does not accord with the fact that Lippard wrote about it from a feminist perspective in "Making Up," in *From the Center*, which was first published in *Ms.* 4, no. 4 (October 1975), as did Tickner in "The Body Politic," which was first published in *Art History* 1, no. 2 (June 1978): 236–51.

34 See also Lippard, "Sexual Politics: Art Style," in *From the Center*, 36–7.

35 For an analysis of the relationship between Antoni's work and Robert Morris's, see Lajer-Burcharth, "Antoni's Difference," 129–70.

36 Janine Antoni, "Lick and Lather," interview by Art:21, http://www.pbs.org/art21/artists/antoni/clip2.html.

37 Schor, "This Essentialism Which Is Not One," 51.

38 Betterton, "Body Horror?" 131.

39 Creed, *The Monstrous-Feminine.*

40 Bordo, *Unbearable Weight.*

41 Hart, *Between the Body and the Flesh*, 36–82.

42 Dolan, "Practicing Cultural Disruptions," 265–6.

43 See Krane, *Lynda Benglis*, 100; and Jones, "Interpreting Feminist Bodies," 227.
44 Lasch, *The Culture of Narcissism*, 31. Lasch does not specifically associate narcissism with women at all, even in his discussion of the feminist movement (187–206), of which he was mainly supportive.
45 Freud, "On Narcissism," 88–9.
46 Jacobus, *Reading Woman*, 105, italics in the original.
47 Isaak, *Feminism and Contemporary Art*, 13.
48 Freud, "On Humour," 162.
49 Jones, "Interpreting Feminist Bodies," 228; see also Jones, *Body Art*, 151–95.
50 See Berger, *Ways of Seeing*, 46; and Mulvey, "Visual Pleasure and Narrative Cinema," 14–26.
51 Wolff, "Reinstating Corporeality," in *Feminine Sentences*, 128.
52 Jones, *Body Art*, 23–5. For Pollock's theory of "Brechtian distanciation," see "Screening the Seventies: Sexuality and Representation in Feminist Practice – A Brechtian Perspective," in *Vision and Difference*, 155–99. For Kelly's critique of body art, see "Re-Viewing Modernist Criticism," 87–103, italics in the original.
53 Owens, "The Discourse of Others," 62; see also Foster, "Subversive Signs," 88–92.
54 Braidotti, *Nomadic Subjects*, 161.
55 De Lauretis, "The Technology of Gender," 1, 20, 25–6.
56 Lippard, "The Pains and Pleasures of Rebirth," in *From the Center*, 129.
57 Antin, quoted in Roth, ed., *The Amazing Decade*, 19.
58 Lippard, "The Pains and Pleasures of Rebirth," in *From the Center*, 130.
59 Wilson and Apple, "Correspondence between Jacki Apple and Martha Wilson," 43.
60 Mulvey, "Visual Pleasure and Narrative Cinema," 19–21.
61 Doane, "Film and the Masquerade," 81.
62 Irigaray, *This Sex Which Is Not One*, 84. In Doane's subsequent reworking of her concept of masquerade, she drew more directly on Irigaray's theorizing of it in terms of women's relation to language; see Doane, "Masquerade Reconsidered," 33–43.
63 Irigaray, *Speculum of the Other Woman*, 54.
64 Diamond, "Brechtian Theory/Feminist Theory," 120–35.
65 Diamond, "Mimesis, Mimicry, and the 'True-Real,'" 375.
66 Braidotti, "Of Bugs and Women," 134.
67 Lippard, "The Pains and Pleasures of Rebirth," in *From the Center*, 124, italics in the original.
68 Lacan, "Guiding Remarks for a Congress on Feminine Sexuality," 90, italics in the original.
69 Wilke, script for *Intercourse with …* (performed at the London Regional Art Gallery, London, Ontario, 17 February 1977), in Kochheiser, ed., *Hannah Wilke*, 139.
70 See Frueh, "Hannah Wilke," in Kochheiser, ed., *Hannah Wilke*, 56.
71 Lippard, "The Pains and Pleasures of Rebirth," in *From the Center*, 126.
72 Jones, *Body Art*, 174–5.

73 Lippard, "The Pains and Pleasures of Rebirth," in *From the Center*, 127.
74 Barry and Flitterman, "Textual Strategies," 39.
75 Jones, *Body Art*, 176.
76 Marshall, "Video Art," 244–5.
77 Lacan, "The Mirror Stage," 1–7.
78 See Tong, *Feminist Thought*, 220–2.
79 Marshall, "Video Art," 245–6.
80 Krauss, "Video: The Aesthetics of Narcissism," 58–9.
81 Jonas, "Untitled," 367.
82 Mulvey, "Visual Pleasure and Narrative Cinema" 21–2.
83 Peacock, *Corpus Loquendi,* loose insert on Dorit Cypis, n.p.
84 Wagner, "Performance, Video, and the Rhetoric of Presence," 69.
85 Piper, quoted in Goldberg, "Public Performance: Private Memory," 23.
86 Irigaray, *Speculum of the Other Woman*, 232; quoted in Tenhaaf, "Of Monitors and Men," 28.
87 Tenhaaf, "Of Monitors and Men," 34.
88 See Harrison and Wood, "Modernity and Modernism Reconsidered," 221–6.
89 Rosler, "A Conversation with Martha Rosler," 45. See also her article "For an Art Against the Mythology of Everyday Life," 12–15.
90 Alexander Alberro notes that Rosler's decision to re-do the work as a video came from her concern that the presence of a naked woman in the live performance added to the objectification. Through mediatization, she moved from the physically close to the conceptually removed; see Alberro, "The Dialectics of Everyday Life," 98–9.
91 Sayre, *The Object of Performance*, 82–3.
92 See, for example, Spelman, *Inessential Woman*; and Ahmed, *Differences that Matter*. For a moderation of these critiques, see Martin and Mohanty, "Feminist Politics," 517–39.
93 O'Grady, quoted in Withers, "Feminist Performance Art," 173.
94 O'Grady, e-mail message to author, 13 September 2005.
95 Rosler, "Place, Position, Power, Politics," 67.
96 For a more detailed discussion of this work, see my article "Wendy Geller's *48-Hour Beauty Blitz*," 41–7.
97 Peacock, *Corpus Loquendi*, loose insert on Wendy Geller, n.p.
98 Freud, "On Humour," 162–3.
99 Blondeau, "High Tech Storyteller," 28.
100 Lori Weidenhammer was curator of "Virtual Postcards from the Feminist Utopia," presented in 1997 by the Winnipeg organization Mentoring Artists for Women's Art (MAWA). For information and images from the exhibition, see the MAWA website: http://www.mawa.ca/archives/postcards/contents.html.
101 Baert, "Three Dresses, Tailored to the Times," 81.
102 These live performances by Dempsey and Millan have been documented in their video compilation *A Live Decade: 1989–1999*, available from Finger-in-the-Dyke Productions, Winnipeg. See also Dempsey and Millan's descriptions of their work in "Shawna Dempsey and Lorri Millan," in May, ed., *The Feminist Reconstruction of Space*, 66–83.

103 For an in-depth analysis of how humour can enact a feminist politics, see Auslander, "'Brought to You by Fem-Rage,'" in *From Acting to Performance*, 108–25.

104 Braidotti, "Of Bugs and Women," 134.

**CONCLUSION**

1 See, for example, Spark and Watkins, eds, *Everyday: The 11th Biennale of Sydney*. "Sensation" was the name of an exhibition of so-called "Young British Artists" first shown at the Royal Academy of Arts, London, 1997.

2 Shottenkirk, "First Person Painting," 31.

3 The complex and often overlapping relationship between postfeminism and third-wave feminism is in the process of being sorted out and analyzed by young feminist scholars. For one of the most insightful studies, see Pinterics, "Riding the Feminist Waves," 15–21. See also Heywood and Drake, eds, *Third Wave Agenda*; and Karaian, Rundle, and Mitchell, eds, *Turbo Chicks*.

4 Anderson, "Contemporary Canadian Women's Performance Art," 39–43.

5 Ibid., 49–67.

6 Lippard, "Sweeping Exchanges," 362, italics in the original.

7 Hamilton, *Gendering the Vertical Mosaic*, 70.

8 Pollock, "Preface," in Pollock, ed., *Generations and Geographies in the Visual Arts*, xii.

9 Ibid., xii–xiii.

10 Rhodes, "Shining a Light on the Everyday."

11 See Jameson, "Postmodernism," 59–92; Foster, *The Return of the Real*, 99–124, and *Design and Crime*, 123–43; Hopkins, *After Modern Art, 1945–2000*, 197–203; and Sheppard, *Modernism—Dada—Postmodernism*, 355–62.

12 Sheppard, *Modernism—Dada—Postmodernism*, 360.

13 I am indebted to my student Krista Davis for drawing my attention to this work. For a profile of this installation, see Alaez, "Beauty Cabinet Prototype."

14 Anderson, "Happy F.O. to You," 7–8.

15 See McKay, "Allyson Mitchell: The Fluff Stands Alone," 46–9.

16 For the Pretty Porky and Pissed Off website, see http://www.stumptuous.com/ppp.

17 Steenbergen, "Feminism and Young Women," 9.

# Bibliography


Ahmed, Sara. *Differences That Matter: Feminist Theory and Postmodernism.* Cambridge: Cambridge University Press, 1999.

Alaez, Ana Laura. "Beauty Cabinet Prototype." Palais de Tokyo, 2002. http://www.palaisdetokyo.com/fr/prog/expo/alaez.html.

Alberro, Alexander. "The Dialectics of Everyday Life: Martha Rosler and the Strategy of the Decoy." In M. Catherine de Zegher, ed., *Martha Rosler: Positions in the Life World,* 73–112. Exhibition catalogue. Birmingham, England: Ikon Gallery; Vienna: Generali Foundation; Cambridge, MA: MIT Press, 1998.

– "Mel Bochner: Thought Made Visible, 1966–1973." Review of the exhibition "Mel Bochner: Thought Made Visible, 1966–1973." *Artforum* 34, no. 6 (February 1996): 80–1.

– and Blake Stimson, eds. *Conceptual Art: A Critical Anthology*. Cambridge, MA:MIT Press, 1999.

Alloway, Lawrence, Max Kozloff, Rosalind Krauss, Joseph Macheck, and Annette Michelson. Letter from editors. *Artforum* 13, no. 4 (December 1974): 9.

Althusser, Louis. "Ideology and Ideological State Apparatuses." In *Lenin and Philosophy and Other Essays,* 121–73. London: New Left Books, 1971.

Anderson, Bonnie S., and Judith Zinsser. *A History of Their Own: Women in Europe from Prehistory to the Present.* 2 vols. New York: Harper and Row, 1988.

Anderson, Heather. "Contemporary Canadian Women's Performance Art: Reading Postfeminism and Third-Wave Feminism." Master's thesis, Dalhousie University, 2003.

– "Happy F.O. To You." *Arts Atlantic* 78 (Winter 2004): 7–9.

Andre, Carl. "Carl Andre: Artworker, in an Interview with Jeanne Siegel." *Studio International* 180, no. 927 (November 1970): 175–9.

Antin, Eleanor. *The Angel of Mercy*. Exhibition catalogue. La Jolla, CA: La Jolla Museum of Contemporary Art, 1977.
– *Being Antinova*. Los Angeles: Astro Artz, 1983.
– "Dialogue with a Medium." *Art-Rite* 7 (Autumn 1974): 23–4.
– "Interview with Eleanor Antin." By Dinah Portner. *Journal: Southern California Art Journal* 26 (February–March 1980): 34–7.
Antoni, Janine. "Lick and Lather." Interview by Art:21. http://www.pbs.org/art21/artists/antoni/clip2.html.
Arat-Koc, Sedef. "In the Privacy of Our Own Home: Foreign Domestic Workers as a Solution to the Crisis in the Domestic Sphere in Canada." *Studies in Political Economy* 28 (Spring 1989): 33–58.
Arbour, Rose-Marie. "Art et féminisme." In *Art et féminisme*, 3–14. Exhibition catalogue. Quebec: Ministère des affaires culturelles; Montreal: Musée d'art contemporain de Montréal, 1982.
Arnold, Grant. "Kate Craig: Skin." In Grant Arnold, ed., *Kate Craig: Skin*, 1–16. Exhibition catalogue. Vancouver: Vancouver Art Gallery, 1998.
"The Artist and Politics: A Symposium." *Artforum* 9, no. 1 (September 1970): 35–9.
Ashton, Dore. "Response to Crisis in American Art." *Art in America* 57, no. 1 (January–February 1969): 24–35.
Auslander, Philip. *From Acting to Performance: Essays in Modernism and Postmodernism*. London and New York: Routledge, 1997.
– *Liveness: Performance in a Mediatized Culture*. London and New York: Routledge, 1999.
Austin, J.L. *How to Do Things with Words*. Cambridge, MA: Harvard University Press, 1962.
Babuscio, Jack. "Camp and Gay Sensibility." In Richard Dyer, ed., *Gays and Film*, 40–57. New York: Zoetrope, 1984.
Baert, Renée. "Three Dresses, Tailored to the Times." In Ingrid Bachmann and Ruth Scheuing, eds, *Material Matters: The Art and Culture of Contemporary Textiles*, 75–91. Toronto: YYZ Books, 1998.
Banes, Sally. *Democracy's Body: Judson Dance Theatre, 1962–1964*. Ann Arbor: UMI Research Press, 1983.
– *Greenwich Village, 1963: Avant–Garde Performance and the Effervescent Body*. Durham, NC: Duke University Press, 1993.
Barber, Bruce. "Indexing: Conditionalism and Its Heretical Equivalents." In A.A. Bronson and Peggy Gale, eds, *Performance by Artists*, 184–204. Toronto: Art Metropole, 1979.
– ed. *Conceptual Art: The NSCAD Connection, 1967–1973*. Exhibition catalogue. Halifax: The Anna Leonowens Gallery of the Nova Scotia College of Art and Design, 2001.
Barker, Francis. *The Tremulous Private Body: Essays on Subjection*. London and New York: Methuen, 1984.
Barry, Judith. "Women, Representation, and Performance Art: Northern California." In Carl E. Loeffler and Darlene Tong, eds, *Performance Anthology:*

*Source Book of California Performance Art*, 439–68. San Francisco: Last Gasp Press and Contemporary Arts Press, 1989.

– and Sandy Flitterman. "Textual Strategies: The Politics of Art-Making." *Screen* 21, no. 2 (Summer 1980): 35–48.

Barthes, Roland. *Camera Lucida: Reflections on Photography*. Translated by Richard Howard. New York: Hill and Wang, 1981.

– "The Death of the Author." In *Image, Music, Text*, 142–8. New York: Hill and Wang, 1977.

Bellour, Raymond. "Video Writing." In Doug Hall and Sally Jo Fifer, eds, *Illuminating Video: An Essential Guide to Video Art*, 421–43. New York: Aperture Foundation in association with the Bay Area Video Coalition, 1990.

Berger, John. *Ways of Seeing*. Harmondsworth, Middlesex: Penguin Books, 1972.

Berger, Maurice. *Labyrinths: Robert Morris, Minimalism, and the 1960s*. New York: Harper and Row, 1989.

– "Styles of Radical Will: Adrian Piper and the Indexical Present." In Maurice Berger, ed., *Adrian Piper: A Retrospective*, 12–32. Exhibition catalogue. Baltimore: Fine Arts Gallery, University of Maryland, 1999.

– ed. *Adrian Piper: A Retrospective*. Exhibition catalogue. Baltimore: Fine Arts Gallery, University of Maryland, 1999.

Bergeron, Michèle, Danielle Binet, Ginette Déziel, Norman Forget, Suzanne Joly, Francis LaPan, Sylvie Tourangeau, and Jocelyne Tremblay. *Parcours désordonné (Propos d'artistes sur la collection)*. Exhibition catalogue. Joliette, QC: Les Ateliers Convertibles, 1996.

Betterton, Rosemary. "Body Horror? Food (and Sex and Death) in Women's Art." In *An Intimate Distance: Women, Artists and the Body*, 130–60. London and New York: Routledge, 1996.

Bezanson, Kathryn, Meg Luxton, and Katherine Side, eds. "Never Done: The Challenge of Unpaid Work." Special issue, *Atlantis* 28, no. 2 (Spring 2004).

Blondeau, Lori. "High Tech Storyteller: A Conversation with Performance Artist Lori Blondeau." By Lynne Bell and Janice Williamson. *Fuse* 24, no. 4 (December 2001): 27–34.

Bloom, Lisa. "Rewriting the Script: Eleanor Antin's Feminist Art." In Howard N. Fox, ed., *Eleanor Antin*, 159–89. Exhibition catalogue. Los Angeles: Los Angeles County Museum of Art, 1999.

Bordo, Susan. *Unbearable Weight: Feminism, Western Culture, and the Body*. Berkeley and Los Angeles: University of California Press, 1993.

Braidotti, Rosi. *Nomadic Subjects: Embodiment and Sexual Difference in Contemporary Feminist Theory*. New York: Columbia University Press, 1994.

– "Of Bugs and Women: Irigaray and Deleuze on the Becoming Woman." In Carolyn Burke, Naomi Schor, and Margaret Whitford, eds, *Engaging with Irigaray: Feminist Theory and Modern European Thought*, 111–37. New York: Columbia University Press, 1994.

Brentano, Robyn. "Outside the Frame: Performance, Art, and Life." In Robyn Brentano and Olivia Georgia, *Outside the Frame: Performance and the Object, a Survey History of Performance Art in the USA since 1970*, 31–61. Exhibition catalogue. Cleveland: Cleveland Center for Contemporary Art, 1994.

– and Olivia Georgia. *Outside the Frame: Performance and the Object, a Survey History of Performance Art in the USA since 1970*. Exhibition catalogue. Cleveland: Cleveland Center for Contemporary Art, 1994.

Broude, Norma, and Mary D. Garrard, eds. *The Power of Feminist Art: The American Movement of the 1970s, History and Impact*. New York: Harry N. Abrams, 1994.

Brown, Wendy. "Where Is the Sex in Political Theory?" *Women and Politics* 7, no. 1 (1987): 3–23.

Buchloh, Benjamin H.D. "Conceptual Art, 1962–1969: From the Aesthetic of Administration to the Critique of Institutions." *October* 55 (Winter 1990): 105–43.

– "Robert Watts: Animate Objects – Inanimate Subjects." In Benjamin H.D. Buchloh and Judith Rodenbeck, eds, *Experiments in the Everyday: Allan Kaprow and Robert Watts; Events, Objects, Documents*, 7–26. Exhibition catalogue. New York: Miriam and Ira D. Wallach Art Gallery, Columbia University, 1999.

– "Theorizing the Avant-Garde." Review of *Theory of the Avant Garde*, by Peter Bürger. *Art in America* 72, no. 10 (November 1984): 19–21.

– Rosalind Krauss, Alexander Alberro, Thierry de Duve, Martha Buskirk, and Yves-Alain Bois. "Conceptual Art and the Reception of Duchamp." *October* 70 (Fall 1994): 127–46.

– and Judith Rodenbeck, eds. *Experiments in the Everyday: Allan Kaprow and Robert Watts; Events, Objects, Documents*. Exhibition catalogue. New York: Miriam and Ira D. Wallach Art Gallery, Columbia University, 1999.

Buhle, Mari Jo. *Feminism and Its Discontents: A Century of Struggle with Psychoanalysis*. Cambridge, MA: Harvard University Press, 1998.

Bürger, Peter. *Theory of the Avant-Garde*. Translated by Michael Shaw. 1984. Reprint, Minneapolis: University of Minnesota Press, 1992.

Burnham, Linda F. "Performance Art in Southern California: An Overview." In Carl E. Loeffler and Darlene Tong, eds, *Performance Anthology: Source Book of California Performance Art*, 390–438. San Francisco: Last Gasp Press and Contemporary Arts Press, 1989.

Butler, Judith. *Bodies That Matter: On the Discursive Limits of "Sex."* London and New York: Routledge, 1993.

– *Gender Trouble: Feminism and the Subversion of Identity*. London and New York: Routledge, 1990.

– "Gender Trouble, Feminist Theory, and Psychoanalytic Discourse." In Linda J. Nicholson, ed., *Feminism/Postmodernism*, 324–40. New York and London: Routledge, 1990.

– "Performative Acts and Gender Constitution: An Essay in Phenomenology and Feminist Theory." In Katie Conboy, Nadia Medina, and Sarah Stanbury, eds, *Writing on the Body: Female Embodiment and Feminist Theory,* 401–17. New York: Columbia University Press, 1997.
– "Sex and Gender in Simone de Beauvoir's *Second Sex.*" *Yale French Studies* 72 (1986): 35–49.
Cameron, Eric. "Structural Videotape in Canada." In Ira Schneider and Beryl Korot, eds, *Video Art: An Anthology,* 188–95. New York: Harcourt Brace Jovanovich, 1976.
Carr, C. "Roped: A Saga of Art in Everyday Life." In *On Edge: Performance at the End of the Twentieth Century,* 3–9. Middletown, CT: Wesleyan University Press; Hanover, NH: The University Press of New England, 1993.
Case, Sue-Ellen. "Toward a Butch-Femme Aesthetic." In Lynda Hart, ed., *Making a Spectacle: Feminist Essays on Contemporary Women's Theatre,* 282–99. Ann Arbor: University of Michigan Press, 1989.
– ed. *Performing Feminisms: Feminist Critical Theory and Theatre.* Baltimore: Johns Hopkins University Press, 1990.
– ed. *Split Britches: Lesbian Practice/Feminist Performance.* London and New York: Routledge, 1996.
Chadwick, Whitney. *Women, Art, and Society.* 3rd ed. London: Thames and Hudson, 2002.
Chicago, Judy. *Through the Flower: My Struggle as a Woman Artist.* Garden City, NY: Doubleday, 1975.
Cixous, Hélène. "The Laugh of the Medusa." In Elaine Marks and Isabelle de Courtivron, eds, *New French Feminisms: An Anthology,* 245–64. Amherst, MA: University of Massachusetts Press, 1980.
– *The Newly Born Woman.* Translated by Betsy Wing. Minneapolis: University of Minnesota Press, 1986.
Collins, Marie, and Sylvie Weil Sayre, eds. *Les femmes en France.* New York: Simon and Schuster, 1974.
Côté, Diane-Jocelyne, ed. *Réseau art-femme.* Exhibition catalogue. Quebec: Éditions Intervention, 1983.
Cottingham, Laura. "Eating from the *Dinner Party* Plates and Other Myths, Metaphors, and Moments of Lesbian Enunciation in Feminism and Its Art Movement." In Amelia Jones, ed., *Sexual Politics: Judy Chicago's* Dinner Party *in Feminist Art,* 133–59. Exhibition catalogue. Los Angeles: The Armand Hammer Museum of Art and Cultural Center; Berkeley and Los Angeles: University of California Press, 1996.
– "The Inadequacy of Seeing and Believing: The Art of Martha Rosler." In M. Catherine de Zegher, ed., *Martha Rosler: Positions in the Life World,* 157–63. Exhibition catalogue. Birmingham, England: Ikon Gallery; Vienna: Generali Foundation; Cambridge, MA: MIT Press, 1998.
– *Seeing through the Seventies: Essays on Feminism and Art.* Australia: G & B International, 2000.

Craig, Kate. "Personal Perspectives, 1970–1979." In Luke Rombout, ed., *Vancouver: Art and Artists, 1931–1983*, 261–2. Exhibition catalogue. Vancouver: Vancouver Art Gallery, 1993.

Creed, Barbara. *The Monstrous-Feminine: Film, Feminism, Psychoanalysis.* London and New York: Routledge, 1993.

Crenshaw, Kimberlè Williams. "Beyond Racism and Misogyny: Black Feminism and 2 Live Crew." In Mari J. Matsuda, Charles R. Lawrence III, Richard Delgado, and Kimberlè Williams Crenshaw, *Words That Wound: Critical Race Theory, Assualtive Speech and the First Amendment*, 111–32. Boulder, CO: Westview Press, 1993.

Crow, Thomas. *The Rise of the Sixties: American and European Art in the Era of Dissent.* New York: Harry N. Abrams, 1996.

Daly, Mary. *Beyond God the Father: Toward a Philosophy of Women's Liberation.* Boston: Beacon Press, 1973.

– *Gyn/Ecology: The Metaethics of Radical Feminism.* Boston: Beacon Press, 1978.

Damon, Betsy. "The 7,000 Year Old Woman." *Heresies* 3 (Fall 1977): 11–13.

Darling-Wolf, Fabienne. "From Airbrushing to Liposuction: The Technological Reconstruction of the Female Body." In Baukje Miedema, Janet M. Stoppard, and Vivienne Anderson, eds, *Women's Bodies/Women's Lives*, 277–93. Toronto: Sumach Press, 2000.

Davis, Elizabeth Gould. *The First Sex.* New York: Putnam, 1971.

Davy, Kate. "Fe/male Impersonation: The Discourse of Camp." In Janelle G. Reinelt and Joseph R. Roach, eds, *Critical Theory and Performance*, 231–47. Ann Arbor: University of Michigan Press, 1992.

– "From Lady Dick to Ladylike: The Work of Holly Hughes." In Lynda Hart and Peggy Phelan, eds, *Acting Out: Feminist Performances*, 55–84. Ann Arbor: University of Michigan Press, 1994.

– "Reading Past the Heterosexual Imperative: Dress Suites to Hire." In Carol Martin, ed., *A Sourcebook of Feminist Theatre and Performance: On and Beyond the Stage*, 136–56. London and New York: Routledge, 1996.

de Beauvoir, Simone. *The Second Sex.* Translated and edited by H.M. Parshley. 1952. Reprint, New York: Alfred A. Knopf, 1964.

de Lauretis, Teresa. "Sexual Indifference and Lesbian Representation." In Sue-Ellen Case, ed., *Performing Feminisms: Feminist Critical Theory and Theatre*, 17–39. Baltimore: Johns Hopkins University Press, 1990.

– "The Technology of Gender." In *Technologies of Gender: Essays on Theory, Film, and Fiction*, 1–30. Bloomington: Indiana University Press, 1987.

– ed. *Feminist Studies/Critical Studies.* Bloomington: Indiana University Press, 1986.

de Zegher, M. Catherine, ed. *Inside the Visible: An Elliptical Traverse of Twentieth-Century Art in, of, and from the Feminine.* Exhibition catalogue. Kortrijk, Flanders: The Kanaal Art Foundation; Boston: The Institute of Contemporary Art, 1994.

– ed. *Martha Rosler: Positions in the Life World.* Exhibition catalogue. Birmingham, England: Ikon Gallery; Vienna: Generali Foundation; Cambridge, MA: MIT Press, 1998.

del Rio, Petra Barreras. "Ana Mendieta: A Historical Overview." In Petra Barreras del Rio and John Perreault, eds, *Ana Mendieta: A Retrospective*, 28–51. Exhibition catalogue. New York: The New Museum of Contemporary Art, 1987.
– and John Perreault, eds. *Ana Mendieta: A Retrospective*. Exhibition catalogue. New York: The New Museum of Contemporary Art, 1987.
Dempsey, Shawna, and Lorri Millan. "Shawna Dempsey and Lorri Millan." In Louise May, ed., *The Feminist Reconstruction of Space*, 66–83. Exhibition catalogue. St Norbert, MB: St Norbert Arts and Cultural Centre, 1996.
Derrida, Jacques. *Of Grammatology*. Translated by Gayatri Chakravorty Spivak. Baltimore: Johns Hopkins University Press, 1976.
– "Signature Event Context." In *Margins of Philosophy*, 321–7. Translated by Alan Bass. Chicago: University of Chicago Press, 1982.
– *Spurs: Nietzsche's Styles = Eperons: Les styles de Nietzsche*. Translated by Barbara Harlow. Chicago: University of Chicago Press, 1978.
Descartes, René. *Discourse on Method, Optics, Geometry, and Meteorology*. 1637. Translated by Paul J. Olscamp, 1937. Reprint, Indianapolis: Bobbs-Merrill, 1965.
Di Stefano, Christine. "Dilemmas of Difference." In Linda J. Nicholson, ed., *Feminism/Postmodernism*, 63–82. New York and London: Routledge, 1990.
Diamond, Elin. "Brechtian Theory/Feminist Theory: Toward a Gestic Feminist Criticism." In Carol Martin, ed., *A Sourcebook of Feminist Theatre and Performance: On and Beyond the Stage*, 120–35. London and New York: Routledge, 1996.
– "Mimesis, Mimicry, and the 'True-Real.'" In Lynda Hart and Peggy Phelan, eds, *Acting Out: Feminist Performances*, 363–82. Ann Arbor: University of Michigan Press, 1994.
– *Unmaking Mimesis: Essays on Feminism and Theatre*. London and New York: Routledge, 1997.
Diamond, Sara. "Daring Documents: The Practical Aesthetics of Early Vancouver Video." In Peggy Gale and Lisa Steele, eds, *Video Re/View: The (Best) Source for Critical Writings on Canadian Artists' Video*, 180–4. Toronto: Art Metropole and V Tape, 1996.
Doane, Mary Ann. "Film and the Masquerade: Theorising the Female Spectator." *Screen* 23, nos 3–4 (September-October 1982): 74–87.
– "Masquerade Reconsidered: Some Thoughts on the Female Spectator." In *Femmes Fatales: Feminism, Film Theory, Psychoanalysis*, 33–43. New York: Routledge, 1991.
Dolan, Jill. "The Dynamics of Desire: Sexuality and Gender in Pornography and Performance." *Theatre Journal* 39, no. 2 (1987): 156–74.
– *The Feminist Spectator as Critic*. Ann Arbor: UMI Research Press, 1988.
– "Gender Impersonation Onstage: Destroying or Maintaining the Mirror of Gender Roles." In Laurence Senelick, ed., *Gender in Performance: The Presentation of Difference in the Performing Arts*, 3–13. Hanover, NH: The University Press of New England, 1992.
– "Practicing Cultural Disruptions: Gay and Lesbian Representation and

Sexuality." In Janelle G. Reinelt and Joseph R. Roach, eds, *Critical Theory and Performance*, 263–75. Ann Arbor: University of Michigan Press, 1992.
–*Presence and Desire: Essays on Gender, Sexuality and Performance*. Ann Arbor: University of Michigan Press, 1993.

Douglas, Mary. *Purity and Danger: An Analysis of the Concepts of Pollution and Taboo*. London: Routledge and Kegan Paul, 1984.

Dragu, Margaret. "Confessions." In Brenda L. Brown, ed., *Bringing It Home: Women Talk About Feminism in Their Lives*, 89–105. Vancouver: Arsenal Pulp Press, 1996.

Dumont, Micheline. "The Origins of the Women's Movement in Quebec." In Veronica Strong-Boag and Anita Clair Fellman, eds, *Rethinking Canada: The Promise of Women's History*, 3rd ed., 462–78. Toronto: Oxford University Press, 1997.

– *The Women's Movement: Then and Now*. Ottawa: Canadian Research Institute for the Advancement of Women/Institut canadien de recherches sur les femmes, 1986.

Dykhuis, Peter. *Gillian Collyer: hand-held*. Exhibition catalogue. Halifax: Art Gallery of Nova Scotia, 2000.

Eddershaw, Margaret. "Acting Methods: Brecht and Stanislavsky." In Graham Bartam and Anthony Waine, eds, *Brecht in Perspective*, 128–44. London: Longman, 1982.

Edelson, Mary Beth. "Pilgrimage/See for Yourself: A Journey to a Neolithic Goddess Cave, 1977. Grapčeva, Hvar Island, Yugoslavia." *Heresies* 5 (Spring 1978): 96–9.

– *Seven Cycles: Public Rituals*. New York: Self-published, 110 Mercer Street, New York City, NY 10012, 1980.

Edelstein, Susan. "Tonia Di Risio: *Parlare*." In Tonia Di Risio, *Tonia Di Risio:* Parlare, n.p. Exhibition catalogue. Kamloops, BC: Kamloops Art Gallery, 1999.

Eisenstein, Hester, and Alice Jardine, eds. *The Future of Difference*. 1980. Reprint, New Brunswick, NJ: Rutgers University Press, 1985.

Elias, Norbert. *The History of Manners*. Vol. 1, *The Civilizing Process*. Oxford: Blackwell, 1978.

Elwes, Catherine. "Floating Femininity: A Look at Performance Art by Women." In Sarah Kent and Jacqueline Morreau, eds, *Women's Images of Men*, 164–93. Published following the 1980 exhibition "Women's Images of Men," Institute of Contemporary Arts in London. 1985. Reprint, London: Pandora, 1990.

– "On Performance and Performativity: Women Artists and Their Critics." *Third Text* 18, no. 2 (March 2004): 193–7.

England, Barbara. "An Examination of Masculinism at NSCAD." Unpublished paper, 1976. Photocopy in The Women's File, Nova Scotia College of Art and Design, Halifax.

Evans, Sara. *Personal Politics: The Roots of Women's Liberation in the Civil Rights Movement and the New Left*. New York: Vintage Books, 1979.

Eyland, Cliff. "Introduction." In Cliff Eyland, ed., *Charmaine*. Exhibition catalogue. Winnipeg: Gallery 1.1.1., University of Manitoba, MB, 2001.

Felski, Rita. *Beyond Feminist Aesthetics: Feminist Literature and Social Change*. Cambridge, MA: Harvard University Press, 1989.

Feminist Art Program. *Womanhouse*. Valencia: California Institute of the Arts, Feminist Art Program, 1972.

Firestone, Shulamith. *The Dialectic of Sex: The Case for Feminist Revolution*. New York: Bantam Books, 1970.

Fischer, Barbara. "Of Children's Rhymes, Spiders and Other Entrapments." In Barbara Fischer and Colleen O'Neill, eds, *Colette Urban*, 23–34. Exhibition catalogue. Corner Brook, NF: Sir Wilfred Grenfell College Art Gallery, 1992.

Fisher, Jennifer. "*Seven Years of Living Art*: Linda Montano." *Parachute* 64 (October-December 1991): 23–8.

Flax, Jane. "Re-Membering the Selves: Is the Repressed Gendered?" *Michigan Quarterly Review* 26, no. 1 (1987): 92–110.

Forte, Jeanie. "Women's Performance Art: Feminism and Postmodernism." In Sue-Ellen Case, ed., *Performing Feminisms: Feminist Critical Theory and Theatre*, 251–69. Baltimore: Johns Hopkins University Press, 1990.

Fortin, Jocelyne. *Attitudes et comportements, Suzy Lake*. Exhibition catalogue. Rimouski, QC: Musée régional de Rimouski, 2002.

Foster, Hal. *Design and Crime (and Other Diatribes)*. London: Verso, 2002.

– *The Return of the Real: The Avant-Garde at the End of the Century*. Cambridge, MA: MIT Press, 1996.

– "Subversive Signs." *Art in America* 70, no. 10 (November 1982): 88–92.

Foucault, Michel. *Discipline and Punish: The Birth of the Prison*. Translated by Alan Sheridan. New York: Pantheon Books, 1977.

– *The History of Sexuality*. Translated by Robert Hurley. New York: Pantheon Books, 1978.

– "Of Other Spaces." Translated by Jay Miskowiec. *Diacritics* 16, no. 1 (Spring 1896): 22–7.

Fox, Howard N. "Waiting in the Wings: Desire and Destiny in the Art of Eleanor Antin." In Howard N. Fox, ed., *Eleanor Antin*, 15–157. Exhibition catalogue. Los Angeles: Los Angeles County Museum of Art, 1999.

– ed. *Eleanor Antin*. Exhibition catalogue. Los Angeles: Los Angeles County Museum of Art, 1999.

Frank, Peter. "Auto-Art: Self-Indulgent? And How!" *Art News* 75, no. 7 (September 1976): 43–8.

Frascina, Francis. "The Politics of Representation." In Paul Wood, Francis Frascina, Jonathan Harris, and Charles Harrison, *Modernism in Dispute: Art since the Forties*, 77–169. New Haven and London: Yale University Press in association with The Open University, 1993.

Fraser, Nancy, and Linda J. Nicholson. "Social Criticism without Philosophy: An Encounter between Feminism and Postmodernism." In Linda J. Nicholson, ed., *Feminism/Postmodernism*, 19–38. New York and London: Routledge, 1990.

Frenkel, Vera, Dot Tuer, and Clive Robertson. "The Story Is Always Partial: A Conversation with Vera Frenkel." *Art Journal* 57, no. 4 (Winter 1998): 3–15.
Freud, Sigmund. "On Humour." 1927. In James Strachey, ed. and trans., *The Standard Edition of the Complete Psychological Works of Sigmund Freud,* 161–6. Vol. 21. London: The Hogarth Press, 1961.
– "On Narcissism: An Introduction." 1914. In James Strachey, ed. and trans., *The Standard Edition of the Complete Psychological Works of Sigmund Freud,* 73–102. Vol. 14. London: The Hogarth Press, 1957.
Fried, Michael. "Art and Objecthood." *Artforum* 5, no. 10 (Summer 1967): 12–23.
Friedan, Betty. *The Feminine Mystique*. New York: Dell Books, 1963.
Frueh, Joanna. "Hannah Wilke." In Thomas H. Kochheiser, ed., *Hannah Wilke: A Retrospective,* 10–103. Exhibition catalogue. Columbia: University of Missouri Press, 1989.
Fuchs, Elinor. "Staging the Obscene Body." *The Drama Review* 33, no. 1 (1989): 33–58.
Fuss, Diana. *Essentially Speaking: Feminism, Nature and Difference*. London and New York: Routledge, 1989.
Gagnon, Monika Kin. "Work in Progress: Canadian Women in the Visual Arts, 1975–1987." In Rhea Tregebov, ed., *Work in Progress: Building Feminist Culture,* 101–27. Toronto: The Women's Press, 1987.
Garnett, Leah. "Homemade: A Showcase of Fine Family Homes." In Tonia Di Risio, *Homemade: A Showcase of Fine Family Homes,* n.p. Halifax: Bella Publications, 2002.
Gaulke, Cheri. "Performance Art of the Woman's Building." *High Performance* 3, nos 3–4 (Fall-Winter 1980): 156–63.
Gimbutus, Marija. *The Goddesses and Gods of Old Europe*. Berkeley and Los Angeles: University of California Press, 1982.
Gitlin, Todd. *The Sixties: Years of Hope, Days of Rage*. 2nd ed. New York: Bantam, 1993.
Goldberg, Roselee. *Performance Art from Futurism to the Present*. 2nd ed. London: Thames and Hudson, 1988.
– *Performance: Live Art since 1960*. London: Thames and Hudson, 1998.
– "Public Performance: Private Memory." *Studio International* 192, no. 982 (1976): 19–23.
Goldstein, Ann, and Anne Rorimer, eds. *Reconsidering the Object of Art: 1965–1975*. Exhibition catalogue. Los Angeles: Los Angeles Museum of Contemporary Art; Cambridge, MA: MIT Press, 1995.
Goodnough, Robert. "Pollock Paints a Picture." *Art News* 50, no. 3 (May 1951): 38–41.
Gornick, Vivian. "Toward a Definition of Female Sensibility." In *Essays in Feminism,* 108–27. New York: Harper and Row, 1978.
– "Woman as Outsider." In Vivian Gornick and Barbara K. Moran, eds, *Woman in Sexist Society: Studies in Power and Powerlessness,* 70–84. New York: Basic Books, 1971.

Gouma-Peterson, Thalia, and Patricia Matthews. "The Feminist Critique of Art History." *Art Bulletin* 69, no. 3 (September 1987): 332–43.
Greenberg, Blue. "Vito Acconci: The State of the Art, 1985." *Arts Magazine* 59, no. 10 (1985): 120–3.
Greenberg, Clement. *Art and Culture: Critical Essays*. Boston: Beacon Press, 1961.
– "Avant-Garde and Kitsch." 1939. In John O'Brian, ed., *Perceptions and Judgments, 1939–1944*. Vol. 1, *The Collected Essays and Criticism*, 5–22. Chicago: University of Chicago Press, 1986.
– "Modernist Painting." 1961. In John O'Brian, ed., *Modernism with a Vengeance, 1957–1969*. Vol. 3, *The Collected Essays and Criticism*, 85–93. Chicago: University of Chicago Press, 1993.
Grey, Alex, and Allyson Grey. "Linda Montano and Tehching Hsieh's *One-Year Art/Life Performance*." *High Performance* 7, no. 3 (1984): 24–9.
Griffin, Susan. *Women and Nature: The Roaring inside Her*. New York: Harper and Row, 1978.
Grimm, Reinhold. "Alienation in Context: On the Theory and Practice of Brechtian Theatre." In Siegfried Mews, ed., *A Bertolt Brecht Reference Companion*, 35–46. Westport, CT: Greenwood Press, 1997.
Grosz, Elizabeth. *Jacques Lacan: A Feminist Introduction*. London and New York: Routledge, 1990.
Guilbaut, Serge. *How New York Stole the Idea of Modern Art*. Translated by Arthur Goldhammer. Chicago: University of Chicago Press, 1983.
Hadley, Karen. "'And We Still Ain't Satisfied': A Report on Gender and Income Inequality in Canada." *Atlantis* 28, no. 1 (Fall-Winter 2003): 3–18.
Hall, Doug, and Sally Jo Fifer, eds. *Illuminating Video: An Essential Guide to Video Art*. New York: Aperture Foundation in association with the Bay Area Video Coalition, 1990.
Hamilton, Roberta. *Gendering the Vertical Mosaic: Feminist Perspectives on Canadian Society*. 2nd ed. Toronto: Pearson Prentice Hall, 2004.
Hanley, JoAnn. "The First Generation: Women and Video, 1970–75." In JoAnn Hanley, ed., *The First Generation: Women and Video, 1970–75*, 8–18. Exhibition catalogue. New York: Independent Curators Incorporated, 1993.
– ed. *The First Generation: Women and Video, 1970–75*. Exhibition catalogue. New York: Independent Curators Incorporated, 1993.
Haraway, Donna. "A Manifesto for Cyborgs: Science, Technology, and Socialist Feminism in the 1980s." In Linda J. Nicholson, ed., *Feminism/Postmodernism*, 190–233. New York and London: Routledge, 1990.
Harding, Sandra. "Feminism, Science, and the Anti-Enlightenment Critiques." In Linda J. Nicholson, ed., *Feminism/Postmodernism*, 83–106. New York and London: Routledge, 1990.
Harris, Ann Sutherland, and Linda Nochlin. *Women Artists, 1550–1950*. Exhibition catalogue. Los Angeles: Los Angeles County Museum of Art; New York: Random House, 1976.

Harris, Geraldine. *Staging Femininities: Performance and Performativity.* Manchester: Manchester University Press, 1999.

Harris, Jonathan. "Modernism and Culture in the USA, 1930–1960." In Paul Wood, Francis Frascina, Jonathan Harris, and Charles Harrison, *Modernism in Dispute: Art since the Forties,* 3–76. New Haven and London: Yale University Press in association with the Open University, 1993.

Harrison, Charles, and Paul Wood. "Modernity and Modernism Reconsidered." In Paul Wood, Francis Frascina, Jonathan Harris, and Charles Harrison, *Modernism in Dispute: Art since the Forties,* 170–260. New Haven and London: Yale University Press in association with the Open University, 1993.

Hart, Lynda. *Between the Body and the Flesh: Performing Sadomasochism.* New York: Columbia University Press, 1998.

– "Identity and Seduction: Lesbians in the Mainstream." In Lynda Hart and Peggy Phelan, eds, *Acting Out: Feminist Performances,* 119–37. Ann Arbor: University of Michigan Press, 1994.

– ed. *Making a Spectacle: Feminist Essays on Contemporary Women's Theatre.* Ann Arbor: University of Michigan Press, 1989.

– and Peggy Phelan, eds. *Acting Out: Feminist Performances.* Ann Arbor: University of Michigan Press, 1994.

Hartsock, Nancy. "Rethinking Modernism: Minority vs. Majority Theories." *Cultural Critique* 7 (1987): 187–206.

Haskell, Barbara. *Blam! The Explosion of Pop, Minimalism and Performance, 1958–1964.* Exhibition catalogue. New York: Whitney Museum of American Art, 1984.

Haywood, Robert. "Critique of Instrumental Labor: Meyer Schapiro's and Allan Kaprow's Theory of Avant-Garde Art." In Benjamin H.D. Buchloh and Judith Rodenbeck, eds, *Experiments in the Everyday: Allan Kaprow and Robert Watts; Events, Objects, Documents,* 27–46. Exhibition catalogue. New York: Miriam and Ira D. Wallach Art Gallery, Columbia University, 1999.

Hendricks, Jon, ed. *Fluxus Etc.* Exhibition catalogue. Bloomfield Hills, MI: Cranbrook Academy of Art Museum, 1981.

Henes, Donna. "Cocoon Ceremony." *High Performance* 1, no. 2 (September 1978): 38–9.

– "Spider Woman: Donna Henes Interviewed by Linda Burnham." *High Performance* 2, no. 2 (June 1979): 24–9.

– "Spider Woman Series." *High Performance* 2, no. 1 (March 1979): 61.

Hershman, Lynn. "Roberta Breitmore: An Alchemical Portrait Begun in 1975." *La Mamelle Magazine: Art Contemporary* 5 (Fall 1976): 24–7.

Heywood, Leslie, and Jennifer Drake, eds. *Third Wave Agenda: Being Feminist, Doing Feminism.* Minneapolis: University of Minnesota Press, 1997.

Hobsbawm, Eric. *The Age of Extremes: The Short Twentieth Century.* 1994. Reprint, London: Abacus, 1995.

hooks, bell. "bell hooks." Interview by Andrea Juno. In Andrea Juno and V.

Vale, eds, *Angry Women*, 78–93. San Francisco: Re/Search Publications, 1991.

Hopkins, David. *After Modern Art, 1945–2000*. Oxford: Oxford University Press, 2000.

Houser, Craig, Leslie C. Jones, and Simon Taylor, eds. *Abject Art: Repulsion and Desire in American Art*. Exhibition catalogue. New York: Whitney Museum of American Art, 1993.

Howells, Coral Ann. *Private and Fictional Words: Canadian Women Novelists of the 1970s and 1980s*. London: Methuen, 1987.

Hutcheon, Linda. "Splitting Images: The Postmodern Ironies of Women's Art." In Shirley Neuman and Glennis Stephenson, eds, *ReImaging Women: Representations of Women in Culture*, 256–70. Toronto: University of Toronto Press, 1993.

– *A Theory of Parody: The Teachings of Twentieth-Century Art Forms*. New York: Methuen, 1985.

Information Canada. *Report of the Royal Commission on the Status of Women in Canada*. Ottawa: Information Canada, 1970.

Irigaray, Luce. *Speculum of the Other Woman*. Translated by Gillian C. Gill. Ithaca, NY: Cornell University Press, 1985.

– *This Sex Which Is Not One*. Translated by Catherine Porter with Carolyn Burke. Ithaca, NY: Cornell University Press, 1985.

Isaak, Jo Anna. *Feminism and Contemporary Art: The Revolutionary Power of Women's Laughter*. London and New York: Routledge, 1996.

Jacobs, Mary Jane. "Introduction." In Moira Roth, ed., *The Amazing Decade: Women and Performance Art in America, 1970–1980*, 10–12. Los Angeles: Astro Artz, 1983.

Jacobus, Mary. *Reading Woman: Essays in Feminist Criticism*. New York: Columbia University Press, 1986.

Jameson, Fredric. "Postmodernism, or The Cultural Logic of Late Capitalism." *New Left Review* 146 (July-August 1984): 59–92.

Jay, Martin. *Downcast Eyes: The Denigration of Vision in Twentieth-Century French Thought*. Berkeley and Los Angeles: University of California Press, 1993.

Johnston, Jill. "Meat Joy." *Village Voice*, 26 November 1964, 13.

Jonas, Joan. "Untitled." In Doug Hall and Sally Jo Fifer, eds, *Illuminating Video: An Essential Guide to Video Art*, 366–74. New York: Aperture Foundation in association with the Bay Area Video Coalition, 1990.

Jones, Amelia. *Body Art: Performing the Subject*. Minneapolis: University of Minnesota Press, 1998.

– "Interpreting Feminist Bodies: The Unframeability of Desire." In Paul Duro, ed., *The Rhetoric of the Frame: Essays on the Boundaries of the Artwork*, 223–314. Cambridge: Cambridge University Press, 1996.

– *Postmodernism and the En-Gendering of Marcel Duchamp*. Cambridge: Cambridge University Press, 1994.

– "'Presence' in Absentia: Experiencing Performance as Documentation." *Art Journal* 56, no. 4 (Winter 1997): 11–18.

– "The 'Sexual Politics' of *The Dinner Party*: A Critical Context." In Amelia Jones, ed., *Sexual Politics: Judy Chicago's* Dinner Party *in Feminist Art,* 84–118. Exhibition catalogue. Los Angeles: The Armand Hammer Museum of Art and Cultural Center; Berkeley and Los Angeles: University of California Press, 1996.

– "Sexual Politics: Feminist Strategies, Feminist Conflicts, Feminist Histories." In Amelia Jones, ed., *Sexual Politics: Judy Chicago's* Dinner Party *in Feminist Art,* 20–38. Exhibition catalogue. Los Angeles: The Armand Hammer Museum of Art and Cultural Center; Berkeley and Los Angeles: University of California Press, 1996.

– ed. *Sexual Politics: Judy Chicago's* Dinner Party *in Feminist Art.* Exhibition catalogue. Los Angeles: The Armand Hammer Museum of Art and Cultural Center; Berkeley and Los Angeles: University of California Press, 1996.

Juno, Andrea, and V. Vale, eds. *Angry Women.* San Francisco: Re/Search Publications, 1991.

Kandel, Susan. "Beneath the Green Veil: The Body in/of New Feminist Art." In Amelia Jones, ed., *Sexual Politics: Judy Chicago's* Dinner Party *in Feminist Art,* 184–200. Exhibition catalogue. Los Angeles: The Armand Hammer Museum of Art and Cultural Center; Berkeley and Los Angeles: University of California Press, 1996.

Kant, Immanuel. *Critique of Judgment.* 1790. Translated by James Creed Meredith. Oxford: Clarendon Press, 1952.

Kaprow, Allan. *Assemblages, Environments and Happenings.* New York: Harry N. Abrams, 1966.

– "The Legacy of Jackson Pollock." *Art News* 57, no. 6 (October 1958): 24–6, 55–7.

– "Performing Life." In Jeff Kelley, ed., *Essays on the Blurring of Art and Life,* 195–8. Berkeley and Los Angeles: University of California Press, 1993.

Karaian, Lara, Lisa Bryn Rundle, and Allyson Mitchell, eds. *Turbo Chicks: Talking Young Feminism.* Toronto: Sumach Press, 2001.

Katz, Robert. *Naked by the Window: The Fatal Marriage of Carl Andre and Ana Mendieta.* New York: Atlantic Monthly Press, 1990.

Kaye, Nick. "Theatricality and the Corruption of the Modernist Work." In *Postmodernism and Performance,* 24–45. New York: St Martin's Press, 1994.

Kazuko, Zarina, and Ana Mendieta. *Dialectics of Isolation: An Exhibition of Third World Women Artists of the United States, September 2–20, 1980.* Exhibition catalogue. New York: AIR Gallery, 1980.

Kelly, Mary. "Re-Viewing Modernist Criticism." In Brian Wallis, ed., *Art after Modernism: Rethinking Representation,* 87–103. New York: New Museum of Contemporary Art, 1984.

Kibbins, Gary. "Elizabethan." *Fuse* 9, no. 6 (May-June 1986): 14–17.

Klein, Yves. "Truth Becomes Reality." Translated by Howard Beckman. In *Yves Klein, 1928–1962: A Retrospective,* 230. Exhibition catalogue. Houston: Institute for the Arts, Rice University, 1982.

Kleinhans, Chuck. "Taking out the Trash: Camp and the Politics of Parody." In Moe Meyer, ed., *The Politics and Poetics of Camp*, 182–201. London and New York: Routledge, 1994.
Kochheiser, Thomas H. ed. *Hannah Wilke: A Retrospective*. Exhibition catalogue. Columbia: University of Missouri Press, 1989.
Kosuth, Joseph. "1975." In Alexander Alberro and Blake Stimson, eds, *Conceptual Art: A Critical Anthology*, 334–48. Cambridge, MA: MIT Press, 1999.
Kozloff, Joyce. "The Women's Movement: Still a 'Source of Strength' or 'One Big Bore'?" *Art News* 75, no. 4 (April 1976): 48–50.
Kozloff, Max. "Pygmalion Reversed." *Artforum* 14, no. 3 (November 1975): 30–7.
Krane, Susan. *Lynda Benglis: Dual Natures*. Exhibition catalogue. Atlanta, GA: High Museum of Art, 1991.
Krauss, Rosalind. "Notes on the Index: Seventies Art in America." In *The Originality of the Avant-Garde and Other Modernist Myths*, 196–219. Cambridge, MA: MIT Press, 1984.
– "Video: The Aesthetics of Narcissism." *October* 1 (Spring 1976): 50–64.
Kristeva, Julia. *Desire in Language: A Semiotic Approach to Literature and Art*. Translated by Alice Jardine, Thomas Gora, and Leon S. Roudiez. New York: Columbia University Press, 1980.
– *Polylogue*. Paris: Éditions du Seuil, 1977.
– *Powers of Horror*. Translated by Leon S. Roudiez. New York: Columbia University Press, 1982.
– "Women's Time." In Nanneri O. Ceohane, Michelle Z. Rosaldo, and Barbara C. Gelpi, eds, *Feminist Theory, a Critique of Ideology*, 31–53. Chicago: University of Chicago Press, 1982.
Kurtz, Bruce. "Video Is Being Invented." *Arts Magazine* 47, no. 3 (December 1972-January 1973): 37–44.
Kwon, Miwon. "Bloody Valentines: Afterimages by Ana Mendieta." In M. Catherine de Zegher, ed., *Inside the Visible: An Elliptical Traverse of Twentieth-Century Art in, of, and from the Feminine*, 165–71. Exhibition catalogue. Kortrijk, Flanders: Kanaal Art Foundation; Boston: Institute of Contemporary Art, 1994.
"La Sfida del Sistema." *Metro* 14 (1968): 38–45.
Lacan, Jacques. *The Four Fundamental Concepts of Psycho-Analysis*. Translated by Alan Sheridan. Edited by Jacques-Alain Miller. New York: W.W. Norton, 1978.
– "Guiding Remarks for a Congress on Feminine Sexuality." In Juliet Mitchell and Jacqueline Rose, eds, *Feminine Sexuality: Jacques Lacan and the école freudienne*, 86–98. Translated by Jacqueline Rose. New York: W.W. Norton, 1983.
– "The Mirror Stage as Formative of the Function of the I as Revealed in Psychoanalytic Experience." In Alan Sheridan, ed., *Écrits: A Selection*, 1–7. London: Tavistock Publications, 1980.

Lacy, Suzanne. "Visions and Re-Visions: A Conversation with Suzanne Lacy." Interview by Lucy R. Lippard. *Artforum* 19, no. 3 (November 1980): 42–5.
– and Lucy R. Lippard. "Political Performance: A Discussion by Suzanne Lacy and Lucy R. Lippard." *Heresies* 17 (1983): 21–5.
Lajer-Burcharth, Ewa. "Antoni's Difference." *Differences* 10, no. 2 (Summer 1998): 129–70.
Lasch, Christopher. *The Culture of Narcissism: American Life in an Age of Diminishing Expectations*. New York: W.W. Norton, 1978.
Lefebvre, Henri. *Everyday Life in the Modern World*. New York: Harper and Row, 1971.
Leider, Philip. "How I Spent My Summer Vacation, or Art and Politics in Nevada, Berkeley, San Francisco and Utah." *Artforum* 9, no. 1 (September 1970): 40–9.
Lessard, Denis, and Sylvie Tourangeau. *Performances + artefacts*. Exhibition catalogue. Longueuil, QC: La Galerie d'art du Collège Éduard-Montpetit, 1989.
Licht, Ira. *Bodyworks*. Exhibition catalogue. Chicago: Museum of Contemporary Art, 1975.
Lippard, Lucy R. "The Dilemma." *Arts Magazine* 45, no. 2 (November 1970): 27–9.
– "Escape Attempts." In Ann Goldstein and Anne Rorimer, eds, *Reconsidering the Object of Art: 1965–1975*, 17–38. Exhibition catalogue. Los Angeles: Los Angeles Museum of Contemporary Art; Cambridge, MA: MIT Press, 1995.
– *From the Center: Feminist Essays on Women's Art*. New York: E.P. Dutton, 1976.
– *Overlay: Contemporary Art and the Art of Prehistory*. New York: Pantheon, 1983.
– "Quite Contrary: Body, Nature, Ritual in Women's Art." *Chrysalis* 2 (1977): 31–47.
– *Six Years: The Dematerialization of the Art Object from 1966 to 1972*. New York: Praeger, 1972.
– "Sweeping Exchanges: The Contribution of Feminism to the Art of the 1970s." *Art Journal* 40, nos 1–2 (Fall-Winter 1980): 362–5.
– "Two Proposals: Lucy Lippard Presents the Ideas of Adrian Piper and Eleanor Antin." *Art and Artists* 6, no. 12 (March 1972): 44–7.
Loeffler, Carl E. "From the Body into Space: Post-Notes on Performance Art in North America." In Carl E. Loeffler and Darlene Tong, eds, *Performance Anthology: Source Book of California Performance Art*, 369–89. San Francisco: Last Gasp Press and Contemporary Arts Press, 1989.
– and Darlene Tong, eds. *Performance Anthology: Source Book of California Performance Art*. San Francisco: Last Gasp Press and Contemporary Arts Press, 1989.
Lum, Ken. "Canadian Cultural Policy." *Canadian Art* 16, no. 3 (Fall 1999): 76–83.

Lyotard, Jean-François. *The Postmodern Condition: A Report on Knowledge.* Translated by Geoffrey Bennington and Brian Massumi. Minneapolis: University of Minnesota Press, 1984.

MacPherson, Kay, and Meg Sears. "The Voice of Women: A History." In Gwen Matherson, ed., *Women in the Canadian Mosaic,* 71–92. Toronto: Peter Martin Associates, 1976.

Marchessault, Janine. "Is the Dead Author a Woman?: Some Thoughts on Feminist Authorship." *Parallélogramme* 15, no. 4 (Spring 1990): 10–18.

Marcuse, Herbert. *One Dimensional Man.* Boston: Beacon Press, 1964.

Marks, Elaine, and Isabelle de Courtivron, eds. *New French Feminisms.* Amherst, MA: University of Massachusetts Press, 1980.

Marshall, Stuart. "Video Art, the Imaginary and the Parole Vide." *Studio International* 191, no. 981 (May-June 1976): 243–7.

Martin, Biddy, and Chandra Talpade Mohanty. "Feminist Politics: What's Home Got to Do with It?" In Morag Shiach, ed., *Feminism and Cultural Studies,* 517–39. Oxford: Oxford University Press, 1999.

Martin, Carol, ed. *A Sourcebook of Feminist Theatre and Performance: On and Beyond the Stage.* London and New York: Routledge, 1996.

Mayer, Rosemary. "Performance and Experience." *Arts Magazine* 47, no. 3 (December 1972-January 1973): 33–6.

McKay, Sally. "Allyson Mitchell: The Fluff Stands Alone." *Canadian Art* 21, no. 2 (Summer 2004): 46–9.

McTavish, Lianne. "Body Narratives in Canada, 1968–99: Sarah Maloney, Catherine Heard, and Kathleen Sellers." *Woman's Art Journal* 21, no. 2 (Fall-Winter 2000–2001): 5–11.

Meehan, Johanna. "Introduction." In Johanna Meehan, ed., *Feminists Read Habermas: Gendering the Subject of Discourse,* 1–20. London and New York: Routledge, 1995.

Mendieta, Raquelin. "Ana Mendieta: Self-Portrait of a Goddess." *Review: Latin American Literature and Arts* 39 (1988): 38–9.

Merleau-Ponty, Maurice. "The Intertwining – the Chiasm," in Claude Lefort, ed., *The Visible and the Invisible,* 130–55. Translated by Alphonso Lingis. Evanston, IL: Northwestern University Press, 1968.

– *Phenomenology of Perception.* Translated by Colin Smith. New York: Humanities Press, 1962.

Metcalfe, Robin. *Cozy.* Exhibition catalogue. London, ON: London Regional Art Gallery, 2001.

Meyer, Moe. "Introduction: Reclaiming the Discourse of Camp." In Moe Meyer, ed., *The Politics and Poetics of Camp,* 1–22. London and New York: Routledge, 1994.

– ed. *The Politics and Poetics of Camp.* London and New York: Routledge, 1994.

Miller, Nancy K. "Changing the Subject: Authorship, Writing, and the Reader." In Teresa de Lauretis, ed., *Feminist Studies/Critical Studies,* 102–20. Bloomington: Indiana University Press, 1986.

Millett, Kate. *Sexual Politics*. Garden City, NY: Doubleday, 1970.
Million, Dian. "Telling Secrets: Sex, Power and Narratives in Indian Residential School Histories." *Canadian Woman Studies/les cahiers de la femme* 20, no. 2 (2000): 92–104.
Milroy, Sarah. "Mars Attack." *Globe and Mail*, 10 June 2004, national edition, sec. R, 1, 9.
Mitchell, Juliet. "Introduction." In Juliet Mitchell and Jacqueline Rose, eds, *Feminine Sexuality: Jacques Lacan and the école freudienne,* 1–26. Translated by Jacqueline Rose. New York: W.W. Norton, 1983.
Modleski, Tania. *Feminism without Women: Culture and Criticism in a "Postfeminist" Age*. London and New York: Routledge, 1991.
Montano, Linda. *Art in Everyday Life*. Los Angeles: Astro Artz, 1981.
– *Letters from Linda M. Montano*. New York: Routledge, 2005.
– "Linda Montano." Interview by Andrea Juno. In Andrea Juno and V. Vale, eds, *Angry Women,* 50–63. San Francisco: Re/Search Publications, 1991.
– "Matters of Life and Death: Linda Montano Interviewed by Moira Roth." *High Performance* 1, no. 4 (December 1978): 2–7.
Moraga, Cherríe, and Gloria Anzaldúa, eds. *This Bridge Called My Back: Writings by Radical Women of Color*. Watertown, MA: Persephone Press, 1981.
Morgan, Robin. *Going Too Far: The Personal Chronicle of a Feminist*. New York: Random House, 1968.
Morris, Cerise. "Determination and Thoroughness: The Movement for a Royal Commission on the Status of Women in Canada." *Atlantis* 5, no. 2 (Spring 1980): 1–21.
Morris, Robert. "Notes on Sculpture, Part 3: Notes and Non Sequiturs." *Artforum* 5, no. 10 (Summer 1967): 24–9.
Mulvey, Laura. "Visual Pleasure and Narrative Cinema." In *Visual and Other Pleasures,* 14–26. Bloomington: Indiana University Press, 1989.
Munroe, Alexandra, and Jon Hendricks, eds. *Yes Yoko Ono*. Exhibition catalogue. Minneapolis: Walker Art Center, 2001.
Murchie, John. "A Third Language." In Tonia Di Risio, *Tonia Di Risio:* Progresso, 6–14. Exhibition catalogue. Halifax: Art Gallery of Nova Scotia, 1998.
Nash, Joanna. "Montréal's Powerhouse Gallery." In Marie Fraser and Lesley Johnstone, eds, *Instabili: La question du sujet,* 85–91. Montreal: La Galerie Powerhouse (La Centrale) and Artextes, 1990.
Native American Women Playwrights Archive. "Origins." *Spiderwoman Theatre*. http://staff.lib.muohio.edu/nawpa/origins.html.
Nemser, Cindy. "Subject-Object: Body Art." *Arts Magazine* 46, no. 1 (September 1971): 38–42.
Nicholson, Linda J., ed. *Feminism/Postmodernism*. New York and London: Routledge, 1990.
Nochlin, Linda. "Why Have There Been No Great Women Artists?" In Thomas B. Hess and Elizabeth C. Baker, eds, *Art and Sexual Politics,* 1–39. New York: Macmillan, 1971.

O'Dell, Kathy. *Contract with the Skin: Masochism, Performance Art and the 1970s*. Minneapolis: University of Minnesota Press, 1998.
– "Toward a Theory of Performance Art: An Investigation of Its Sites." PhD thesis, City University of New York, 1992.
O'Grady, Lorraine. "Olympia's Maid." In Joanna Frueh, Cassandra Langer, and Arlene Raven, eds, *New Feminist Criticism: Art, Identity, Action*, 152–70. New York: Harper Collins, 1994.
Orenstein, Gloria Feman. "Recovering Her Story: Feminist Artists Reclaim the Great Goddess." In Norma Broude and Mary D. Garrard, eds, *The Power of Feminist Art: The American Movement of the 1970s, History and Impact*, 174–89. New York: Harry N. Abrams, 1994.
Ortner, Sherry. "Is Female to Male as Nature Is to Culture?" In Michelle Zimbalist Rosaldo and Louise Lamphere, eds, *Women, Culture and Society*, 67–87. Stanford: Stanford University Press, 1974.
Osaki, Shinichiro. "Body and Place." In Paul Schimmel, ed., *Out of Actions: Between Performance and the Object, 1949–1979*, 121–57. Exhibition catalogue. Los Angeles: The Museum of Contemporary Art; London: Thames and Hudson, 1998.
Ostriker, Alicia Suskin. *Stealing the Language: The Emergence of Women's Poetry in America*. Boston: Beacon Press, 1986.
Owens, Craig. "The Discourse of Others: Feminists and Postmodernism." In Hal Foster, ed., *The Anti-Aesthetic: Essays on Postmodern Culture*, 57–82. Seattle: Bay Press, 1983.
– "The Medusa Effect, or The Spectacular Ruse." *Art in America* 72, no. 1 (January 1984): 97–105.
Parker, Rozsika, and Griselda Pollock. *Old Mistresses: Women, Art and Ideology*. London: Pandora, 1981.
– eds. *Framing Feminism: Art and the Women's Movement*. London: Pandora, 1987.
Patraka, Vivian M. "Binary Terror and Feminist Performance: Reading Both Ways." *Discourse* 14, no. 2 (Spring 1992): 163–85.
– "Split Britches in *Split Britches*: Performing History, Vaudeville, and the Everyday." In Lynda Hart and Peggy Phelan, eds, *Acting Out: Feminist Performances*, 215–24. Ann Arbor: University of Michigan Press, 1994.
Peacock, Jan. *Corpus Loquendi/Body for Speaking: Body-Centred Video in Halifax, 1972–1982*. Exhibition catalogue. Halifax: Dalhousie University Art Gallery, 1994.
Perreault, John. "Earth and Fire: Mendieta's Body of Work." In Petra Barreras del Rio and John Perreault, eds, *Ana Mendieta: A Retrospective*, 10–17. Exhibition catalogue. New York: The New Museum of Contemporary Art, 1987.
Petersen, Karen, and J.J. Wilson. *Women Artists: Recognition and Reappraisal from the Early Middle Ages to the Twentieth Century*. New York: Harper and Row, 1976.
Phelan, Peggy. "Reciting the Citation of Others, or A Second Introduction."

In Lynda Hart and Peggy Phelan, eds, *Acting Out: Feminist Performances*, 13–31. Ann Arbor: University of Michigan Press, 1994.
– "Survey." In Helena Reckitt, ed., *Art and Feminism*, 14–49. New York: Phaidon, 2001.
– *Unmarked: The Politics of Performance*. London and New York: Routledge, 1993.
Philip, Margaret. "Breadwinner Now Likely to Be a Woman." *Globe and Mail*, 15 September 2000, metro edition, sec. A, 3.
Pincus-Witten, Robert. "Lynda Benglis: The Frozen Gesture." *Artforum* 13, no. 3 (November 1974): 54–9.
Pinterics, Natasha. "Riding the Feminist Waves: In with the Third?" *Canadian Woman Studies/les cahiers de la femme* 20–21, nos 4–1 (Winter-Spring): 15–21.
Piper, Adrian. "Catalysis: An Interview with Adrian Piper." In Lucy Lippard, *From the Center: Feminist Essays on Women's Art*, 167–71. New York: E.P. Dutton, 1976.
– "The Critique of Pure Racism: An Interview with Adrian Piper." By Maurice Berger. In Maurice Berger, ed., *Adrian Piper: A Retrospective*, 76–98. Exhibition catalogue. Baltimore: Fine Arts Gallery, University of Maryland, 1999.
– "Food for the Spirit, July 1971." *High Performance* 4, no. 1 (Spring 1981): 34–5.
– "Supplementary Material, No. 17." Unpublished manuscript in Adrian Piper file, John Weber Gallery, New York.
– *Talking to Myself: The Ongoing Autobiography of an Art Object*. Bari, Italy: Marilena Bonomo, 1975.
– "*Untitled*." *0 to 9* (January 1969): 49–52.
– "*Untitled*." *0 to 9* (July 1969): 79–81.
– "Xenophobia and the Indexical Present." In Craig B. Little and Mark O'Brian, eds, *Reimaging America: The Arts of Social Change*, 285–95. Philadelphia: New Society Publishers, 1990.
Podheiser, Linda. "Ilene Segalove, Girl Video Artist." *Boston Review* 9, no. 3 (1984): 11–14.
Poggioli, Renato. *The Theory of the Avant-Garde*. Translated by Gerald Fitzgerald. Cambridge, MA: Belknap Press of Harvard University, 1968.
Pollock, Griselda, "The Politics of Theory: Generations and Geographies in Feminist Theory and the Histories of Art Histories." In Griselda Pollock, ed., *Generations and Geographies in the Visual Arts: Feminist Readings*, 3–21. London and New York: Routledge, 1996.
– *Vision and Difference: Femininity, Feminism and the Histories of Art*. London and New York: Routledge, 1988.
– ed. *Generations and Geographies in the Visual Arts: Feminist Readings*. London and New York: Routledge, 1996.
Potkin, Helen. "Performance Art." In Fiona Carson and Claire Pajaczkowska, eds, *Feminist Visual Culture*, 75–88. London and New York: Routledge, 2001.

Rae, Bob. "Canada: As Good as It Gets." Review of *The Efficient Society: Why Canada Is as Close to Utopia as It Gets*, by Joseph Heath. *Globe and Mail*, 19 May 2001, national edition, sec. D, 2.

Raven, Arlene. "At Home." In *Crossing Over: Feminism and Art of Social Concern*, 83–153. Ann Arbor: UMI Research Press, 1988.

– *Crossing Over: Feminism and Art of Social Concern*. Ann Arbor: UMI Research Press, 1988.

– "The New Culture: Women Artists of the Seventies." In *Crossing Over: Feminism and Art of Social Concern*, 3–11. Ann Arbor: UMI Research Press, 1988.

–"Womanhouse." In Norma Broude and Mary D. Garrard, eds, *The Power of Feminist Art: The American Movement of the 1970s, History and Impact*, 48–65. New York: Harry N. Abrams, 1994.

Reid, Stuart. *15 Minutes: Michael Buckland, Suzy Lake, Sasha Yungju Lee, Mitch Robertson*. Exhibition catalogue. Mississauga, ON: Art Gallery of Mississauga, 2000.

Reinelt, Janelle G., and Joseph R. Roach, eds. *Critical Theory and Performance*. Ann Arbor: University of Michigan Press, 1992.

Rhodes, Richard. "Shining a Light on the Everyday." *Globe and Mail*, 1 November 2003, national edition, sec. V, 10.

Rich, Adrienne. "Compulsory Heterosexuality and Lesbian Existence." *Signs: Journal of Women in Culture and Society* 5 (Summer 1980): 631–60.

– *Diving into the Wreck: Poems 1971–1972*. New York: W.W. Norton, 1973.

Richard, Alain-Martin, and Clive Robertson, eds. *Performance au/in Canada, 1970–1990*. Quebec: Éditions Intervention; Toronto: Coach House Press, 1991.

Riley, Denise. *"Am I That Name?" Feminism and the Category of "Women" in History*. Minneapolis: University of Minnesota Press, 1988.

Robertson, Clive. "The Complete Clichettes." *Fuse* 9, no. 4 (December 1985–January 1986): 9–15.

Rodney, Lee. "Deflecting the Blind Spot: Suzy Lake and Martha Wilson (1972–1975)." Master's curatorial project thesis paper, Art Gallery of York University, 1996.

"The Role of the Artist in Today's Society." *Art Journal* 34, no. 4 (Summer 1975): 327–31.

Rose, Barbara. "Vaginal Iconology." *New York Magazine*, 20 May 1974, 59.

Rosenberg, Harold. "The American Action Painters." *Art News* 51, no. 8 (December 1952): 22–3, 48–50.

Rosler, Martha. "A Conversation with Martha Rosler." By Benjamin H.D. Buchloh. In M. Catherine de Zegher, ed., *Martha Rosler: Positions in the Life World*, 23–55. Exhibition catalogue. Birmingham, England: Ikon Gallery; Vienna: Generali Foundation; Cambridge, MA: MIT Press, 1998.

– "For an Art against the Mythology of Everyday Life." *Journal: Southern California Art Journal* 23 (June-July 1979): 12–15.

– "In, Around, and Afterthoughts (on Documentary Photography)." In 3

*Works: Critical Essays on Photography and Photographs*, 59–86. Halifax: The Press of the Nova Scotia College of Art and Design, 1981.
– "Interview with Martha Rosler." By Jane Weinstock. *October* 17 (Summer 1981): 77–98.
– "An Interview with Martha Rosler." By Martha Gever. *Afterimage* 9, no. 3 (October 1981): 10–17.
– "Place, Position, Power, Politics." In Carol Becker, ed., *The Subversive Imagination: Artists, Society, and Social Responsibility*, 55–76. London and New York: Routledge, 1994.
– "The Private and the Public: Feminist Art in California." *Artforum* 16, no. 1 (September 1977): 66–74.
– *Service, a Trilogy on Colonization: A Budding Gourmet, McTowers Maid, Tijuana Maid*. New York: Printed Matter, 1978.
– "Shedding the Utopian Moment." *Block* 11 (Winter 1985–86): 27–33.
– "Well, *Is* the Personal Political?" In Hilary Robinson, ed., *Feminism-Art-Theory: An Anthology, 1968–2000*, 95–6. Oxford: Blackwell, 2001.
Roth, Moira. *Linda Montano: Seven Years of Living Art*. Exhibition catalogue. New York: The New Museum of Contemporary Art, 1984.
– "Toward a History of California Performance: Part Two." *Arts Magazine* 52, no. 10 (June 1978): 114–23.
– ed. *The Amazing Decade: Women and Performance Art in America, 1970–1980*. Los Angeles: Astro Artz, 1983.
Roy, Marina. "Corporeal Returns: Feminism and Phenomenology in Vancouver Video and Performance, 1968–1983." *Canadian Art* 18, no. 2 (Summer 2001): 58–65.
Said, Edward. *Culture and Imperialism*. New York: Alfred A. Knopf, 1993.
Sandler, Irving. *American Art of the 1960s*. New York: Harper and Row, 1988.
Sartre, Jean-Paul. *Being and Nothingness*. Translated by Hazel Barnes. New York: Washington Square Press, 1956.
Sayre, Henry. *The Object of Performance: The American Avant-Garde since 1970*. Chicago: University of Chicago Press, 1989.
Schapiro, Miriam. "The Education of Women as Artists: Project Womanhouse." *Art Journal* 31, nos 3–4 (Spring 1972): 268–70.
Schechner, Richard. *Environmental Theater*. 2nd ed. New York: Applause Books, 1994.
– "What Is Performance Studies Anyway?" In Peggy Phelan and Jill Lane, eds, *The Ends of Performance*, 357–66. New York: New York University Press, 1998.
Schimmel, Paul, ed. *Out of Actions: Between Performance and the Object, 1949–1979*. Exhibition catalogue. Los Angeles: The Museum of Contemporary Art; London: Thames and Hudson, 1998.
Schneemann, Carolee. *More Than Meat Joy: Complete Performance Works and Selected Writings*. Edited by Bruce McPherson. New Paltz, NY: Documentext, 1979.

– ed. *Imaging Her Erotics: Essays, Interviews, Projects*. Cambridge, MA: MIT Press, 2002.
Schneider, Rebecca. "After Us the Savage Goddess." In Elin Diamond, ed., *Performance and Cultural Politics*, 155–76. New York and London: Routledge, 1996.
– *The Explicit Body in Performance*. London and New York: Routledge, 1997.
– "See the Big Show: Spiderwoman Theatre Doubling Back." In Lynda Hart and Peggy Phelan, eds, *Acting Out: Feminist Performances*, 227–55. Ann Arbor: University of Michigan Press, 1994.
Schor, Mira. "Representations of the Penis." *M/E/A/N/I/N/G* 4 (November 1988): 3–17.
Schor, Naomi. "The Essentialism Which Is Not One: Coming to Grips with Irigaray." In Naomi Schor and Elizabeth Weed, eds, *The Essential Difference*, 40–62. Bloomington: Indiana University Press, 1994.
– and Elizabeth Weed, eds. *The Essential Difference*. Bloomington: Indiana University Press, 1994.
Schwartz, Therese. "The Politicalization of the Avant-Garde." Parts 1–4. *Art in America* 59, no. 6 (November 1971): 97–105; 60, no. 2 (March-April 1972): 70–9; 61, no. 2 (March-April 1973): 67–71; and 62, no. 1 (February 1974): 80–4.
Sharp, Willoughby. "Body Works." *Avalanche* 1 (1970): 14–17.
Sheppard, Richard. *Modernism—Dada—Postmodernism*. Evanston, IL: Northwestern University Press, 2000.
Shottenkirk, Dena. "First Person Painting: Reflections on Recent New York Painting." *C Magazine* 66 (Summer 2000): 31.
Siegel, Jerold. *Bohemian Paris: Culture, Politics, and the Boundaries of Bourgeois Life, 1830–1930*. Harmondsworth, Middlesex: Penguin Books, 1987.
Smithson, Robert. "Cultural Confinement." *Artforum* 11, no. 2 (October 1972): 2.
– "Production for Production's Sake." In Alexander Alberro and Blake Stimson, eds, *Conceptual Art: A Critical Anthology*, 284–5. Cambridge, MA: MIT Press, 1999.
Solomon, Alisa. *Re-Dressing the Canon: Essays on Theater and Gender*. London and New York: Routledge, 1997.
– "The WOW Café." In Carol Martin, ed., *A Sourcebook of Feminist Theatre and Performance: On and Beyond the Stage*, 42–51. London and New York: Routledge, 1996.
Sontag, Susan. "Notes on Camp." In *A Susan Sontag Reader*, 105–19. New York: Vintage Books, 1983.
– *On Photography*. New York: Farrar, Straus and Giroux, 1978.
Spark, Jo, and Jonathan Watkins, eds. *Everyday: The 11th Biennale of Sydney*. Exhibition catalogue. Sydney: The Biennale of Sydney, 1998.
Spelman, Elizabeth V. *Inessential Woman: Problems of Exclusion in Feminist Thought*. Boston: Beacon Press, 1988.

Spivak, Gayatri Chakravorty. "Subaltern Studies: Deconstructing Historiography." In *In Other Worlds: Essays in Cultural Politics*, 197–221. New York: Methuen, 1987.

Spretnak, Charlene. *The Politics of Women's Spirituality: Essays on the Rise of Spiritual Power within the Feminist Movement*. Garden City, NY: Anchor Books, 1982.

Stallybrass, Peter, and Allon White. *The Politics and Poetics of Transgression*. Ithaca, NY: Cornell University Press, 1986.

Steele, Valerie. *Fetish: Fashion, Sex and Power*. Oxford University Press, 1996.

Steenbergen, Candis. "Feminism and Young Women: Alive and Well and Still Kicking." *Canadian Woman Studies/les cahiers de la femme* 20–21, nos 4–1 (Winter-Spring 2001): 6–14.

Stiles, Kristine. "Between Water and Stone: Fluxus Performance, A Metaphysics of Acts." In Elizabeth Armstrong and Joan Rothfuss, eds, *In the Spirit of Fluxus*, 63–99. Exhibition catalogue. Minneapolis: Walker Art Center, 1993.

– "Uncorrupted Joy: International Art Actions." In Paul Schimmel, ed., *Out of Actions: Between Performance and the Object, 1949–1979*, 227–329. Exhibition catalogue. Los Angeles: The Museum of Contemporary Art; London: Thames and Hudson, 1998.

Stimson, Blake. "The Promise of Conceptual Art." In Alexander Alberro and Blake Stimson, eds, *Conceptual Art: A Critical Anthology*, xxxviii–lii. Cambridge, MA: MIT Press, 1999.

Stone, Merlin. *When God Was a Woman*. New York: Dial Press, 1976.

Straayer, Chris. "I Say I Am: Feminist Performance Video in the '70s." *Afterimage* 13, no. 4 (November 1985): 8–12.

Strauss, David Levi. "Love Rides Aristotle through the Audience: Body, Image, and Idea in the Work of Carolee Schneemann." In Carolee Schneemann, ed. *Imaging Her Erotics: Essays, Interviews, Projects*, 316–25. Cambridge, MA: MIT Press, 2002.

Strong-Boag, Veronica. "Home Dreams: Women and the Suburban Experiment in Canada, 1945–60." In Veronica Strong-Boag and Anita Clair Fellman, eds, *Rethinking Canada: The Promise of Women's History*, 375–401. 3rd ed. Toronto: Oxford University Press, 1997.

– and Anita Clair Fellman, eds. *Rethinking Canada: The Promise of Women's History*. 3rd ed. Toronto: Oxford University Press, 1997.

Tenhaaf, Nell. "A History, or A Way of Knowing." In Marie Fraser and Lesley Johnstone, eds, *Instabili: La question du sujet*, 77–84. Montreal: La Galerie Powerhouse (La Centrale) and Artextes, 1990.

– "Of Monitors and Men and Other Unsolved Mysteries: Video Technology and the Feminine." *Parallélogramme* 18, no. 3 (Winter 1992): 24–37.

Thornham, Sue. "Postmodernism and Feminism (or: Repairing Our Own Cars)." In Stuart Sim, ed., *The Routledge Critical Dictionary of Postmodern Thought*, 41–52. New York: Routledge, 1999.

Tickner, Lisa. "The Body Politic: Female Sexuality and Women Artists since 1970." In Rosemary Betterton, ed., *Looking On: Images of Femininity in the Visual Arts and Media,* 235–53. London: Pandora, 1987.

Tippett, Maria. *By a Lady: Celebrating Three Centuries of Art by Canadian Women*. Toronto: Viking, 1992.

Tong, Rosemarie. *Feminist Thought: A Comprehensive Introduction*. Boulder, CO: Westview Press, 1989.

Tourangeau, Sylvie. "An Art of Manner." In Alain-Martin Richard and Clive Robertson, eds, *Performance au/in Canada, 1970–1990,* 152. Quebec: Éditions Intervention; Toronto: Coach House Press, 1991.

– *Objet(s) de présence*. Exhibition catalogue. Joliette, QC: Musée d'art de Joliette, 1998.

Tuer, Dot. "The Women Men Love to Hate, or Anatomy Is Not Quite Destiny in Pure Hell." In Barbara Fischer, ed., *Tanya Mars: Pure Hell,* 9–26. Exhibition catalogue. Toronto: The Power Plant, 1990.

Tufts, Eleanor. *Our Hidden Heritage: Five Centuries of Women Artists*. New York: Paddington Press, 1974.

Vergine, Lea. *Il corpo come linguaggio*. Milan: Giampaolo Prearo Editore, 1974.

Video Data Bank. *Early Video Art in the United States, 1968–1980*. Chicago: Video Data Bank, 1993.

Wagner, Anne M. "Performance, Video and the Rhetoric of Presence." *October* 91 (Winter 2000): 59–80.

Wallace, Keith, ed. *Whispered Art History: Twenty Years at the Western Front*. Vancouver: Arsenal Pulp Press, 1993.

Wallis, Brian, ed. *Hans Haacke: Unfinished Business*. Exhibition catalogue. New York: New Museum of Contemporary Art; Cambridge, MA: MIT Press, 1986.

Ward, Frazer. "Some Relations between Conceptual and Performance Art." *Art Journal* 56, no. 4 (Winter 1997): 36–40.

Wark, Jayne. "Conceptual Art and Feminism: Martha Rosler, Adrian Piper, Eleanor Antin, and Martha Wilson." *Woman's Art Journal* 22, no. 1 (Spring-Summer 2001): 44–50.

– "Gillian Collyer: Second Skin." In Gillian Collyer, *Gillian Collyer: hand-held,* n.p. Exhibition catalogue. Annapolis Royal, NS: ARTsPLACE, 2001.

– "Martha Wilson: Not Taking It at Face Value." *Camera Obscura* 15, no. 3 (2001): 1–33.

– "Wendy Geller's *48-Hour Beauty Blitz*: Gender, Class and the Pleasures of Popular Culture." *Art Journal* 56, no. 4 (Winter 1997): 41–7.

Watson, Scott. "Hand of the Spirit." In Scott Watson, ed., *Hand of the Spirit: Documents of the Seventies from the Morris/Trasov Archive,* 5–28. Exhibition catalogue. Vancouver: University of British Columbia Fine Arts Gallery, 1992.

– "Return to Brutopia." In Scott Watson, ed., *Return to Brutopia: Eric*

*Metcalfe Works and Collaborations*, 7–45. Exhibition catalogue. Vancouver: University of British Columbia Fine Arts Gallery, 1992.

[Weatherman]. "Look at It: America 1969." In Harold Jacobs, ed., *Weatherman*, 167–8, 172. Berkeley: Ramparts Press, 1970.

Weidenhammer, Lori. *Virtual Postcards from the Feminist Utopia*. Internet exhibition. http://www.mawa.ca/archives/postcards/contents.html. Winnipeg, MB: Mentoring Artists for Women's Art, 1997.

Wilding, Faith. *By Our Own Hands: The Women Artist's Movement*. Santa Monica: Double X, 1977.

– "*The Feminist Art Programs at Fresno and Calarts.*" In Norma Broude and Mary D. Garrard, eds, *The Power of Feminist Art: The American Movement of the 1970s, History and Impact*, 32–47. New York: Harry N. Abrams, 1994.

Wilke, Hannah. "*Intercourse with …*" In Thomas H. Kochheiser, ed., *Hannah Wilke: A Retrospective*, 139. Exhibition catalogue. Columbia: University of Missouri Press, 1989.

Wilson, Judith. "In Memory of the News and of Our Selves: The Art of Adrian Piper." *Third Text* 16–17 (Autumn-Winter 1991): 39–64.

Wilson, Martha. "Artist's Book Beat." Interview by Nancy Princenthal. *Print Collector's Newsletter* 22, no. 1 (March-April 1991): 61–4.

– and Jacki Apple. "Correspondence between Jacki Apple and Martha Wilson, 1973–1974." *Heresies* 2 (May 1977): 43–7.

Winnicott, D.W. *Playing and Reality*. London and New York: Routledge, 1982.

Withers, Josephine. "Feminist Performance Art: Performing, Discovering, Transforming Ourselves." In Norma Broude and Mary D. Garrard, eds, *The Power of Feminist Art: The American Movement of the 1970s, History and Impact*, 158–73. New York: Harry N. Abrams, 1994.

Wittig, Monique. *The Straight Mind and Other Essays*. New York: Harvester Wheatsheaf, 1992.

Wolff, Janet. *Feminine Sentences: Essays on Women and Culture*. Berkeley and Los Angeles: University of California Press, 1990.

Wollen, Peter. "Bitter Victory: The Art and Politics of the Situationist International." In Elizabeth Sussmann, ed., *On the Passage of a Few People through a Rather Brief Moment in Time: The Situationist International, 1957–1972*, 20–61. Exhibition catalogue. Boston: Institute of Contemporary Art; Cambridge, MA: MIT Press, 1989.

Women's History Research Center. *Female Artists Past and Present*. Berkeley: Women's History Research Center, 1974.

Wordsworth, William. "The World Is Too Much with Us; Late and Soon." In *The Complete Poetical Works of William Wordsworth*, 353–54. London: MacMillan, 1913.

Wood, Paul, Francis Frascina, Jonathan Harris, and Charles Harrison. *Modernism in Dispute: Art since the Forties*. New Haven and London: Yale University Press in association with the Open University, 1993.

Wooster, Ann-Sargent. "The Way We Were." In JoAnn Hanley, ed., *The First Generation: Women and Video, 1970–75*, 20–44. Exhibition catalogue. New York: Independent Curators Incorporated, 1993.

Young, Iris Marion. "The Ideal of Community and the Politics of Difference." In Linda J. Nicholson, ed., *Feminism/Postmodernism*, 300–23. New York and London: Routledge, 1990.

Zemel, Carol. "Women and Video: An Introduction to the Community of Video." *Artscanada* 30, no. 4 (October 1973): 30–40.

# Index

Page numbers of illustrations and captions are in bold. There may be textual references on the same page.